INGENIX®

ShopIngenix.com

Shop Faster. Shop Smarter.
Experience ShopIngenix.com.

- **Network with industry peers when you join the Ingenix Coding Circle.** The new ShopIngenix.com eCommunity allows health care professionals to access the latest industry news, share ideas, test coding skills, and connect with colleagues.

- **Navigate the site more efficiently.** Start your product search by selecting either your market type or narrow down resource offerings by specific category.

- **Experience a hassle-free online purchase process.** The new streamlined, easy-to-follow checkout options also give you access to Live Help and a wide variety of self-paced instructions at every step, if needed.

- **Get eSmart:** the ShopIngenix.com frequent buyer program rewards you for every $500 you spend online.**

- **Access your Order History or outstanding Product Renewals.**

- **Create a Wish List.** Create and maintain a Wish List and send it along in an email to others that may need to preapprove purchases, or suggest titles to colleagues or anyone else in your professional network.

- **Get customized product recommendations.** Based on your selections, these recommendations show you items other shoppers have purchased along with the product you've just added to your cart.

CPT is a registered trademark of the American Medical Association.

SAVE UP TO 20%

with source code FOBAW9

Visit **www.shopingenix.com** and enter the source code in the lower right-hand corner and save 20%.

(*)Offer valid online only and not to be combined with other promotions or discounts and cannot be used with Partner accounts. This offer cannot be used for online applications, conferences, updateable products, package items, Customized Fee Products and AMA CPT® products, bookstore items, specialty credential products, or Workers' Compensation items.

(**) Offer valid only for Ingenix customers who are NOT part of Medallion or Partner Accounts programs. You must be registered at ShopIngenix.com to have your online purchases tracked for rewards purposes. Shipping charges and taxes still apply and cannot be used for rewards. eSmart reward offers valid online only.

Ingenix | Intelligence for Health Care | Call toll-free 1.800.INGENIX (464.3649), option 1.

100% Money Back Guarantee If our merchandise ever fails to meet your expectations, please contact our Customer Service Department toll-free at 1.800.INGENIX (464.3649), option 1, for an immediate response. Software: Credit will be granted for unopened packages only.

FOBA09

INGENIX®

Four simple ways to place an order.

Call
1.800.ingenix (464.3649), option 1. Mention source code FOBA09 when ordering.

Mail
PO Box 27116
Salt Lake City, UT 84127-0116
With payment and/or purchase order.

Fax
801.982.4033
With credit card information and/or purchase order.

Click
www.shopingenix.com
Save 20% when you order online today—use source code FOBAW9.

ingenix e smart
Shopingenix.com frequent buyer program

GET REWARDS FOR SHOPPING ONLINE!
To find out more, visit www.shopingenix.com

eSmart program available only to Ingenix customers who are not part of Medallion, Gold Medallion or Partner Accounts programs. You must be registered at ShopIngenix.com to have your online purchases tracked for rewards purposes. Shipping charges and taxes still apply and cannot be used for rewards. Offer valid online only.

100% Money Back Guarantee
If our merchandise* ever fails to meet your expectations, please contact our Customer Service Department toll-free at 1.800.ingenix (464.3649), option 1 for an immediate response.

*Software: Credit will be granted for unopened packages only.

Customer Service Hours
7:00 am - 5:00 pm Mountain Time
9:00 am - 7:00 pm Eastern Time

Shipping and Handling

no. of items	fee
1	$10.95
2-4	$12.95
5-7	$14.95
8-10	$19.95
11+	Call

Order Form

Information

Customer No. _____ Contact No. _____

Source Code _____

Contact Name _____

Title _____ Specialty _____

Company _____

Street Address _____
NO PO BOXES, PLEASE

City _____ State _____ Zip _____

Telephone (___) _____ Fax (___) _____
IN CASE WE HAVE QUESTIONS ABOUT YOUR ORDER

E-mail _____ @ _____
REQUIRED FOR ORDER CONFIRMATION AND SELECT PRODUCT DELIVERY.

Ingenix respects your right to privacy. We will not sell or rent your e-mail address or fax number to anyone outside Ingenix and its business partners. If you would like to remove your name from Ingenix promotion, please call 1.800.ingenix (464.3649), option 1.

Product

Item No.	Qty	Description	Price	Total

Subtotal _____

UT, VA, TN, OH, CT, IA, MD, MN, NC & NJ residents, please add applicable Sales tax _____

(See chart on the left) Shipping & handling charges _____

All foreign orders, please call for shipping costs

Total _____

Payment

○ Please bill my credit card ○ MasterCard ○ VISA ○ Amex ○ Discover

Card No. | | | | | | | | | | | | | | | | Expires | |
MONTH   YEAR

Signature _____

○ Check enclosed, made payable to: Ingenix, Inc.   ○ Please bill my office

Purchase Order No. _____
ATTACH COPY OF PURCHASE ORDER

FOBA09

Ingenix Learning: Implementing ICD-10

INGENIX.

ACKNOWLEDGMENTS

Julie Orton Van, CPC, CPC-P, *Product Manager*
Stacy Perry, *Manager, Desktop Publishing*
Lisa Singley, *Project Manager*
Beth Ford, RHIT, CCS, *Clinical/Technical Editor*
Temeka Lewis, MBA, CCS, *Clinical/Technical Editor*
Hope M. Dunn, *Desktop Publishing Specialist*
Kate Holden, *Editor*

ABOUT THE AUTHORS

BETH FORD, RHIT, CCS

Ms. Ford is a clinical/technical editor for Ingenix. She has extensive background in both the professional and technical components of CPT/HCPCS and ICD-9-CM coding. Ms. Ford has served as a coding supervisor and coding consultant, as well as a health information management director. She is an active member of the American Heath Information Management Association (AHIMA).

TEMEKA LEWIS, MBA, CCS

Ms. Lewis is a clinical/technical editor for Ingenix with expertise in hospital inpatient and outpatient coding. Her areas of expertise include ICD-9-CM, CPT, and HCPCS coding. Ms. Lewis's past experience includes conducting coding audits and physician education, teaching ICD-9-CM and CPT coding, functioning as a member of a revenue cycle team, chargemaster maintenance, and writing compliance newsletters. Most recently she was responsible for coding and compliance in a specialty hospital. She is an active member of the American Health Information Management Association (AHIMA).

Contents

Introduction

It is a reality in today's modern medical science that the codes within ICD-9-CM fall woefully short of today's medical reporting needs. ICD-9-CM was created more than 25 years ago as a modern and expansive system that was then only partially filled. Thousands of codes have been added to ICD-9-CM to classify new procedures and diseases over the years, and today the remaining space in ICD-9-CM procedure and diagnosis coding systems cannot accommodate our new technologies or our new understanding of diseases. An overhaul of our coding systems is needed.

New coding systems have been developed. Through the World Health Organization (WHO), ICD-10 was created and adopted in 1994. This is the system upon which the new U.S. diagnosis coding system, ICD-10-CM, is based. Concurrent to the clinical modification of ICD-10 by the National Center for Health Statistics (NCHS), the Centers for Medicare and Medicaid Services (CMS) commissioned 3M Health Information Management to develop a new procedure coding system to replace volume 3 of ICD-9-CM, used for inpatient procedure coding.

Now that the coding systems have been designed and written, they need only be implemented; but progress is slow. The government is moving very cautiously toward implementation, partly because (1) the medical reimbursement industry is already reeling under the impact of the Health Insurance Portability and Accountability Act of 1996; (2) the scope of change is massive and will have a profound effect upon all care providers, payers, and government agencies; and (3) the change is big enough and costly enough to carry considerable political impact.

Two important events occurred late in 2002 that affected ICD-10-CM and ICD-10-PCS and their implementation: First, a subcommittee on coding for the National Committee on Vital and Health Statistics (NCVHS) forwarded a recommendation to the full committee that ICD-10-CM and ICD-10-PCS be adopted by the secretary of Health and Human Services (HHS). The recommendation of the subcommittee is important and will most likely pass the full committee and be sent to the secretary of HHS. That takes ICD-10-CM and ICD-10-PCS one step closer to national rule making, which normally opens up a formal public comment period. The second event was the posting of a near-final draft of ICD-10-CM on the CMS website. While an earlier draft included only the tabular section of ICD-10-CM, this draft included the index as well. (The final draft of ICD-10-PCS has been available for more than two years.)

In June 2003, NCHS posted a pre-release draft of ICD-10-CM on the NCHS website. This pre-release draft, containing both index and tabular sections, a table of drugs and chemicals, as well as a preface and coding guidelines can be downloaded at the following URL: http://www.cdc.gov/nchs/about/otheract/icd9/icd10cm.htm. Ingenix has published updated versions of the complete text.

On August 22, 2008, HHS published a notice of proposed rulemaking (NPRM) to adopt the ICD-10 coding systems (ICD-10-CM and ICD-10-PCS) to replace ICD-9-CM in transactions under the Health Insurance Portability and Accountability Act (HIPAA).

Proposed rule NPRM CMS-0013-P called for updated versions of HIPAA electronic transaction standards. Specifically, the rule urged adoption of version 5010 to facilitate electronic health care transactions to accommodate the ICD-10 code sets. This NPRM

 DEFINITIONS

CMS. Centers for Medicare and Medicaid Services, formerly the Health Care Financing Administration (HCFA). A federal agency that provides health insurance for more than 74 million Americans through Medicare, Medicaid, and Child Health. CMS contracted for the development of a new procedure coding system by 3M HIS. Find CMS at: http://www.cms.hhs.gov/

NCHS. National Center for Health Statistics. The U.S. government agency that, jointly with CMS, refines the diagnostic portion of ICD-9-CM and is responsible for the clinical modification of ICD-10. NCHS holds several hearings a year to consider changes or additions in diagnostic coding. Find NCHS at: http://www.cdc.gov/nchs

WHO. World Health Organization. The international agency that maintains an international nomenclature of diseases, causes of death, and public health practices. WHO, with advice from participating countries, developed ICD-9 to track morbidity and mortality statistics worldwide. It recently updated diagnostic coding with ICD-10. Find WHO at: http://www.who.org/

also proposed implementing ICD-10-CM for diagnosis coding and ICD-10-PCS for inpatient hospital procedure coding, effective October 1, 2011. The comment period for this proposed rule was closed on October 21, 2008.

On January 16, 2009, the Department of Health and Human Services published a final rule in the *Federal Register*, 45 CFR part 162, "HIPAA Administrative Simplification: Modifications to Medical Data Code Set Standards to Adopt ICD-10-CM and ICD-10-PCS." This rule may be downloaded at http://edocket.access.gpo.gov/2009/pdf/E9-743.pdf.

This final rule adopts modifications to standard medical data code sets for coding diagnoses and inpatient hospital procedures by adopting ICD-10-CM for diagnosis coding, including the Official ICD-10-CM Guidelines for Coding and Reporting, and ICD-10-PCS for inpatient hospital procedure coding, effective October 1, 2013. The most current 2009 draft update release is available for public viewing, and additional updates are expected prior to implementation. At this time, ICD-10 codes are not valid for any purpose or use other than for reporting mortality data for death certificates.

The purpose of this book is to explain those issues. First, *Ingenix Learning: Implementing ICD-10* provides a comprehensive introduction to ICD-10-CM. This reference analyzes the similarities and differences between ICD-9-CM and ICD-10-CM and provides a preview of ICD-10-PCS. Most importantly, *Ingenix Learning: Implementing ICD-10* teaches you how to prepare your office, practice, department, or facility for the significant changes the new coding systems will bring. Everyone in your facility will be affected: human resources staff, accountants, information systems staff, physicians—just to name a few. The proposed codes provide tremendous opportunities for disease and procedure tracking, but also create enormous challenges. Computer hardware and software, medical documentation, and the reimbursement cycle are just three elements of medical reimbursement that will be shaken when implementation occurs.

You can take many actions today to help reduce the impact of implementation in the years to come. This book will guide you in identifying the strategies you can employ to make implementation easier for your organization. A heightened awareness of the issues surrounding ICD-10 coding systems can:

- Prevent your organization from investing in potentially obsolete equipment
- Guide you in cultivating the right skill sets required for ICD-10-CM implementation
- Allow your financial managers to prepare for the added capital and personnel investments required by the change
- Minimize the overall impact of the change for your organization

HISTORY OF MODIFICATIONS TO ICD

WHO's original intent for ICD was as a statistical tool for the international exchange of mortality data. A subsequent revision was expanded to accommodate data collection for morbidity statistics. An eventual seventh revision, published by WHO in 1955, was clinically modified for use in the United States based upon a joint study on the efficiency of hospital diseases indexing by the American Hospital Association (AHA) and the American Association of Medical Record Librarians (AAMRL). Results of that study led to the 1959 publication of the International Classification of Diseases, Adapted for Indexing Hospital Records (ICDA), by the federal Public Health Service. The ICDA uniformly modified ICD-7, and it gave the United States a way to classify operations and treatments.

KEY POINT

Two federal agencies, NCHS and CMS, are responsible for the development of the ICD-9-CM replacement, i.e., ICD-10-CM and ICD-10-PCS.

Hospitals were initially slow in their acceptance of ICDA, though momentum picked up. An eighth edition of ICD, published by WHO in 1965, lacked the depth of clinical data required for America's emerging health care system. In 1968, two widely accepted modifications were published in the United States: the Eighth Revision International Classification of Diseases Adapted for Use in the United States (ICDA-8) and the Hospital Adaptation of ICDA (H-ICDA). Hospitals used either of these two systems through the latter years of the next decade.

ICD-9

The ninth revision by WHO in 1975 prompted the typical American response: clinical modification. This time the impetus flowed from a process initiated in 1977 by NCHS to modify ICD-9 for hospital indexing and retrieving case data for clinical studies. The NCHS and the newly created Council on Clinical Classifications modified ICD-9 according to U.S. clinical standard, and developed a companion procedural classification. This classification, published as volume 3 of ICD-9-CM, revised a portion of WHO's International Classification of Procedure Modification (ICPM). In 1978, the three-volume set was published in the United States for use one year later. There were no further changes in the direction to ICD-9-CM until the October 1983 implementation of diagnosis related groups (DRGs), which gave ICD-9-CM a new significance. After almost 30 years since ICD's arrival in the United States, the classification system proves indispensable to hospitals interested in payment schedules for health care services.

ICD-10

The evolution of ICD took another turn in 1994 when WHO published ICD-10. Again, the NCHS wanted to modify the latest revision, but with an emphasis on problems that had been identified in the current ICD-9-CM and resolved by the improvements to ICD-10 for classifying mortality and morbidity data. The Center for Health Policy Studies (CHPS) was awarded the NCHS contract to analyze ICD-10 and to develop the appropriate clinical modifications.

ICD-10-CM

Phase I provided the analysis for clinical modification. According to CHPS, ICD-10 must be modified to do the following:

- Return the level of specificity found in ICD-9-CM
- Facilitate an alphabetic index to assign codes
- Provide code titles and language that complement accepted clinical practice
- Remove codes unique to mortality coding

Phase II followed protocol. CHPS developed modifications based on the analysis, including the following:

- Increasing the five-character structure to six characters
- Incorporating common fourth- and fifth-digit subclassifications
- Creating laterality
- Combining certain codes
- Adding trimesters to obstetric codes
- Creating combined diagnosis/symptoms codes
- Deactivating procedure codes

In the second phase, CHPS expanded the codes for alcohol/drug abuse, diabetes mellitus, and injuries.

KEY POINT

NCHS is responsible for developing the diagnostic portion of the ICD-10 coding system, ICD-10-CM. CMS is responsible for developing the procedure portion of the ICD-10 coding system, ICD-10-PCS.

DEFINITIONS

Morbidity. The disease rate—or number of cases of a particular disease—in a given age range, gender, occupation, or other relevant population-based grouping.

Mortality. The death rate reflected by the population in a given region, age range, or other relevant statistical grouping.

The Centers for Disease Control in Atlanta publishes a weekly epidemiologic report on the incidence of communicable diseases and deaths (morbidity and mortality) in selected urban areas of the United States.

KEY POINT

WHO's seventh edition of ICD was the first edition modified by the United States. Two versions of a modified ICD-8 were published in 1968. A procedure classification was created by the U.S. government and accompanied the clinical modification of ICD-9, which was published here in 1978.

A draft of ICD-10-CM for public comment was released at the conclusion of Phase II. The final version will draw on an analysis of the comments by NCHS and Phase III reviewers.

ICD-10-PCS

ICD-10-PCS was developed to replace ICD-9-CM volume 3 under a three-year contract with CMS, beginning in 1995. PCS was developed with these CMS objectives in mind: completeness, expandability, uniform structure, and standardized terminology. The contract included completion of the first draft in year one; training and testing in inpatient and outpatient facilities with revision of the system to accommodate problems revealed in testing; and formal testing in the third year. The testing has been completed and results have been reviewed by specialty groups independent of CMS and tested at Clinical Data Abstractions Centers (CDAC). Their work resulted in a final version now standing ready as a replacement for ICD-9-CM volume 3.

The issue of replacing ICD-9-CM volume 3 with ICD-10-PCS has become somewhat politicized, and inpatient implementation has been clouded by other issues. In June 1997, the National Center for Vital and Health Statistics recommended a single procedure classification rather than two. Currently CPT is used for physician coding, and volume 3 for inpatient. NCVHS stated, "We recommend that you advise the industry to build and modify their information systems to accommodate ... [a] major change to a unified approach to coding procedures...[We] recommend that you identify and implement an approach for procedure coding that addresses deficiencies in the current systems, including issues of specificity and aggregation, unnecessary redundancy, and incomplete coverage of health care providers and settings." It is the concern of some that implementation of ICD-10-PCS could jeopardize the position of the American Medical Association's CPT codes for physician coding.

The American Health Information Management Association, in testimony at the May 2001 Coordination and Maintenance Committee hearing on ICD-10-PCS, suggested that before ICD-10-PCS is implemented, the issue of one or two procedure coding systems should be decided.

In November 2003, the NCVHS sent a letter to HHS recommending adoption of ICD-10-CM and ICD-10-PCS as HIPAA standards for national implementation as replacements for the current uses of ICD-9-CM. The letter requested that the regulatory process for the national adoption be initiated by HHS with an implementation period of at least two years following issuance of a final rule.

Since that time, the CMS NPRM (CMS-0013-P) published in the August 22, 2008, *Federal Register* calls for replacing ICD-9-CM volume 3 procedures only in inpatient hospital settings. According to this NPRM, providers who currently use CPT to report procedures in their health care settings would continue to do so.

Regulatory Process

This section outlines the regulatory process as defined by HIPAA for adoption of a new standard code set. Recently, legislation has been introduced in both houses of Congress that address national health information issues. A few bills that have been introduced include provisions for adopting ICD-10. Both the House and Senate must approve legislation before the bill advances to the President for signature. At this time, no legislation has passed joint conference compromise. The inclusion of ICD-10 adoption provisions within current legislation is separate from the process outlined in HIPAA. Should a bill pass both the House and Senate and be signed by the President, the regulatory process outlined here must still take place.

 FOR MORE INFO

NCHS has posted a final draft of ICD-10-CM on the Web at www.cdc.gov/nchs/about/otheract/icd9/abticd10.htm.

The final draft of ICD-10-PCS is available on the CMS home page (http://www.cms.hhs.gov).

Background

On Wednesday, November 5, 2003, the National Committee on Vital and Health Statistics (NCVHS) voted to recommend that the secretary of HHS take steps toward national adoption of ICD-10-CM and ICD-10-PCS as replacements under HIPAA standards for the current uses of ICD-9-CM, volumes 1, 2, and 3.

Administrative Simplification

Congress addressed the need for a consistent framework for electronic transactions and other administrative simplification issues in the Health Insurance Portability and Accountability Act of 1996 (HIPAA), which became part of Social Security Act titled "Administrative Simplification." Administrative Simplification sections 1171 through 1179 require any standard adopted by the secretary of the Department of Health and Human Services (including the standard code sets):

- To be developed, adopted, or modified by a standard-setting organization
- To adopt code standards applicable to health plans, health care clearinghouses, and health care providers who transmit any health information in electronic form
- To adopt transaction standards and data elements for the electronic exchange of health information for certain health care transactions
- To ensure that procedures exist for the routine maintenance, testing, enhancement, and expansion of code sets
- To set a compliance date not later than 24 months after the date on which an initial standard or implementation specification is adopted for all covered entities except small health plans

The transactions and code sets final rule (2000) adopted a number of standard medical data code sets for use in those transactions, including:

- ICD-9-CM volumes 1 and 2 for coding and reporting diseases, injuries, impairments, other health problems and their manifestations, and causes of injury, disease, impairment, or other health problems
- ICD-9-CM volume 3 for the following procedures reported by hospitals: prevention, diagnosis, treatment, and management
- CPT for physician services and all other health care services
- HCPCS for other substances, equipment, supplies, and other items used in health care

The rule also included adoption of a procedure for maintaining existing standards, for adopting modifications to existing standards, and for adopting new standards.

Process

The committee formulated a letter of recommendation requesting that the secretary of HHS initiate the regulatory process for the concurrent national adoption of the two classification systems with an implementation period of at least two years following issuance of a final rule.

The NCVHS recommendation was the first step of the regulatory process. The next step was the acceptance of the recommendation by the secretary of Health and Human Services. In the meantime, AHIMA had urged the secretary of HHS to issue a notice of proposed rule making (NPRM).

On August 22, 2008, the NPRM was published in the *Federal Register* with a proposed implementation date of October 1 of 2011. A two-year implementation period after establishment of the final rule is required under the HIPAA two-year window for compliance.

The comment period for the NPRM closed on October 21, 2008. However, a final rule was not published at that time.

Upon publishing the ICD-10 and version 5010/NCPDP version D.0 (electronic transaction standards) final rules both CMS and the industry will begin documenting the requirements for both ICD-10 and version 5010 system changes, initiate and/or complete any gap analyses, and then undertake design and system changes. Version 5010 is progressing first, based on the need to have this transaction standard in place prior to ICD-10 implementation to accommodate the increase in the size of the fields for the ICD-10 code sets.

In the United States, the clinical modification of the code set is maintained by the ICD-9-CM Coordination and Maintenance Committee (National Center for Health Statistics [NCHS], CMS, American Hospital Association [AHA], and American Health Information Management Association [AHIMA]). However, the code set standard is approved by legislative process.

The Administrative Simplification provision of HIPAA encourages the development of health care information systems by establishing standards, including code sets for each data element for health care services. HIPAA requires the secretary of HHS to adopt the code set standards, who then tasked the NCVHS with studying and recommending the standard code sets. These impact studies have been completed, and reports have been made to Congress and HHS.

In summary, the necessary steps to implementation include:

1. Development of recommendations for standards to be adopted by HHS/NCVHS

2. Publication of the proposed rule in the *Federal Register* with a 60-day public comment period

3. Analysis of the public comments and publication of the final rule in the *Federal Register* with the effective date of the rule being 60 days after publication

4. Distribution of standards and coordinated preparation and distribution of implementation guidelines and crosswalks. Implementation is 24 months from the effective date, excluding small health plans (fewer than 50 participants), which have 36 months to comply.

Step 1 of this process ended up lasting until 2008. Cost/benefit analyses were performed. According to the regulatory process, implementation was no sooner than October 1, 2009. However, the NPRM was not released before May 1, 2007, making the 2009 implementation date impossible.

On August 22, 2008, HHS published an NPRM to adopt the ICD-10 coding systems (ICD-10-CM and ICD-10-PCS) to replace ICD-9-CM in HIPAA transactions.

Proposed rule NPRM CMS-0013-P called for updated versions of HIPAA electronic transaction standards. Specifically, the rule urged adoption of version 5010 to facilitate electronic health care transactions to accommodate the ICD-10 code sets. This NPRM also proposed implementing ICD-10-CM for diagnosis coding and ICD-10-PCS for inpatient hospital procedure coding, effective October 1, 2011. The comment period for this proposed rule was closed on October 21, 2008.

On January 16, 2009, the Department of Health and Human Services published a final rule in the *Federal Register*, 45 CFR part 162, "HIPAA Administrative Simplification: Modifications to Medical Data Code Set Standards to Adopt ICD-10-CM and ICD-10-PCS." This final rule adopts modifications to standard medical data code sets for coding diagnoses and inpatient hospital procedures by adopting ICD-10-CM for diagnosis coding, including the Official ICD-10-CM Guidelines for Coding and Reporting, and ICD-10-PCS for inpatient hospital procedure coding, effective October 1, 2013.

Ingenix Learning: Implementing ICD-10

Pending passage of legislation before Congress at the time of this publication, the following timeline for ICD-10 coding systems is a distinct possibility.

Potential ICD-10 Implementation Timeline

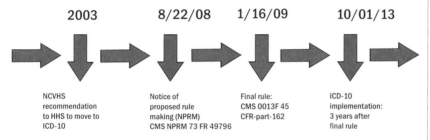

2003	8/22/08	1/16/09	10/01/13
NCVHS recommendation to HHS to move to ICD-10	Notice of proposed rule making (NPRM) CMS NPRM 73 FR 49796	Final rule: CMS 0013F 45 CFR-part-162	ICD-10 implementation: 3 years after final rule

Chapters and appendixes in the book address these pertinent issues about ICD-10-CM:

- **Chapter 1** provides an introduction to ICD-10-CM, including comparisons between clinical modifications from the WHO 10th revision of ICD, and ICD-9-CM.
- **Chapter 2** reviews the differences and similarities in coding rules and conventions found in ICD-10-CM, as compared with ICD-9-CM.
- **Chapter 3** explores each code family in ICD-10-CM and organizational changes made to disease classification.
- **Chapter 4** provides an introduction to the intended use, structure, and conventions of ICD-10-PCS, including comparisions to ICD-9-CM.
- **Chapter 5** provides an introduction to the general equivalence mappings (GEMs) for both ICD-10 coding systems.
- **Chapter 6** describes the impact of national standards under HIPAA on coding systems.
- **Chapter 7** examines documentation issues and considerations for ICD-10-CM.
- **Chapter 8** addresses various implementation issues inherent in the transition to ICD-10.
- **Appendix A** contains the ICD-10-CM Official Guidelines for Coding and Reporting.
- **Appendix B** contains the ICD-10-PCS Draft Coding Guidelines.
- **The glossary** provides definitions for terms and phrases frequently used throughout the book.
- **The index** facilitates easy lookups.

Chapter 1: Introduction to ICD-10-CM

OVERVIEW OF CHANGES

Before the clinical modifications to ICD-10 are reviewed and understood, you must first become familiar with the changes made by the World Health Organization when it moved from ICD-9 to ICD-10. The first clue to the revisions is in the full title: International Statistical Classification of Diseases and Related Health Problems. WHO felt this change would not only clarify the classification's content and purpose, but show how the scope of the classification has moved beyond the classification of disease and injuries to the coding of ambulatory care conditions and risk factors frequently encountered in primary care.

Overall, the tenth revision results in an increase in clinical detail and addresses information about previously classified diseases as well as those diseases discovered since the last revision. Conditions are grouped according to the most appropriate for general epidemiological purposes and the evaluation of health care. Organizational changes are made and new features added. However, for the most part the format and conventions of the classification remain unchanged.

Other adaptations of the ICD include:

- International Classification of Diseases for Oncology, third edition (ICD-O-3)
- International Classification of External Causes of Injury (ICECI)
- International Classification of Primary Care, second edition (ICPC-2)
- The ICD-10 for Mental and Behavioural Disorders Diagnostic Criteria for Research
- The ICD-10 for Mental and Behavioral Disorders Clinical Descriptions and Diagnostic Guidelines

In the United States, the clinical modification of ICD-10, ICD-10-CM, will replace the clinical modification of ICD-9, ICD-9-CM. The parent classification system, the International Classification of Disease (ICD), is owned and copyrighted by the World Health Organization (WHO), which publishes the classification. As with ICD-9-CM, the WHO authorized the development of an adaptation of ICD-10 for use in the United States. This adaptation, the Clinical Modification (CM), must conform to WHO conventions for the ICD.

Many of the codes considered new in ICD-10 may seem familiar to users of ICD-9-CM. This is because ICD-10 is a further evolution of the ICD-9 classification, as the ICD-10-CM is a further evolution of the ICD-9-CM. The underlying basic structure, conventions, and philosophy remain the same. The clinical modification in use in the United States (ICD-9-CM) has been maintained and updated annually since 1985. The following example illustrates the evaluation of these systems by showing how angina pectoris classifications have changed from the preclinical modification ICD-9 version to the current 2009 version of ICD-10-CM:

ICD-9

413	Angina pectoris

ICD-9-CM

411.1	Intermediate coronary syndrome (includes unstable angina)
413.0	Angina decubitus
413.1	Prinzmetal angina

OBJECTIVES

In this chapter you will learn:

- The purpose of ICD-10-CM
- The motivations for clinically modifying ICD-10
- About the many important uses of ICD-10 and ICD-10-CM beyond reimbursement

KEY POINT

This publication refers to the 2009 ICD-10-CM update.

| 413.9 | Other and unspecified angina pectoris — (includes angina of effort and stenocardia) |

ICD-10 and ICD-10-CM

All diseases of the circulatory system appear under the letter "I" in ICD-10.

I20.0	Unstable angina
I20.1	Angina pectoris with documented spasm — (includes Prinzmetal angina)
I20.8	Other forms of angina pectoris — (includes angina of effort and stenocardia)
I20.9	Angina pectoris, unspecified

No further additions have been made to the ICD-10 entries for angina pectoris in ICD-10-CM at the time of this publication.

ICD Structure

The WHO published ICD-10 in three volumes: an index, an instructional manual, and a tabular list. ICD-10-CM will be published in two volumes: an index and a tabular list.

Volume 1: Tabular List

Volume 1 contains the listing of alphanumeric codes. The same hierarchical organization of ICD-9 applies to ICD-10: All codes with the same first three digits have common traits. Each digit beyond three adds more specificity. In ICD-10, valid codes can contain anywhere from three to five digits. However, ICD-10-CM for use in the United States has been expanded with valid codes containing anywhere from three to seven characters. In some instances, the final character may be a lower case letter, known as an alpha extension, and not a number. In some cases, the use of a "reserve" subclassification (identified as an "x") has been incorporated into codes that continue with greater specificity beyond the fifth digit to allow for built-in expansion within that established level of specificity:

H83.3	Noise effects on inner ear
	Acoustic trauma of inner ear
	Noise-induced hearing loss of inner ear
H83.3x	Noise effects on inner ear
H83.3x1	Noise effects on right inner ear
H83.3x2	Noise effects on left inner ear
H83.3x3	Noise effects on inner ear, bilateral
H83.3x9	Noise effects on inner ear, unspecified ear

The same ICD-9-CM hierarchical organization is at work in ICD-10-CM notes and instructions. When a note appears under a three-character code, it applies to all codes within that rubric. For example, see the instructional note under category W22. The instructional notes at the category level apply to codes within the entire W22 category. Instructions under a specific code apply only to that single code. For example, see the Excludes1 note under code W22.041 which applies only to code W22.041.

W22	Striking against or struck by other objects
	Excludes1: striking against or struck by object with subsequent fall (W18.09)
	The following 7th character extensions are to be added to each code from category W22:
	A initial encounter
	D subsequent encounter
	Q sequelaes
W22.0	Striking against stationary object
	Excludes1: striking against stationary sports equipment (W21.8)
W22.01	Walked into wall
W22.02	Walked into lamppost
W22.03	Walked into furniture
W22.04	Striking against wall of swimming pool

KEY POINT

In ICD-10-CM, all codes and descriptions appear in bold font in the text.

W22.041   Striking against wall of swimming pool causing drowning and submersion

Excludes1:   drowning and submersion while swimming without striking against wall (W67)

W22.042   Striking against wall of swimming pool causing other injury

W22.09   Striking against other stationary object

The following is an example of the tabular listing in ICD-10, for international use:

Other Disorders of the Skin and Subcutaneous Tissue (L80-L99)

L80   Vitiligo

L81   Other disorders of pigmentation

Excludes: birthmark NOS (Q82.5)
naevus — see Alphabetic Index
Peutz-Jeghers syndrome (Q85.8)

L81.0   Postinflammatory hyperpigmentation

L81.1   Chloasma

L81.2   Freckles

L81.3   Café au lait spots

L81.4   Other melanin hyperpigmentation
Lentigo

L81.5   Leukoderma, not elsewhere classified

L81.6   Other disorders of diminished melanin formation

L81.7   Pigmented purpuric dermatosis
Angioma serpiginosum

L81.8   Other specified disorders of pigmentation
Iron pigmentation
Tattoo pigmentation

L81.9   Disorder of pigmentation, unspecified

L82   Seborrhoeic keratosis
Dermatosis papulosa nigra
Leser-Trélat disease

L83   Acanthosis nigricans
Confluent and reticulated papillomatosis

L84   Corns and callosities
Callus
Clavus

This is how the tabular list looks in ICD-10-CM for use in the United States:

Other Disorders of the Skin and Subcutaneous Tissue (L80-L99)

L80   Vitiligo

Excludes2:   vitiligo of eyelids (H02.73-)
vitiligo of vulva (N90.8)

L81   Other disorders of pigmentation

Excludes1:   birthmark NOS (Q82.5)
Peutz-Jeghers syndrome (Q85.8)

Excludes2:   nevus — see Alphabetic Index

L81.0   Postinflammatory hyperpigmentation

L81.1   Chloasma

L81.2   Freckles

L81.3   Café au lait spots

L81.4   Other melanin hyperpigmentation
Lentigo

L81.5   Leukoderma, not elsewhere classified

L81.6   Other disorders of diminished melanin formation

L81.7   Pigmented purpuric dermatosis
Angioma serpiginosum

KEY POINT

When an instructional note appears under a three-digit code, it applies to all codes within that rubric. However, an instructional note under a specific code applies only to that single code.

L81.8   Other specified disorders of pigmentation
     Iron pigmentation
     Tattoo pigmentation

L81.9   Disorder of pigmentation, unspecified

L82   **Seborrheic keratosis**
    Includes: dermatosis papulosa nigra
                Leser-Trélat disease
    Excludes2:   seborrheic dermatitis (L21.-)

L82.0   **Inflamed seborrheic keratosis**

L82.1   **Other seborrheic keratosis**
     Seborrheic keratosis NOS

L83   **Acanthosis nigricans**
    Includes: confluent and reticulated papillomatosis

L84   **Corns and callosities**
    Includes: callus
               clavus

KEY POINT

The current version of ICD-10-CM, code mappings, and coding guidelines are posted on the NCHS website: http://www.cdc.gov/nchs/about/otheract/icd9/icd10cm.htm.

Coding Guidelines/Instructional Manual

While ICD-10 is published in three volumes, it is expected that volume 2, the instructional manual for ICD-10, will not be used in the United States for morbidity coding. Instead, the NCHS will continue to post current versions of the official ICD-10-CM coding guidelines on the NCHS website. The NCHS will continue to release the official ICD-10-CM on CD, and private publishers will produce the ICD-10-CM books. At the time of this publication, the Cooperating Parties (CMS, NCHS, AHA, and AHIMA) are preparing to revise and finalize a 2009 version of the Official ICD-10-CM Coding Guidelines to accompany the 2009 code update. These updated guidelines will be posted to the NCHS website, similar to the previous July 2007 version. They are expected to be revised regularly (usually annually) by the Cooperating Parties, as were the ICD-9-CM guidelines. Additionally, these guidelines will continue to be published in the *AHA Coding Clinic for ICD-10-CM*.

Section I of the draft official ICD-10-CM guidelines address ICD-10-CM conventions, the general rules for use of the ICD-10-CM classification system, independent of the guidelines. These conventions include instructional notes and other features inherent to the index and tabular sections, which universally apply to all health care settings.

See chapter 2 of this publication for further information on ICD-10-CM coding conventions and guidelines.

See appendix A of this publication for the complete draft of the official ICD-10-CM guidelines.

Alphabetic Index

The alphabetic index provides a listing of the codes in the tabular list. As in the ICD-9-CM index, terms in the ICD-10 index are found alphabetically, by diagnosis. This is no different for ICD-10-CM. Therefore, a code for a supernumerary nipple would be accessed by looking under Supernumerary, then nipple. This is how the alphabetic index appears in ICD-10-CM:

Alphabetical Index to Diseases and Nature of Injury

Supernumerary (congenital)
    aortic cusps Q23.8
    auditory ossicles Q16.3
    bone Q79.8
    breast Q83.1
    carpal bones Q74.0
    cusps, heart valve NEC Q24.8
       aortic Q23.8

KEY POINT

The alphabetic index in ICD-10-CM functions similarly to the alphabetic index in ICD-9-CM, as the initial point of reference for proper code selection. Always refer to the tabular list to complete accurate code assignment.

```
    mitral Q23.2
    pulmonary Q22.3
digit(s) Q69.9
ear (lobule) Q17.0
fallopian tube Q50.6
finger Q69.0
hymen Q52.4
kidney Q63.0
lacrimonasal duct Q10.6
lobule (ear) Q17.0
mitral cusps Q23.2
muscle Q79.8
nipple(s) Q83.3
organ or site not listed - see Accessory
ossicles, auditory Q16.3
ovary Q50.31
oviduct Q50.6
pulmonary, pulmonary cusps Q22.3
rib Q76.6
    cervical or first (syndrome) Q76.5
roots (of teeth) K00.2
spleen Q89.09
tarsal bones Q74.2
teeth K00.1
    causing crowding M26.3
testis Q55.29
thumb Q69.1
toe Q69.2
uterus Q51.2
vagina Q52.1
vertebra Q76.49
```

ICD-10 Code Structure

All codes in ICD-10 and ICD-10-CM are alphanumeric, (i.e., one letter followed by two numbers at the three-character level), as opposed to the strictly numeric characters in the main classification of ICD-9-CM. Of the 26 available letters, all but the letter U is used, which was reserved for additions and changes that may need to be incorporated in the future or for classification difficulties that may arise between revisions. Codes for terrorism were created after September 11, 2001, within the framework of ICD-10 and ICD-9-CM. They have been incorporated into ICD-9-CM for 2002 and proposed for implementation in ICD-10 as U codes. The new U codes for terrorism have not officially been adopted by WHO yet and will be identified as U.S. codes by an asterisk to distinguish them from official ICD codes.

In ICD-10-CM, external causes due to acts of terrorism are classified to code category Y38. This category includes seven-character codes that identify injuries resulting from acts of terrorism, defined as "the unlawful use of force or violence against persons or property to intimidate or coerce a government, the civilian population, or any segment thereof, in furtherance of political or social objective." An additional code from category Y92 should be assigned to specify place of occurrence. The seventh character reports the encounter as A (Initial encounter), D (Subsequent encounter), or S (Sequela).

Some three-character categories have been left vacant for future expansion and revision. A listing of all ICD-10-CM three-digit categories is presented in the appendix to Ingenix Learning: ICD-10 Implementation.

 KEY POINT

While ICD-10 is published in three volumes, it is expected that volume 2, Instruction Manual, will not be used in the United States for purposes of morbidity coding. Coding guidelines are posted on the NCHS website. Check periodically for new and revised guidelines published before implementation and on an ongoing basis.

ICD-9-CM

Diseases of Arteries, Arterioles, and Capillaries (440–449)

440	Atherosclerosis
441	Aortic aneurysm and dissection
442	Other aneurysm
443	Other peripheral vascular disease
444	Arterial embolism and thrombosis
445	Atheroembolism
446	Polyarteritis nodosa and allied conditions
447	Other disorders of arteries and arterioles
448	Disease of capillaries
449	Septic arterial embolism

ICD-10-CM

Diseases of Arteries, Arterioles and Capillaries (I70-I79)

I70	Atherosclerosis
I71	Aortic aneurysm and dissection
I72	Other aneurysm
I73	Other peripheral vascular diseases
I74	Arterial embolism and thrombosis
I75	Atheroembolism
I76	Septic arterial embolism
I77	Other disorders of arteries and arterioles
I78	Diseases of capillaries
I79	Disorders of arteries, arterioles and capillaries in diseases classified elsewhere

The code structures of ICD-9-CM and ICD-10-CM are similar in that each classification system is maintained to be as congruent with the other as possible, pending transition. As ICD-9-CM expands its classification and code structure, ICD-10-CM is similarly expanded and maintained.

Though the use of alpha characters I and O may be confused with numbers 1 and 0, coders should remember that the first character in the ICD-10 system is always a letter, and the following characters are always numerical. Within ICD-10-CM, there is the exception of those codes containing an alpha extension in the final character position or a reserve subclassification, denoted as "x."

ICD-10 Category Restructuring

The review of the different diseases and how they are classified in ICD-9 resulted in the restructuring of some of the categories in ICD-10.

ICD-9-CM

In ICD-9-CM, a fifth digit in categories 433 and 434 identifies whether cerebra infarction is present. The three-digit category description identifies the condition to general anatomic sites as precerebral or cerebral. The fourth-digit subclassifications either further specify type of occlusion (434) or anatomic site (433).

The following fifth-digit subclassification is for use with category 433:

0	without mention of cerebral infarction
1	with cerebral infarction

433	Occlusion and stenosis of precerebral arteries
433.2	Vertebral artery

KEY POINT

It will be important for both providers of care and coders to understand how diseases are classified differently in ICD-10-CM as this change may affect the specific documentation that will be needed for coding.

For example, ICD-10-CM requires that coders capture specific anatomic sites and laterality, where documented.

ICD-10

In ICD-10, category I63 includes occlusion and stenosis of cerebral and precerebral arteries, resulting in cerebral infarction.

I63   Cerebral infarction
     I63.0   Cerebral infarction due to thrombosis of precerebral arteries
     I63.1   Cerebral infarction due to embolism of precerebral arteries
     I63.2   Cerebral infarction due to unspecified occlusion or stenosis of precerebral arteries
     I63.3   Cerebral infarction due to thrombosis of cerebral arteries
     I63.4   Cerebral infarction due to embolism of cerebral arteries
     I63.5   Cerebral infarction due to unspecified occlusion or stenosis of cerebral arteries
     I63.6   Cerebral infarction due to cerebral venous thrombosis, nonpyogenic
     I63.8   Other cerebral infarction
     I63.9   Cerebral infarction, unspecified

ICD-10-CM

In ICD-10-CM, further data granularity is incorporated to identify the affected artery (specific anatomic site) and laterality (left, right, or unspecified).

I63.0   Cerebral infarction due to thrombosis of precerebral arteries
     I63.00   Cerebral infarction due to thrombosis of unspecified precerebral artery
     I63.01   Cerebral infarction due to thrombosis of vertebral artery
         I63.011   Cerebral infarction due to thrombosis of right vertebral artery
         I63.012   Cerebral infarction due to thrombosis of left vertebral artery
         I63.019   Cerebral infarction due to thrombosis of unspecified vertebral artery

GENERAL ORGANIZATION OF ICD-10

In ICD-10, a chapter may encompass more than one letter and more than one chapter may share a letter.

- Chapter 2—Neoplasms (C00-D48)
- Chapter 3—Diseases of the Blood and Blood-Forming Organs and Certain Disorders Involving the Immune System (D50-D89)

Organizational Changes

The tabular list comprises 22 chapters versus the 17 main chapters and two supplementary classifications (V and E codes) for ICD-9-CM. As in ICD-9-CM, many of the chapters classify diseases of an organ or system. Others are devoted to specific types of conditions grouped according to etiology or nature, e.g., neoplasms, referred to in ICD-10 as "special group" chapters. Three chapters do not fall into either of these categories.

ICD-9-CM

Classification of Diseases and Injuries

1. Infectious and Parasitic Diseases (001–139)

2. Neoplasms (140–239)

3. Endocrine, Nutritional and Metabolic Diseases, and Immunity Disorders (240–279)

4. Diseases of the Blood and Blood-Forming Organs (280–289)

5. Mental Disorders (290–319)

6. Diseases of the Nervous System and Sense Organs (320–389)

 KEY POINT

E codes of ICD-9-CM become V codes, W codes, X codes, and Y codes in ICD-10.

And ICD-9-CM's V codes become Z codes in ICD-10.

ICD-10-CM CODES

V03.10xA	Pedestrian on foot injured in collision with car, pick-up truck or van in traffic accident, initial encounter
W52.xxxS	Crushed, pushed or stepped on by crowd or human stampede, sequelae
X37.0xxA	Hurricane, initial encounter
Y65.2	Failure in suture or ligature during surgical operation
Z80.49	Family history of malignant neoplasm of other genital organs

7. Diseases of the Circulatory System (390–459)

8. Diseases of the Respiratory System (460–519)

9. Diseases of the Digestive System (520–579)

10. Diseases of the Genitourinary System (580–629)

11. Complications of Pregnancy, Childbirth, and the Puerperium (630–679)

12. Diseases of the Skin and Subcutaneous Tissue (680–709)

13. Diseases of the Musculoskeletal System and Connective Tissue (710–739)

14. Congenital Anomalies (740–759)

15. Certain Conditions Originating in the Perinatal Period (760–779)

16. Symptoms, Signs, and Ill-Defined Conditions (780–799)

17. Injury and Poisoning (800–999)

18. Classification of Factors Influencing Health Status and Contact with Health Services (V Codes) (V01–V89)

19. Classification of External Causes of Injury and Poisoning (E Codes) (E800–E999)

ICD-10-CM

Classification of Diseases and Injuries

1. Certain Infectious and Parasitic Diseases (A00–B99)

2. Neoplasms (C00–D48)

3. Diseases of the Blood and Blood-Forming Organs and Certain Disorders Involving the Immune Mechanism (D50–D89)

4. Endocrine, Nutritional and Metabolic Diseases (E00–E90)

5. Mental and Behavioral Disorders (F01–F99)

6. Diseases of the Nervous System (G00–G99)

7. Diseases of the Eye and Adnexa (H00–H59)

8. Diseases of the Ear and Mastoid Process (H60–H95)

9. Diseases of the Circulatory System (I00–I99)

10. Diseases of the Respiratory System (J00–J99)

11. Diseases of the Digestive System (K00–K99)

12. Diseases of the Skin and Subcutaneous Tissue (L00–L99)

13. Diseases of the Musculoskeletal System and Connective Tissue (M00–M99)

14. Diseases of the Genitourinary System (N00–N99)

15. Pregnancy, Childbirth, and the Puerperium (O00–O99)

16. Certain Conditions Originating in the Perinatal Period (P00–P99)

17. Congenital Malformations, Deformations and Chromosomal Abnormalities (Q00–Q99)

18. Symptoms, Signs and Abnormal Clinical and Laboratory Findings, Not Elsewhere Classified (R00–R99)

19. Injury, Poisoning and Certain Other Consequences of External Causes (S00–T98)

 KEY POINT

The three chapters that do not fall into either the body system or the "special groups" are: "Symptoms, Signs and Abnormal Clinical and Laboratory Findings, Not Elsewhere Classified"; "External Causes of Morbidity and Mortality"; and "Factors Influencing Health Status and Contact with Health Services."

The revision of a chapter's title occurs for a variety of reasons. For example, the term "Complications of ..." had been removed from the title of the pregnancy chapter as a number of categories in chapter 15 describe uncomplicated deliveries.

20. External Causes of Morbidity and Mortality (V01–Y98)

21. Factors Influencing Health Status and Contact with Health Services (Z00–Z99)

In contrast to ICD-10-CM, ICD-10 contains the following chapter:

22. Codes for Special Purposes (U00–U99)

Chapter 20, "External Causes of Morbidity and Mortality," and chapter 21, "Factors Influencing Health Status and Contact with Health Services," are no longer considered to be supplementary, but are a part of the core classification.

Certain chapter titles have undergone revisions in ICD-10. For example, in ICD-9-CM, the title of chapter 5 is "Mental Disorders." In ICD-10-CM, it is "Mental and Behavioral Disorders." The term "certain" is added to the title of chapter 1, "Infectious and Parasitic Diseases" to stress the fact that localized infections are classified with the diseases of the pertinent body system. The title of the ICD-9-CM chapter of congenital anomalies is expanded to include "Congenital Malformations, Deformations and Chromosomal Abnormalities."

There also is a rearrangement of the chapter order from ICD-9-CM to ICD-10. This includes expanding the number of categories for disorders of the immune mechanism and placing them with diseases of the blood and blood-forming organs. In ICD-9-CM, these disorders are included with "Endocrine, Nutritional and Metabolic Diseases." The chapters for "Diseases of the Genitourinary System," "Pregnancy, Childbirth and the Puerperium," "Certain Conditions Originating in the Perinatal Period," and "Congenital Malformations, Deformations and Chromosomal Abnormalities" are placed sequentially in ICD-10.

Also, some conditions are reassigned to a different chapter due to advances in medical technology that have led to insights into the origins of those conditions. For example, in ICD-9-CM, gout is classified to chapter 3, "Endocrine, Nutritional, and Metabolic Diseases and Immunity Disorders," and in ICD-10, it is classified to chapter 13, "Diseases of the Musculoskeletal System and Connective Tissue." See chapter 3 for more information on disease reclassifications.

NEW FEATURES TO ICD-10-CM

There are a number of new features to ICD-10-CM with which users will need to become familiar. These additions provide clarity and facilitate proper use of the classification.

More Complete Descriptions

In ICD-9-CM, often the user must review the description of the category in order to determine the complete intent of the subcategory or subclassification. One needs to review the title of the category to understand the meaning of the code. In ICD-10-CM, the subcategory titles are usually complete, with the exception of some codes in the neoplasm and health circumstances sections.

ICD-9-CM

Typically, in ICD-9-CM, codes are presented in this fashion:

451   Phlebitis and thrombophlebitis
      451.0   of superficial vessels of lower extremities

ICD-10-CM

In ICD-10-CM, most codes have complete descriptions:

I80   Phlebitis and thrombophlebitis

 KEY POINT

One major difference in ICD-10-CM is that codes will have complete descriptions rather than relying on the hierarchy.

I80.0   Phlebitis and thrombophlebitis of superficial vessels of lower extremities

    I80.03   Phlebitis and thrombophlebitis of superficial vessels of lower extremities, bilateral

Postprocedural Disorders

Categories for postprocedural disorders specific to a particular body system have been created at the end of each body system chapter. There has been no change to the classification of those situations in which postprocedural conditions are not specific to a particular body system, such as postoperative hemorrhage. These are found in ICD-10-CM, chapter 19, "Injury, Poisoning and Certain Other Consequences of External Causes," which is compatible to ICD-9-CM.

ICD-9-CM

In ICD-9-CM, complications specific to the digestive system are not located under one category.

564   Functional digestive disorders, not elsewhere classified
    564.2   Postgastric surgery syndromes
    564.3   Vomiting following gastrointestinal surgery
    564.4   Other postoperative functional disorders
569   Other disorders of intestine
    569.6   Colostomy and enterostomy complications
        569.60   Colostomy and enterostomy complications, unspecified
        569.61   Infection of colostomy or enterostomy
        569.62   Mechanical complication of colostomy and enterostomy
        569.69   Other complication
    997.4   Digestive system complications

ICD-10-CM

In ICD-10 and ICD-10-CM, complications specific to the digestive system are located under category K91, with specific fourth- and fifth-digit subclassifications. The fourth-digit subclassifications for category K91 include:

K91   Intraoperative and postprocedural complications and disorders of digestive system, not elsewhere classified
    K91.0   Vomiting following gastrointestinal surgery
    K91.1   Postgastric surgery syndromes
    K91.2   Postsurgical malabsorption, not elsewhere classified
    K91.3   Postoperative intestinal obstruction
    K91.5   Postcholecystectomy syndrome
    K91.6   Intraoperative and postprocedural hemorrhage and hematoma complicating a digestive system procedure
    K91.7   Accidental puncture or laceration during a digestive system procedure
    K91.8   Other postprocedural disorders of digestive system, not elsewhere classified

Notes

The tenth revision contains some changes to instructional notes as well. At the beginning of each chapter, "excludes" notes were expanded to provide guidance on the hierarchy of chapters and to clarify the priority of code assignment.

ICD-10-CM

The following excludes note, found in chapter 14, indicates the priority of the "special group" chapters over the genitourinary system chapter.

DEFINITIONSS

Iatrogenic. Caused by or resulting from medical treatment as in an adverse reaction to a prescribed drug or a postoperative infection. Keep an eye out for this term as physicians may use it to describe a postprocedural disorder.

KEY POINT

"Excludes" notes are expanded in ICD-10 to clarify priority of code assignment and to provide guidance.

Diseases of the Genitourinary System (N00–N99)

Excludes2: certain conditions originating in the perinatal period (P04-P96)
certain infectious and parasitic diseases (A00-B99)
complications of pregnancy, childbirth and the puerperium (O00-O99)
congenital malformations, deformations and chromosomal
   abnormalities (Q00-Q99)
endocrine, nutritional and metabolic diseases (E00-E90)
injury, poisoning and certain other consequences of external causes
   (S00-T98)
neoplasms (C00-D48)
symptoms, signs and abnormal clinical and laboratory findings, not
   elsewhere classified (R00-R94)

ICD-10 Blocks

After the appropriate includes and excludes notes, each chapter starts with a list of the subchapters or "blocks" of three-character categories. These blocks provide an overview of the structure of the chapter.

The blocks for chapter 14 are:

N00–N08	Glomerular diseases
N10–N16	Renal tubulo-interstitial diseases
N17–N19	Acute renal failure and chronic kidney disease
N20–N23	Urolithiasis
N25–N29	Other disorders of kidney and ureter
N30–N39	Other diseases of the urinary system
N40–N51	Diseases of male genital organs
N60–N64	Disorders of breast
N70–N77	Inflammatory diseases of female pelvic organs
N80–N98	Noninflammatory disorders of female genital tract
N99	Intraoperative and postprocedural complications and disorders of genitourinary system, not elsewhere classified

SIGNIFICANT CHANGES TO ICD-10

Historically, three chapters in particular have had significant structural changes in the manner in which codes are "blocked" or grouped in to sections and therefore, classified:

- Chapter 5—Mental and Behavioral Disorders
- Chapter 19—Injury, Poisoning and Certain Other Consequences of External Causes
- Chapter 20—External Causes of Morbidity

Because major changes were made to these chapters, field-testing took place in a number of countries. In addition, WHO depended on technical support from specific groups in the revision. For example, the Nordic Medical Statistics Committee (NOMESCO) and the WHO Global Steering Committee on the Development of Indicators for Accidents had a major influence on the revision of the classification of injuries and external causes.

Chapter 5—Mental and Behavioral Disorders

Chapter 5 has undergone a number of revisions. The title has changed from Mental Disorders in ICD-9-CM, to Mental and Behavioral Disorders in ICD-10. This title remains the same in ICD-10-CM. Next, the number of subchapters was expanded from three to eleven.

ICD-9-CM

Chapter 5—Mental Disorders (290-319)

Psychoses (290-299)
Neurotic Disorders, Personality Disorders, and Other Nonpsychotic Mental Disorders (300-316)
Mental Retardation (317-319)

ICD-10

Chapter 5—Mental and Behavioural Disorders

F00–F09	Organic, including symptomatic, mental disorders
F10–F19	Mental and behavioural disorders due to psychoactive substance use
F20–F29	Schizophrenia, schizotypal and delusional disorders
F30–F39	Mood [affective] disorders
F40–F48	Neurotic, stress-related and somatoform disorders
F50–F59	Behavioural syndromes associated with physiological disturbances and physical factors
F60–F69	Disorders of adult personality and behaviour
F70–F79	Mental retardation
F80–F89	Disorders of psychological development
F90–F98	Behavioural and emotional disorders with onset usually occurring in childhood and adolescence
F99	Unspecified mental disorder

With this expansion, ICD-10 arranges specific disorders differently than they were in ICD-9-CM, and the clinical detail also is expanded.

ICD-10-CM

Chapter 5—Mental and Behavioral Disorders

F01–F09	Mental disorders due to known physiological conditions
F10–F19	Mental and behavioral disorders due to psychoactive substance use
F20–F29	Schizophrenia, schizotypal, delusional, and other non-mood psychotic disorders
F30–F39	Mood [affective] disorders
F40–F48	Anxiety, dissociative, stress-related, somatoform and other nonpsychotic mental disorders
F50–F59	Behavioral syndromes associated with physiological disturbances and physical factors
F60–F69	Disorders of adult personality and behavior
F70–F79	Mental retardation
F80–F89	Pervasive and specific developmental disorders
F90–F98	Behavioral and emotional disorders with onset usually occurring in childhood and adolescence
F99	Unspecified mental disorder

In the development of ICD-10-CM, some of the block titles and ranges within the chapters listed above have been changed.

ICD-9-CM

The ninth revision includes codes for a certain number of conditions that are drug induced.

292	Drug-induced mental disorders	
	292.0	Drug withdrawal
	292.1	Drug induced psychotic disorders
		292.11 Drug induced psycotic disorder with delusions
		292.12 Drug induced psycotic disorder with hallucinations
	292.2	Pathological drug intoxication
	292.8	Other specified drug induced mental disorders
		292.81 Drug induced delirium
		292.82 Drug induced persisting dementia
		292.83 Drug induced persisting amnestic disorder
		292.84 Drug induced mood disorder
		292.85 Drug induced sleep disorders
		292.89 Other
	292.9	Unspecified drug-induced mental disorder

ICD-10

In ICD-10, a number of categories are available to specify the drug induced mental and behavioral disorders due to psychoactive substance use. In addition, there are 10 fourth-character subdivisions to use with these categories to identify the specific mental and behavioral disorder, such as withdrawal state (.3) or withdrawal state with delirium (.4).

Mental and Behavioural Disorders Due to Psychoactive Substance Use (F10–F19)

F10	Mental and behavioural disorders due to use of alcohol
F11	Mental and behavioural disorders due to use of opioids
F12	Mental and behavioural disorders due to use of cannabinoids
F13	Mental and behavioural disorders due to use of sedatives or hypnotics
F14	Mental and behavioural disorders due to use of cocaine
F15	Mental and behavioural disorders due to use of other stimulants, including caffeine
F16	Mental and behavioural disorders due to use of hallucinogens
F17	Mental and behavioural disorders due to use of tobacco
F18	Mental and behavioural disorders due to use of volatile solvents
F19	Mental and behavioural disorders due to multiple drug use and use of other psychoactive substances

ICD-10-CM

ICD-10-CM includes additional revisions to this subchapter: Three other fourth-character subdivisions (except F17) identify abuse (.1), dependence (.2), or unspecified use (.9). Fifth and sixth-character subdivisions further specify the state of the mental and behavioral disorder, such as intoxication, intoxication with delirium, psychotic disorder with hallucinations, remission, or withdrawal.

Mental and Behavioral Disorders Due to Psychoactive Substance Use (F10–F19)

F10	Alcohol-related disorders
F11	Opioid-related disorders
F12	Cannabis-related disorders
F13	Sedative, hypnotic, or anxiolytic-related disorders
F14	Cocaine-related disorders
F15	Other stimulant-related disorders
F16	Hallucinogen-related disorders
F17	Nicotine dependence
F18	Inhalant-related disorders
F19	Other psychoactive substance-related disorders

FOR MORE INFO

ICD-10-CM includes additional revisions to the categories for drug induced mental and behavioral disorders due to psychoactive substance use.

Chapter 19—Injury, Poisoning, and Certain Other Consequences of External Causes

The axis of classification for chapter 19, "Injury, Poisoning and Certain Other Consequences of External Causes" (chapter 17, "Injury and Poisoning," in ICD-9-CM) changed from "type of injury" and "site of injury" in ICD-9-CM to "body region" and "type of injury" in ICD-10.

ICD-9-CM

"Fractures" is the first subchapter in the "Injury and Poisoning" chapter of ICD-9-CM. The breakdown is then by site, e.g., vault of skull, base of skull.

Chapter 17—Injury and Poisoning

	Fractures (800–829)
	Fracture of Skull (800–804)
800	Fracture of vault of skull
801	Fracture of base of skull
802	Fracture of face bones
803	Other and unqualified skull fractures
804	Multiple fractures involving skull or face with other bones

ICD-10

Chapter 19 in ICD-10 is a large chapter. It spans two letters, S00-T88. The S codes cover different injury types in relation to a particular, single body region, and the T codes cover injuries to unspecified or multiple body regions, poisonings, burns, frostbite, complications of care, and other consequences of external causes. The chapter, "Injury, Poisoning and Certain Other Consequences of External Causes" describes injuries to the head (the body region) and then breaks down the injury by type, (e.g., superficial injury of head, open wound of head).

Chapter 19—Injury, Poisoning and Certain Other Consequences of External Causes

	Injuries to the Head (S00–S09)
S00	Superficial injury of head
S01	Open wound of head
S02	Fracture of skull and facial bones
S03	Dislocation, sprain and strain of joints and ligaments of head
S04	Injury of cranial nerves
S05	Injury of eye and orbit
S06	Intracranial injury
S07	Crushing injury of head
S08	Traumatic amputation of part of head
S09	Other and unspecified injuries of head

Categories S03 and S08 have undergone title changes in ICD-10-CM:

S03	Dislocation and sprain of joints and ligaments of head
S08	Avulsion and traumatic amputation of part of head

Chapter 20—External Causes of Morbidity and Mortality

The chapter for external causes of morbidity and mortality also has been changed in a number of ways. In ICD-9-CM, the supplementary classification of external causes of injury and poisoning (E codes) is found at the end of the tabular list. In ICD-10, these codes follow chapter 19, "Injury, Poisoning and Certain Other Consequences of External Causes," and consist of categories V01–Y98. In addition, the transport accidents section of the external causes chapter has been completely revised and extended with blocks of categories identifying the victim's mode of transport.

ICD-9-CM

In ICD-9-CM, the main axis is whether the event was a traffic or non-traffic accident.

Supplementary Classification of External Causes of Injury and Poisoning (E800–E999)
        Railway accidents (E800–E807)
        Motor vehicle traffic accidents (E810–E819)
        Motor vehicle nontraffic accidents (E820–E825)
        Other road vehicle accidents (E826–E829)

ICD-10

In ICD-10 and ICD-10-CM, the main axis is the injured person's mode of transport. For land transport accidents, categories V01–V89, the vehicle of which the injured person is an occupant, or pedestrian status, is identified in the first two characters since it is perceived as the essential issue for prevention purposes. In ICD-10-CM, an additional category, V00, identifies pedestrian conveyance accidents due to falls, collisions with stationary objects, or other accidents not occurring with land transport vehicles.

Chapter 20—External Causes of Morbidity and Mortality (V01–Y98)

V01–X59	Accidents
V01–V99	Transport accidents
V01–V09	Pedestrian injured in transport accident
V10–V19	Pedal cyclist injured in transport accident
V20–V29	Motorcycle rider injured in transport accident
V30–V39	Occupant of three-wheeled motor vehicle injured in transport accident
V40–V49	Car occupant injured in transport accident
V50–V59	Occupant of pick-up truck or van injured in transport accident
V60–V69	Occupant of heavy transport vehicle injured in transport accident
V70–V79	Bus occupant injured in transport accident
V80–V89	Other land transport accidents
V90–V94	Water transport accidents
V95–V97	Air and space transport accidents
V98–V99	Other and unspecified transport accidents

Another change to this chapter is to the codes for sequelae of external causes. Previously, late-effect codes for external causes were located in various subchapters throughout the supplementary classification. In ICD-10, all late effects for each intent, i.e., accidents, suicide, etc., have been brought together in a block (subchapter), "Sequelae of External Causes of Morbidity and Mortality" (Y85–Y89). In ICD-10-CM, these are identified by the use of the alpha extensor for sequelae ("s") added to the code.

ICD-9-CM

E929	Late effects of accidental injury
E959	Late effects of self-inflicted injury
E969	Late effects of injury purposely inflicted by other person
E977	Late effects of injuries due to legal intervention
E989	Late effects of injury, undetermined whether accidentally or purposely inflicted
E999	Late effect of injury due to war operations and terrorism

ICD-10

Sequelae of External Causes of Morbidity and Mortality (Y85–Y89)

Y85	Sequelae of transport accidents
Y86	Sequelae of other accidents
Y87	Sequelae of intentional self-harm, assault and events of undetermined intent
Y88	Sequelae with surgical and medical care as external cause
Y89	Sequelae of other external causes

DEFINITIONS

Classification. The systematic arrangement, based on established criteria, of similar entities. ICD-10 is a disease classification. The particular criterion on which the arrangement is based is called the axis of classification. The primary axis of the disease classification as a whole is by anatomy. Other axes have been used, such as etiology and morphology.

DEFINITIONS

Late effect. A residual or sequela of a previous disease or injury.

ICD-10-CM

T47.7x2s Poisoning by emetics, intentional self-harm, sequela
T48.995s Adverse effect of other agents primarily acting on the respiratory system, sequela
V43.51s Car driver injured in collision with sport utility vehicle in traffic accident, sequela
V90.02s Drowning and submersion due to fishing boat overturning, sequela
W55.01s Bitten by cat, sequela
Y04.0s Assault by unarmed brawl or fight, sequela

MODIFICATION OF ICD-10

At the International Conference for the Tenth Revision of the International Classification of Diseases, a recommendation was made that "WHO should endorse the concept of an updating process between revisions..." Prior to this time there was no provision for updating the ICD between revisions, i.e., every 10 years. In October 1997, a mechanism was finalized to put an update process into operation. The nine WHO collaborating centers for classification of diseases and an update reference committee have been identified as coordinators and reviewers of proposed updates. With a timeline for issuance of amendments established, one should expect to see modifications to ICD-10 coming from the Secretariat at WHO.

History of the Modification

In May of 1994, the Centers for Disease Control and Prevention published an ICD-10 request for proposal (RFP). The contract sought the answer to the following questions:

1. Is ICD-10 such a significant improvement over ICD-9-CM for morbidity classification that it should be implemented in the United States?

2. Are there any codes or concepts in ICD-9-CM that have not been and should be included in ICD-10?

To answer these questions, the RFP required the contractor to perform an in-depth analysis addressing the following issues and to present recommendations in a report:

FOR MORE INFO

The WHO collaborating center for classification of diseases for the United States is the National Center for Health Statistics, 6525 Belcrest Road, Hyattsville, Maryland 20782.

- Strengths and weaknesses of ICD-10 as compared with ICD-9-CM for data collection on:
  - risk factors
  - severity of illness
  - primary care encounters
  - preventive health requirements
  - any other topics important to morbidity, as opposed to mortality, reporting
- Compatibility of the ICD-10 and ICD-9-CM codes for diagnosis, health status (V codes), and external cause (E codes)
- Ease of use of the ICD system
- Adaptability to computerized patient records
- Identification and review of improvements
- Review of and recommendations for change in the tabular notes
- Alternatives to the dagger/asterisk for morbidity application (this system helps identify secondary diagnoses)
- Review of the tabular section and index with an emphasis on whether the category assignments, which are based on mortality, remain appropriate for morbidity
- If the categories are different between ICD-9-CM and ICD-10, determination of what the impact would be on trend analysis

In September 1994, the Center for Health Policy Studies (CHPS) was awarded the contract to perform the in-depth evaluation of ICD-10. Phase One of the contract consisted of describing how significant the modifications to ICD-10 were expected to be and, if made, how such revisions would impact comparability between the two systems. Any problems identified were to be accompanied by solutions. The development of a revised alphabetic index and crosswalk between ICD-9-CM and ICD-10-CM was also a part of Phase One.

Phase One

The contractor formed a Technical Advisory Panel (TAP) to perform the evaluation. The 20 members came from the health care and coding community. They included federal members from the Agency for Health Care Policy and Research (CMS and NCHS), nonfederal members from the hospital and physician environment, and classification experts. After evaluating ICD-10, CHPS provided the following goals for a clinical modification of ICD-10:

- Return to the level of specificity implemented in ICD-9-CM
- Facilitate alphabetic index use to assign codes
- Modify code titles and language to enhance consistency with accepted U.S. clinical practice
- Modify the dagger and asterisk codes
- Remove codes unique to mortality coding and those designed for the needs of emerging nations
- Remove procedure codes included with diagnosis codes
- Remove "multiple codes"

In answer to the main questions posed in the evaluation contract, CHPS indicated that ICD-10 is not a significant improvement over ICD-9-CM for morbidity classification, and that a clinical modification should be implemented in the United States that would include the codes or concepts lacking in ICD-10.

Phase Two

Phase Two consisted of further refinement of the clinical modification based on the draft created under the evaluation study. Since WHO holds a copyright on ICD-10, there are specific rules regarding changes. WHO requirements include the following:

- Title changes cannot alter the meaning of the category or code.
- There must be limited modifications to the three and four character codes.

During this phase, ICD-10 was looked at from the standpoint of creating codes for ambulatory and managed-care encounters, clinical decision-making, and outcomes research. This phase also involved a review by physician groups and others to assure clinical accuracy. The reviewers for this phase included the following:

- American Academy of Pediatrics
- American Academy of Neurology
- American College of Obstetricians and Gynecologists
- American Urological Association
- National Association of Children's Hospitals and Related Institutions
- American Burn Association
- Burn Foundation
- ANSI Z16.2 Workgroup
- American Academy of Dermatology

 KEY POINT

In addition to being a member of the TAP, CMS is also responsible for the replacement to Volume 3, the procedure classification of ICD-9-CM. Chapter 5 provides you with the information on ICD-10-PCS.

- CDC Diabetes Program
- National Center for Injury Prevention and Control
- National Center for Infectious Diseases
- National Center for Chronic Disease and Prevention & Health Promotion
- Veterans Administration's National Diabetes Program

During Phase Two, focused reviews were performed. This examination included the evaluation of residual categories to decide if further specificity was needed. An analysis also was made of previous ICD-9-CM coordination and maintenance committee recommendations where adoption was not possible due to ICD-9-CM space limitations.

Phase Three

The third phase involved a review of the public comments on the proposed ICD-10-CM released to the public in the winter of 1997. More than 1,200 comments from more than 20 organizations were received. Phase Three reviewers included the American Academy of Ophthalmology, American Academy of Orthopedic Surgeons, Johns Hopkins Injury Center, and Pennsylvania Head Injury Center.

As a result of these three phases, there were thousands of clinical modifications made to ICD-10.

Fourth, Fifth, Sixth, and Seventh Character Addition

To be able to have the desired specificity, fifth, sixth, and seventh characters were added throughout the classification. These characters may identify such things as more specificity about a disorder, whether the patient's condition exists on the right or left side, the trimester in which the patient is experiencing problems, and whether the encounter was initial, subsequent, or with sequelae. Here's an example of added specificity at the fifth digit:

ICD-10
P78.8   Other specified perinatal digestive system disorders

ICD-10-CM
P78.8   Other specified perinatal digestive system disorders
      P78.81   Congenital cirrhosis (of liver)
      P78.82   Peptic ulcer of newborn
      P78.89   Other specified perinatal digestive system disorders

Here's a sample of the trimester specified with a sixth digit:

ICD-10
O99.0   Anemia complicating pregnancy, childbirth and the puerperium

ICD-10-CM
O99.0   Anemia complicating pregnancy, childbirth and the puerperium
      O99.01   Anemia complicating pregnancy
            O99.011   Anemia complicating pregnancy, first trimester
            O99.012   Anemia complicating pregnancy, second trimester
            O99.013   Anemia complicating pregnancy, third trimester
            O99.019   Anemia complicating pregnancy, unspecified trimester

The following examples demonstrate laterality at the sixth-digit level and the encounter status in the seventh character:

DEFINITIONS

Residual category. A place for classifying a specified form of a condition that does not have its own specific subdivision.

ICD-10

S72   Fracture of femur
    S72.0   Fracture of neck of femur
        S72.00   Closed fracture of neck of femur

ICD-10-CM

S72   Fracture of femur
    S72.0   Fracture of head and neck of femur
        S72.00   Fracture of unspecified part of neck of femur
            S72.001   Fracture of unspecified part of neck of right femur

S72.001A	Fracture of unspecified part of neck of right femur, initial encounter for closed fracture
S72.001B	Fracture of unspecified part of neck of right femur, initial encounter for open fracture type I or II
S72.001C	Fracture of unspecified part of neck of right femur, initial encounter for open fracture type IIIA, IIIB, or IIIC
S72.001D	Fracture of unspecified part of neck of right femur, subsequent encounter for closed fracture with routine healing
S72.001E	Fracture of unspecified part of neck of right femur, subsequent encounter for open fracture type I or II with routine healing
S72.001F	Fracture of unspecified part of neck of right femur, subsequent encounter for open fracture type IIIA, IIIB, or IIIC with routine healing
S72.001G	Fracture of unspecified part of neck of right femur, subsequent encounter for closed fracture with delayed healing
S72.001H	Fracture of unspecified part of neck of right femur, subsequent encounter for open fracture type I or II with delayed healing
S72.001J	Fracture of unspecified part of neck of right femur, subsequent encounter for open fracture type IIIA, IIIB, or IIIC with delayed healing
S72.001K	Fracture of unspecified part of neck of right femur, subsequent encounter for closed fracture with nonunion
S72.001M	Fracture of unspecified part of neck of right femur, subsequent encounter for open fracture type I or II with nonunion
S72.001N	Fracture of unspecified part of neck of right femur, subsequent encounter for open fracture type IIIA, IIIB, or IIIC with nonunion
S72.001P	Fracture of unspecified part of neck of right femur, subsequent encounter for closed fracture with malunion

S72.001Q   Fracture of unspecified part of neck of right femur, subsequent encounter for open fracture type I or II with malunion

S72.001R   Fracture of unspecified part of neck of right femur, subsequent encounter for open fracture type IIIA, IIIB, or IIIC with malunion

S72.001S   Fracture of unspecified part of neck of right femur, sequela

INCORPORATION OF COMMON SUBCLASSIFICATIONS

In ICD-10, fourth-digit and fifth-digit subdivisions were often provided for optional use. In ICD-10-CM these subdivisions are incorporated into the code listing thus making them a required component of the code's use. In addition, full code titles are adopted in ICD-10-CM to provide a clear understanding of the code's meaning.

ICD-10

S52   Fracture of forearm

The following subdivisions are provided for optional use in a supplementary character position where it is not possible or not desired to use multiple coding to identify fracture and open wound; a fracture not indicated as closed or open should be classified as closed.

    0   closed
    1   open

Excludes: fracture at wrist and hand level (S62.-)

S52.0   **Fracture of upper end of ulna**
    Coronoid process
    Elbow NOS
    Monteggia's fracture-dislocation
    Olecranon process
    Proximal end

ICD-10-CM

S52   Fracture of forearm
    A fracture not identified as displaced or nondisplaced should be coded to displaced.
    Excludes1:   traumatic amputation of forearm (S58.-)
    Excludes2:   fracture at wrist and hand level (S62.-)
    The appropriate seventh character is to be added to each code from category S52
    A fracture not designated as open or closed should be coded to closed.
    The open fracture designations are based on the Gustilo open fracture classification.
    The following extensions are to be added to each code for category S52:
    A   initial encounter for closed fracture
    B   initial encounter for open fracture type I or II
    C   initial encounter for open fracture type IIIA, IIIB, or IIIC
    D   subsequent encounter for closed fracture with routine healing
    E   subsequent encounter for open fracture type I or II with routine healing
    F   subsequent encounter for open fracture type IIIA, IIIB, or IIIC with routine healing
    G   subsequent encounter for closed fracture with delayed healing
    H   subsequent encounter for open fracture type I or II with delayed healing
    J   subsequent encounter for open fracture type IIIA, IIIB, or IIIC with delayed healing
    K   subsequent encounter for closed fracture with nonunion
    M   subsequent encounter for open fracture type I or II with nonunion
    N   subsequent encounter for open fracture type IIIA, IIIB, or IIIC with nonunion
    P   subsequent encounter for closed fracture with malunion
    Q   subsequent encounter for open fracture type I or II with malunion
    R   subsequent encounter for open fracture type IIIA, IIIB, or IIIC with malunion
    S   sequela

 KEY POINT

The modifications to ICD-10 will provide the detail required for morbidity coding in the United States, thereby meeting the goal for more comprehensive and qualitative patient data for all uses and users.

S52.0   Fracture of upper end of ulna
        Fracture of proximal end of ulna
        Excludes2:   fracture of elbow NOS (S42.40-)
                    Fractures of shaft of ulna (S52.2-)

    S52.00   Unspecified fracture of upper end of ulna
        S52.001   Unspecified fracture of upper end of right ulna
        S52.002   Unspecified fracture of upper end of left ulna
        S52.009   Unspecified fracture of upper end of unspecified ulna

    S52.01   Torus fracture of upper end of ulna
        Note: Open fracture seventh characters do not apply to codes under subcategory S52.01
        S52.011   Torus fracture of upper end of right ulna
        S52.012   Torus fracture of upper end of left ulna
        S52.019   Torus fracture of upper end of unspecified ulna

Laterality

In the past, there have been proposals to the ICD-9-CM coordination and maintenance committee to add laterality codes (i.e., right, left, or bilateral). This has been done in ICD-10-CM; however, ICD-10-CM does not add laterality in all cases. The majority of codes affected by this modification are found in the neoplasm and injury chapters.

ICD-10

C56   Malignant neoplasm of ovary

ICD-10-CM

C56   Malignant neoplasm of ovary
    Use additional code to identify any functional activity
    C56.0   Malignant neoplasm of right ovary
    C56.1   Malignant neoplasm of left ovary
    C56.9   Malignant neoplasm of ovary, unspecified side

Trimester Specificity for Obstetrical Coding

Neither ICD-9 nor ICD-10 expands the codes in the "Pregnancy, Childbirth and the Puerperium" chapter to specify circumstances surrounding the pregnancy. In ICD-9-CM, a fifth-digit subdivision denotes the current episode of care. The episode of care is defined as the encounter in which the patient is receiving care, whether delivery occurred during that encounter, or an antepartum or postpartum condition is being treated without delivery occurring during that episode of care. The fifth digits from ICD-9-CM were not adopted for ICD-10-CM. Instead, the last character in the code reports the patient's trimester. Because certain obstetric conditions or complications occur at only one point in the obstetric period, not all codes will include all three trimesters or a character to describe the trimester at all.

ICD-10

O60   Preterm delivery
    Onset (spontaneous) of delivery before 37 completed weeks of gestation.

ICD-10-CM

O60   Preterm labor
    Includes: onset (spontaneous) of labor before 37 completed weeks of gestation
    Excludes1:   false labor (O47.0-)
                 threatened labor NOS (O47.0-)
    O60.0   Preterm labor without delivery
        O60.00   Preterm labor without delivery, unspecified trimester
        O60.02   Preterm labor without delivery, second trimester
        O60.03   Preterm labor without delivery, third trimester

 DEFINITIONS

Trimester. A period of three months. The first trimester is the period of pregnancy from the first day of the last normal menstrual period through the completion of 13 weeks of gestation. The second trimester is the period of pregnancy from the beginning of the 14th through the 27th completed week of gestation. The third trimester is the period of pregnancy from the beginning of the 28th week until delivery.

Expansion of Alcohol & Drug Codes

Although ICD-10 had already made major changes to chapter 5, "Mental and Behavioral Disorders," analysis of the codes for disorders due to alcohol and drug use has resulted in further modifications. The ICD-10 codes were reviewed for ways to better describe these disorders due to psychoactive substance use.

The result is the identification of the effects of use (e.g., abuse and dependence) at the fourth-digit level, the specific aspects to the use (e.g., withdrawal), at the fifth-digit level, and some of the manifestations (e.g., delirium), at the sixth-digit level.

ICD-10

F10.–   Mental and behavioural disorders due to use of alcohol

.0	Acute intoxication
.1	Harmful use
.2	Dependence syndrome
.3	Withdrawal state
.4	Withdrawal state with delirium
.5	Psychotic disorder
.6	Amnesic syndrome
.7	Residual and late-onset psychotic disorder
.8	Other mental and behavioural disorders
.9	Unspecified mental and behavioural disorder

ICD-10-CM

F10   Alcohol-related disorders

    Use additional code for blood alcohol level, if applicable (Y90.-)

    F10.1   Alcohol abuse

       Excludes1:   alcohol dependence (F10.2-)
                    alcohol use, unspecified (F10.9-)

       F10.10   Alcohol abuse, uncomplicated

       F10.12   Alcohol abuse with intoxication

          F10.120   Alcohol abuse with intoxication, uncomplicated

          F10.121   Alcohol abuse with intoxication delirium

          F10.129   Alcohol abuse with intoxication, unspecified

       F10.14   Alcohol abuse with alcohol-induced mood disorder

       F10.15   Alcohol abuse with alcohol-induced psychotic disorder

          F10.150   Alcohol abuse with alcohol-induced psychotic disorder with delusions

          F10.151   Alcohol abuse with alcohol-induced psychotic disorder with hallucinations

          F10.159   Alcohol abuse with alcohol-induced psychotic disorder, unspecified

       F10.18   Alcohol abuse with other alcohol-induced disorders

          F10.180   Alcohol abuse with alcohol-induced anxiety disorder

          F10.181   Alcohol abuse with alcohol-induced sexual dysfunction

          F10.182   Alcohol abuse with alcohol-induced sleep disorder

          F10.188   Alcohol abuse with other alcohol-induced disorder

       F10.19   Alcohol abuse with unspecified alcohol-induced disorder

KEY POINT

In ICD-10-CM, sixth digits may identify:

- Trimester
- Laterality
- Certain manifestations

Expansion of Injury Codes

To further enhance the restructuring of chapter 19, "Injury, Poisoning and Certain Other Consequences of External Causes," ICD-10-CM will provide codes to further specify the type and site of the injury. Also, as mentioned previously, subdivisions have been incorporated into the code listing, thus making them a required component of the code's use.

ICD-10

S51   Open wound of forearm
                Excludes: open wound of wrist and hand (S61.-)
                                        traumatic amputation of forearm (S58.-)

        S51.0   Open wound of elbow

ICD-10-CM

S51   Open wound of elbow and forearm
                Code also any associated wound infection
                Excludes 1:   open fracture of elbow and forearm (S52.- with open fracture
                                        extensions)
                                        traumatic amputation of elbow and forearm (S58.-)
                Excludes 2:   open wound of wrist and hand (S61.-)

                The following extensions are to be added to each code for category S51
                a   initial encounter
                d   subsequent encounter
                s   sequela

        S51.0   Open wound of elbow
                S51.00   Unspecified open wound of elbow
                                S51.001   Unspecified open wound of right elbow
                                S51.002   Unspecified open wound of left elbow
                                S51.009   Unspecified open wound of unspecified elbow
                S51.01   Laceration without foreign body of elbow
                                S51.011   Laceration without foreign body of right elbow
                                S51.012   Laceration without foreign body of left elbow
                                S51.019   Laceration without foreign body of unspecified
                                                  elbow
                S51.02   Laceration with foreign body of elbow
                                S51.021   Laceration with foreign body of right elbow
                                S51.022   Laceration with foreign body of left elbow
                                S51.029   Laceration with foreign body of unspecified
                                                  elbow
                S51.03   Puncture wound without foreign body of elbow
                                S51.031   Puncture wound without foreign body of right
                                                  elbow
                                S51.032   Puncture wound without foreign body of left
                                                  elbow
                                S51.039   Puncture wound without foreign body of
                                                  unspecified elbow
                S51.04   Puncture wound with foreign body of elbow
                                S51.041   Puncture wound with foreign body of right elbow
                                S51.042   Puncture wound with foreign body of left elbow
                                S51.049   Puncture wound with foreign body of unspecified
                                                  elbow
                S51.05   Open bite of elbow
                                Bite of elbow NOS
                                Excludes1:   superficial bite of elbow (S50.36, S50.37)
                                S51.051   Open, bite, right elbow
                                S51.052   Open bite, left elbow
                                S51.059   Open bite, unspecified elbow

 KEY POINT

Health care providers will need to be educated on the additional details required to be documented in the medical record in order to code injuries. For example, with the reporting of laterality, providers will need to document where the injury occurred.

S51.8   Open wound of forearm
           Excludes2:   open wound of elbow (51.0-)
           S51.80   Unspecified open wound of forearm
                        S51.801   Unspecified open wound of right forearm
                        S51.802   Unspecified open wound of left forearm
                        S51.809   Unspecified open wound of unspecified forearm

DEFINITIONS

Principal diagnosis. The Uniform Hospital Discharge Data Set defines as "that condition established after study to be chiefly responsible for occasioning the admission of the patient to the hospital for care." This definition applies only to inpatients in acute, short-term, general hospitals.

Combination Codes

A combination code is a single code used to classify two diagnoses, or a diagnosis with an associated manifestation or complication. Combination codes may be identified by subterm entries in the alphabetic index or by instructional notes in the tabular list. Assign only the combination code that fully identifies the diagnostic conditions documented. Multiple coding should not be used when combination codes clearly identify all of the elements documented in the diagnostic statement. Alternately, if a combination code does not adequately describe the nature of the associated manifestation or complication, an additional code should be assigned.

ICD-10

K50   Crohn's disease [regional enteritis]
         Includes: granulomatous enteritis
         Excludes: ulcerative colitis (K51.-)
         K50.0   Crohn's disease of small intestine
                    Crohn's disease [regional enteritis] of:
                      duodenum
                      ileum
                      jejunum
                      Ileitis:
                      regional
                      terminal
                    Excludes: with Crohn's disease of large intestine (K50.8)

ICD-10-CM

K50   Crohn's disease [regional enteritis]
         Includes: granulomatous enteritis
         Excludes1:   ulcerative colitis (K51.-)
         Use additional code to identify manifestations, such as:
           pyoderma gangrenosum (L88)
         K50.0   Crohn's disease of small intestine
                    Crohn's disease [regional enteritis] of duodenum
                    Crohn's disease [regional enteritis] of ileum
                    Crohn's disease [regional enteritis] of jejunum
                    Regional ileitis
                    Terminal ileitis
                    Excludes1:   Crohn's disease of both small and large intestine (K50.8-)
                    K50.00   Crohn's disease of small intestine without complications
                    K50.01   Crohn's disease of small intestine with complications
                                K50.011   Crohn's disease of small intestine with rectal bleeding
                                K50.012   Crohn's disease of small intestine with intestinal obstruction
                                K50.013   Crohn's disease of small intestine with fistula
                                K50.014   Crohn's disease of small intestine with abscess
                                K50.018   Crohn's disease of small intestine with other complications
                                K50.019   Crohn's disease of small intestine with unspecified complications

Combination of Dagger and Asterisk Codes

In ICD-9 and ICD-10, WHO provides a classification scheme in which certain disease entities may be classified twice, once according to etiology or cause of the disease and once according to its manifestations or symptoms. The coder can choose to use one code or the other. In ICD-9-CM and ICD-10-CM, this dual classification was eliminated. In certain ICD-10-CM classifications, the manifestation merged with the etiology codes.

ICD-10

A02.2†   Localized salmonella infections
       Salmonella:
         arthritis (M01.3*)
         meningitis (G01*)
         osteomyelitis (M90.2*)
         pneumonia (J17.0*)
         renal tubulo-interstitial disease (N16.0*)

ICD-10-CM

A02.2   Localized salmonella infections
     A02.20   Localized salmonella infection, unspecified
     A02.21   Salmonella meningitis
     A02.22   Salmonella pneumonia
     A02.23   Salmonella arthritis
     A02.24   Salmonella osteomyelitis
     A02.25   Salmonella pyelonephritis
         Salmonella tubulo-interstitial nephropathy
     A02.29   Salmonella with other localized infection

Movement of Categories

The ICD-10-CM reviewers identified the need to move additional disease categories from one chapter to another as the types of conditions grouped under the ICD-10 category were better classified elsewhere.

ICD-10

Diseases of the Digestive System (K00–K93)
K07   Dentofacial anomalies [including malocclusion]
K10   Other diseases of jaw

ICD-10-CM

Diseases of the Musculoskeletal System and Connective Tissue (M00–M99)
M26   Dentofacial anomalies [including malocclusion]
M27   Other diseases of jaws

Expansion of Postoperative Complication Codes

Building on ICD-10's new feature of adding codes for postprocedural disorders to particular body system chapters, NCHS expands ICD-10-CM further by deactivating codes found in chapter 19, "Injury, Poisoning and Certain Other Consequences of External Causes," and adding these conditions to the body system chapters.

ICD-10

T81.0   Hemorrhage and hematoma complicating a procedure, not elsewhere classified
T81.2   Accidental puncture and laceration during a procedure, not elsewhere classified

ICD-10-CM

Codes T81.0 and T81.2 have been deactivated in ICD-10-CM. In previous updates, a notation was placed into the tabular list for deactivated codes. For the 2009 update, this notation has been removed from tabular list sections where codes T81.0 and T81.2 were

---

CODING AXIOM

ICD-9 and ICD-10 provide the dual classification scheme in which certain disease entities may be classified twice, once according to etiology of the disease and once according to its manifestations. This is called the dagger and asterisk system.

---

previously classified. However, the following notation is an example of such a notation as listed in the 2009 update:

Categories T00–T06 deactivated. Code to individual injuries.

K91.6   Intraoperative hemorrhage and hematoma of a digestive system organ or structure complicating a procedure
    Excludes1:   intraoperative hemorrhage and hematoma of a digestive system organ or structure due to accidental puncture and laceration during a procedure (K91.7-)
    K91.61   Intraoperative hemorrhage and hematoma of a digestive system organ or structure complicating a digestive system procedure
    K91.62   Intraoperative hemorrhage and hematoma of a digestive system organ or structure complicating other procedure
K91.7   Accidental puncture and laceration of a digestive system organ or structure during a procedure
    K91.71   Accidental puncture and laceration of a digestive system organ or structure during a digestive system procedure
    K91.72   Accidental puncture and laceration of a digestive system organ or structure during other procedure

Deactived Codes

To meet data-gathering goals desired by the federal government for coding in the United States, some codes that are valid in ICD-10 have been deactivated for ICD-10-CM. These codes fall into several categories that are considered by NCHS and CMS to be highly unspecified. To maintain international data-gathering requirements, deactivated ICD-10 codes cannot be reassigned in ICD-10-CM.

Procedure Codes

Some ICD-10 codes actually identify a procedure, rather than a disease or health status. These codes were reviewed and a determination was made to either deactivate them, or in some instances to revise the category title. For example:

ICD-10
Z23   Need for immunization against single bacterial diseases
Z24   Need for immunization against certain single viral diseases
Z25   Need for immunization against other single viral diseases
Z26   Need for immunization against other single infectious diseases
Z27   Need for immunization against combinations of infectious diseases
Z28   Immunization not carried out
Z29   Need for other prophylactic measures

ICD-10-CM
Z23   Encounter for immunization
    Code first any routine childhood examination
    Note: procedure codes are required to identify the types of immunizations given.
Z24   deactivated
Z25   deactivated
Z26   deactivated
Z27   deactivated
Z28   Immunization not carried out
Z29   deactivated

Categories Z24–Z27 and Z29 have been deactivated and category Z23 has been retitled.

Highly Nonspecific Codes

ICD-10 includes codes for "multiple" injuries. In ICD-10-CM, these nonspecific multiple codes have been deactivated. Coders will, instead, be expected to report multiple, individual codes to describe specific injuries.

KEY POINT

Not all codes in ICD-10 are available in ICD-10-CM. Some are deactivated by NCHS to meet federal data-gathering goals.

ICD-10

S30.7   Multiple superficial injuries of abdomen, lower back and pelvis
S49.7   Multiple injuries of shoulder and upper arm

ICD-10-CM

S30.7   deactivated
S49.7   deactivated

Other codes providing overly generalized information have also been deleted, such as:

A16   Respiratory tuberculosis, not confirmed bacteriologically or histologically

For the purpose of tracking disease and health-related issues in the United States, codes associated with conditions in which the death occurs without contact with medical authorities are not appropriate to U.S. reporting. These codes, used in mortality reporting for ICD-10, have been deleted in ICD-10-CM. Some examples include:

R98   Unattended death
S18   Traumatic amputation at neck level
R95   Sudden infant death syndrome

Notes

In addition to the analysis of the codes themselves, the notes in ICD-10 were reviewed. Many of the clinical modifications reflect the addendum to ICD-9-CM published over the years, while others were added as new codes to ICD-10-CM.

ICD-10

C34   Malignant neoplasm of bronchus and lung

ICD-10-CM

This excludes note was added because of the addition of codes C46.50–C46.52 for Kaposi's sarcoma of the lung.

C34   Malignant neoplasm of bronchus and lung
         Excludes1:   Kaposi's sarcoma of lung (C46.5-)

ICD-10

D05   Carcinoma in situ of breast
         Excludes1:   carcinoma in situ of skin of breast (D04.5)
                       melanoma in situ of breast (skin) (D03.5)

ICD-10-CM

The note for Paget's disease is found in ICD-9-CM.

D05   Carcinoma in situ of breast
         Excludes1:   carcinoma in situ of skin of breast (D04.5)
                       melanoma in situ of breast (skin) (D03.5)
                       Paget's disease of breast or nipple (C50.-)

DEFINITIONS

Deactivation. Tthe code will not be available for use in coding. This helps maintain international data-gathering goals.

DISCUSSION QUESTIONS

1. What are some reasons for clinically modifying ICD-10 in the United States?

   _____

   _____

   _____

2. Iatrogenic illnesses have been relocated in ICD-10-CM. Where do they occur?

   _____

   _____

   _____

3. How are dagger and asterisk codes handled in ICD-10-CM?

   _____

   _____

   _____

4. For what reasons would ICD-10 codes would be deactivated in ICD-10-CM?

   _____

   _____

   _____

Chapter 2: ICD-10-CM Coding Conventions

Now that you have an understanding of the overall clinical modifications made to ICD-10, it is time to build on that knowledge and examine the conventions of the ICD-10-CM system. While many of the rules have not changed, there are others that are new, expanded, or deleted. The rules must be understood to accurately apply them and to assign a correct code from ICD-10-CM.

Both the tabular list, volume 1, and the alphabetic index, volume 3, contain conventions. Some of the rules are unique to one volume or the other. For example, the "excludes" note is found only in the tabular list. Other conventions are found in both volumes, such as the use of the term "with" to indicate certain codes that have been provided for diseases in combination.

Prior to reviewing these various conventions, this chapter provides an explanation of the overall arrangement of ICD-10-CM. Chapter 1 introduced you to the contents of ICD-10-CM, while this chapter gives the general order of each volume to help you become more comfortable with the classification system. As you will see, ICD-10-CM is not so foreign. Much of what we are familiar with as users of ICD-9-CM remains a part of ICD-10-CM.

Coding guidelines for ICD-10-CM need to be carefully reviewed as part of orientation and training. Coders will need to be as well versed in application of the guidelines for the new system as they were with coding guidelines for ICD-9-CM. Guidelines for coding and reporting with ICD-10-CM appear on the official government version of the ICD-10-CM and on the NCHS website: http://www.cdc.gov/nchs/about/otheract/icd9/icd10cm.html.

At this point, ICD-10-CM coding guidelines mainly follow logic similar to ICD-9-CM coding guidelines. However, there are some significant differences that correlate to the increased granularity of the new coding system. For example:

- Pre-existing complications from diabetes in a post pancreas transplant patient are classified with codes from the diabetes categories to describe the complications.
- Classification of intrauterine death and stillbirth differs from ICD-9-CM. Code O02.1 Intrauterine death is used on the maternal record only. Code P95 Stillbirth is used on the baby's record only.
- Many manifestations associated with a disease process are included in the code, minimizing or sometimes eliminating the need for dual coding. For example:
  — Angina can now be reported with atherosclerotic heart disease using a single code, negating complex sequencing instructions.
  — Crohn's disease of large intestine with intestinal obstruction is reported with a single code.

It will be necessary to continue to keep current with the guidelines as they are updated. Coders need to review all sections of the guidelines to fully understand all of the rules and instructions to code properly. There are no codes for procedures in ICD-10-CM.

OBJECTIVES

In this chapter, you will learn:

- The general arrangement of ICD-10-CM
- The conventions in the tabular list and alphabetic index of ICD-10-CM
- How these conventions compare and contrast to ICD-9-CM
- How to use these conventions for assigning an ICD-10-CM code

KEY POINT

The Draft ICD-10-CM Official Guidelines for Coding and Reporting can be downloaded at the following URL: http://www.cdc.gov/nchs/about/otheract/icd9/icd10cm.html.

Procedures are coded using the procedure classification appropriate for the encounter setting, such as ICD-10-PCS or CPT.

AXIS OF CLASSIFICATION

The ICD-10-CM is an arrangement of similar entities, diseases, and other conditions on the basis of specific criteria. Diseases can be arranged in a variety of ways: according to etiology, anatomy, or severity. The particular criterion chosen is called the axis of classification.

Anatomy is the primary axis of classification of ICD-10-CM. Thus, there are chapters entitled "Diseases of the Circulatory System" and "Diseases of the Genitourinary System." ICD-10-CM employs other axes as well, such as etiology, as in the chapter, "Certain Infectious and Parasitic Diseases."

Different axes are used in classifying different diseases within the same chapters. The choice is based upon the most important aspects of the disease from both a statistical and clinical point of view. For example:

- Pneumonia: etiology or cause of the pneumonia
- Malignant neoplasm: site
- Cardiac arrhythmia: type
- Leukemia: morphology

ARRANGEMENT OF THE TABULAR LIST

The tabular list consists of chapters, subchapters, three character categories, four character subcategories, and five, six, and seven character subdivisions.

Chapters and Subchapters

As mentioned, the chapter order in ICD-10-CM is not always the same as in ICD-9-CM. Disorders of the immune mechanism in ICD-10-CM are found with diseases of the blood and blood-forming organs. In ICD-9-CM these disorders are included with endocrine, nutritional, and metabolic diseases. Chapters for diseases of the genitourinary system; pregnancy, childbirth and the puerperium; certain conditions originating in the perinatal period; and congenital malformations, deformations and chromosomal abnormalities are placed consecutively in ICD-10. This chapter arrangement is the same in ICD-10-CM.

The ICD-10-CM classification is divided into 21 chapters. The chapter title describes the general content of the chapter. The code range describes the extent of the chapter; for example, chapter 7, "Diseases of the Eye and Adnexa" (H00–H59).

Chapters are subdivided into subchapters or "blocks" containing rubrics that identify closely related conditions. Each chapter begins with a summary of its subchapters to provide an overview of the classification structure at that level.

The title describes the content of the subchapter. The code range describes the extent of the subchapter; for example, "Disorders of Vitreous Body and Globe" (H43–H44).

Three-character Category

Three-character categories are the essential subdivisions of the disease classification. The disease classification begins with category A00 and ends with Z99. Not all letters of the alphabet or all numbers at the second and third positions have been used.

Three-character categories may represent a single disease entity or may represent a group of homogenous or closely related conditions. The three-character category title describes the

DEFINITIONS

Rubric. A grouping of similar conditions. In ICD-10-CM, rubric denotes either a three-character category or a four-character subcategory.

exact content of the category. For example: Category K55 provides codes for a number of vascular disorders, while category R64 is very specific to the condition, cachexia.

K55	Vascular disorders of intestine
R64	Cachexia

Generally the sequence of the categories within a block begins with categories that have specific titles, and progresses to categories with less specific titles. The next-to-the-last three-character category in a series is called the "residual" three-character category. This is the one used for "other specified disease." For example:

Hernia (K40–K46)
K40	Inguinal hernia
K41	Femoral hernia
K42	Umbilical hernia
K43	Ventral hernia
K44	Diaphragmatic hernia
K45	Other abdominal hernia
K46	Unspecified abdominal hernia

Three-character category K45 is the residual category for abdominal hernias.

There are three-character categories that have not been subdivided. These unsubdivided three-character categories describe a disease that needs no further specificity. For example:

L22	Diaper dermatitis	
	Includes:	Diaper erythema
		Diaper rash
		Psoriasiform diaper rash

The majority of three-character categories are subdivided into four-character subcategories. Whenever a three-character category has been subdivided, the three-character category rubric is considered an invalid code and cannot be used. A fourth-digit subcategory (and perhaps a fifth-, sixth-, or seventh-digit subdivision) is required for a valid code. For example, the rubric K35 cannot stand alone as the code for acute appendicitis. A fourth-digit, 0, 1, or 9, must be used, as shown:

K35	Acute appendicitis	
	K35.0	Acute appendicitis with generalized peritonitis
	K35.1	Acute appendicitis with peritoneal abscess
	K35.9	Acute appendicitis, unspecified

Four-character Subcategory
Four-character subcategories are the subdivisions of three-character categories, and define the axis of classification by describing the site, etiology, manifestation, or stage of the disease classified to the three-character category. The four-character subcategory rubric is comprised of the three-character category rubric plus a decimal digit and an additional number.

The axes of the subdivisions vary according to the nature of the condition or conditions included within the three-character category. For example, the subdivisions may describe the stages of the disease (acute, subacute, chronic), the sites of the disease (upper end, shaft, etc.), or the causes of the disease (Streptococcus, rhinovirus, etc.). For example:

N70	Salpingitis and oophoritis		
	N70.0	Acute salpingitis and oophoritis	
		N70.01	Acute salpingitis
		N70.02	Acute oophoritis
		N70.03	Acute salpingitis and oophoritis

 KEY POINT

Some three-character rubrics stand alone as the valid code for the condition. Do not "zero fill" these codes, as that makes them invalid. Valid codes in ICD-10-CM may have three, four, five, six, or seven characters.

N70.1		Chronic salpingitis and oophoritis
		Hydrosalpinx
	N70.11	Chronic salpingitis
	N70.12	Chronic oophoritis
	N70.13	Chronic salpingitis and oophoritis
N70.9		Salpingitis and oophoritis, unspecified
	N70.91	Salpingitis, unspecified
	N70.92	Oophoritis, unspecified
	N70.93	Salpingitis and oophoritis, unspecified

KEY POINT

Decimals and digits .8 and .9 may be used to create the subdivision needed despite nonapplication of rubrics from 0–7.

Four-character subcategories within a three-character category progress in terms of specificity. Often the next-to-the-last four-character subdivision, identified by the fourth digit .8, is the residual category ("other specified") and is the place to classify a specified form of a condition that does not have its own subdivision.

The last four-character subcategory is used for coding the unspecified form (site, cause, etc.) of the condition. Generally this four-character subcategory is identified by the fourth digit .9. For example:

G50		Disorders of trigeminal nerve
		Includes: disorders of 5th cranial nerve
G50.0		Trigeminal neuralgia
		Syndrome on paroxysmal facial pain
		Tic douloureux
G50.1		Atypical facial pain
G50.8		Other disorders of trigeminal nerve
G50.9		Disorder of trigeminal nerve, unspecified

Often four-character subcategories are themselves further subdivided to provide even greater specificity. Whenever a four-character subcategory has been subdivided, that four-character rubric cannot stand alone as the code for the disease to be encoded. The following example of an unsubdivided four-character subcategory shows that code O15.1 can be assigned as the code for eclampsia in labor. The subdivided four-character subcategory O15.0, however, cannot be used as the code for eclampsia in pregnancy. A fifth digit must be used.

O15		Eclampsia
		Includes: convulsions following conditions in O10-14 and O16
O15.0		Eclampsia in pregnancy
	O15.00	Eclampsia in pregnancy, unspecified trimester
	O15.02	Eclampsia in pregnancy, second trimester
	O15.03	Eclampsia in pregnancy, third trimester
O15.1		Eclampsia in labor
O15.2		Eclampsia in the puerperium
O15.9		Eclampsia, unspecified as to time period
		Eclampsia NOS

To retain the same degree of specificity present in ICD-10-CM, manifestations of diseases are identified in the same fashion as in ICD-9-CM. Following are the two ways to identify the diseases, each followed separately by an example:

1. As individual five-character subdivisions of the four-character subcategories to represent the etiology of the disease.

A02.2		Localized salmonella infections
	A02.20	Localized salmonella infection, unspecified
	A02.21	Salmonella meningitis
	A02.22	Salmonella pneumonia
	A02.23	Salmonella arthritis
	A02.24	Salmonella osteomyelitis

A02.25   Salmonella pyelonephritis

As an additional code assigned whenever a three-character category or four-character subcategory is followed by an instructional note to "code first underlying condition." The code for the condition first represents the etiology of the diseases, while the secondary code represents the manifestation of the disease.

The World Health Organization (WHO) did not want manifestations in the primary tabulation of causes for morbidity and mortality. Consequently, the manifestation code never appears as a first diagnosis. For example:

H42   Glaucoma in diseases classified elsewhere
            Code first underlying condition, such as:
                amyloidosis (E85)
                aniridia (Q13.1)
                Lowe's syndrome (E72.03)
                Reiger's anomaly (Q13.81)
                specified metabolic disorder (E70-E90)
            Excludes1:   glaucoma (in):
                            Diabetes mellitus (E08.39, E09.39, E10.39, E11.39, E13.39, E14.39)
                            onchocerciasis (B73.02)
                            syphilis (A52.71)
                            tuberculous (A18.59)

Five-, Six-, and Seven-character Subclassifications

In ICD-9-CM, there are never more than five digits to a code. In ICD-10-CM, there are five-, six-, and seven-character codes. For example:

ICD-9-CM

882   Open wound of hand except finger(s) alone
            882.0   Without mention of complication
            882.1   Complicated
            882.2   With tendon involvement

ICD-10-CM

S61.4   Open wound of hand
            S61.40   Unspecified open wound of hand
                        S61.401   Unspecified open wound of right hand
                        S61.402   Unspecified open wound of left hand
                        S61.409   Unspecified open wound of unspecified hand
            S61.41   Laceration without foreign body of hand
                        S61.411   Laceration without foreign body of right hand
                        S61.412   Laceration without foreign body of left hand
                        S61.419   Laceration without foreign body of unspecified hand

Five-character and six-character subdivisions are used in two ways: first, to provide specific codes for individual inclusion terms within a single four-character subcategory; second, to provide a second axis of classification for an entire three-character category or series of three-character categories. This second axis permits a different cross section of the condition than is provided by the four-character category.

Five- and six-character subclassifications are presented in their natural sequence. When they occur, seventh digits in ICD-10-CM are always presented as an alpha-extension table and referenced in the instructions for that code.

Alpha Extensions

ICD-10-CM has incorporated the use of extension characters to specify the encounter status for that episode of care, or to identify the status of the current condition under care for that specific encounter.

DEFINITIONS

Manifestation. The display or disclosure of characteristic signs or symptoms of an illness, as applied to medicine.

KEY POINT

Use of the fifth, sixth, or seventh digit is not optional. If five-digit subclassifications appear in ICD-9-CM, they must be used. If five-, six-, or seven-digit subclassifications appear in ICD-10-CM, they must be used.

The extensor is a lowercase letter, called an alpha extension or alpha kicker, which may create valid codes that extend to the seventh-character subdivision level. Alpha extensors are not found solely at the seventh-character position; however, they are always the final character in a code, and may be found as the fourth, fifth, sixth, or seventh character in a code:

X75.xxxs   Intentional self-harm by explosive material, sequelae
X73.1xxa   Intentional self-harm by hunting rifle discharge, initial encounter
X95.01xa   Assault by airgun discharge, initial encounter
W22.042s   Striking against wall of swimming pool causing other injury, sequelae

Where applicable, an instructional note appears under the three-digit category, or further divided subcategory, directing the coder to add an extension to each code within the category or subcategory. Every code must have one of these alpha extensions to be valid. The valid codes created by these mandatory alpha extensions are not found listed individually within the tabular list under each subclassification level to which they apply. Instead, the coder must refer to the instructional note and add the appropriate extensor to the available code at its highest specification level within the category:

S59   Other and unspecified injuries of elbow and forearm
  Excludes2:   other and unspecified injuries of wrist and hand (S69.-)
  The appropriate seventh-character extension is to be added to each code for
    subcategories S59.0, S59.1, and S59.2
  A   initial encounter for fracture
  D   subsequent encounter for fracture with routine healing
  G   subsequent encounter for fracture with delayed healing
  K   subsequent encounter for fracture with nonunion
  P   subsequent encounter for fracture with malunion
  S   sequela

  S59.0   Physeal fracture of lower end on ulna
    S59.00   Unspecified physeal fracture of lower end of ulna
      S59.001   Unspecified physeal fracture of lower end of ulna, right arm
      S59.002   Unspecified physeal fracture of lower end of ulna, left arm
      S59.009   Unspecified physeal fracture of lower end of ulna, unspecified arm

Coma Extensions

The convention of using character extensions in ICD-10-CM for more granularity in coding has been implemented in a unique way within the coma subcategory to denote the time. The following seventh-character extensions are to be added to codes R40.21, R40.22, and R40.23:

  1   in the field [EMT or ambulance]
  2   at arrival to emergency department
  3   at hospital admission
  4   24 hours or more after hospital admission

R40.2121   Coma scale, eyes open, to pain, in the field
R40.2222   Coma scale, best verbal response, incomprehensible words, at arrival to emergency department
R40.2334   Coma scale, best motor response, abnormal, 24 hours or more after hospital admission

Fetus Identification in Multiple Gestation

ICD-10-CM provides a specialized group of extensions to be used in chapter 15, "Pregnancy, Childbirth and the Puerperium (O00–O99)," to identify the fetus for which the code applies in multiple gestation pregnancies. These seventh characters are assigned under each category for which an instructional note specifies that the appropriate seventh character is required, as follows:

0	not applicable or unspecified
1	fetus 1
2	fetus 2
3	fetus 3
4	fetus 4
5	fetus 5
9	other fetus

Place Holding X

There are many ways that the hierarchal coding system of ICD-9-CM and ICD-10-CM provides an advantage over other types of coding systems. For collating data and statistical analysis, the hierarchal codes allow disease groups to be monitored easily. Coders using the system become familiar with these hierarchies so code lookup is easy. But despite the system's many advantages, there are disadvantages. Chief among the intrinsic disadvantages is the fixed space within each classification: there can be only 10 divisions of each code at the next level. The creation of an alpha first-character relieved much of the space problems for ICD-10-CM, providing 26 characters instead of 10, but there is still concern that medical advances could outstrip the room left in the coding system. In an effort to plan for these medical advances, some "place-holders" have been added to ICD-10-CM, so that in the future additional detail can be added to the classification. For example:

O45.8	Other premature separation of placenta	
	O45.8x	Other premature separation of placenta
	O45.8x1	Other premature separation of placenta, first trimester
	O45.8x2	Other premature separation of placenta, second trimester
	O45.8x3	Other premature separation of placenta, third trimester
	O45.8x9	Other premature separation of placenta, unspecified trimester

Note that the definition of O45.8 and O45.8x are exactly the same. It is the intention of the creators of ICD-10-CM that if, in the future, there are causes of premature separation of the placenta that should be assigned unique codes, these causes would be assigned numbers that replace the x "place holder." Until then, coders are required to use the x as a place holder. It is not acceptable to drop the x.

TABULAR LIST CONVENTIONS

The ICD-10-CM tabular list employs certain abbreviations, punctuations, symbols, and other conventions that must be clearly understood to use the classification appropriately.

NEC and NOS

Two abbreviations are found in the tabular list: NEC and NOS. The abbreviation NEC means "not elsewhere classified" or "not elsewhere classifiable." NOS means "not otherwise specified."

Exercise caution when using the NEC category. NEC tells you that certain specified forms are classified elsewhere.

In the tabular list, the phrase "not elsewhere classified" is applied to residual categories that do not appear in sequence with (i.e., immediately following) the pertinent specific categories. These residual categories are entitled "other specified." For example, K73 is the residual category for chronic hepatitis. This category is not immediate to the specific categories for forms of chronic hepatitis. The forms of the disease are assigned to various categories throughout the classification. An exclusion note in an NEC category lets you know that the condition is elsewhere classified.

K70	Alcoholic liver disease
K71	Toxic liver disease
K72	Hepatic failure, not elsewhere classified
K73	Chronic hepatitis, not elsewhere classified

Excludes1:	alcoholic hepatitis (chronic) (K70.1-)
	drug-induced hepatitis (chronic) (K71.-)
	granulomatous hepatitis (chronic) NEC (K75.3)
	reactive, nonspecific hepatitis (chronic) (K75.2)
	viral hepatitis (chronic) (B15–B19)

The abbreviation NOS is equivalent to "unspecified." The term is assigned when the documentation does not provide the detail for a specific code. Double check the medical record for information about the condition before selecting an NOS code.

The term "bronchitis" alone means the same as "bronchitis, unspecified" or "bronchitis NOS."

J40	Bronchitis, not specified as acute or chronic
Includes:	bronchitis NOS
	catarrhal bronchitis
	bronchitis with tracheitis NOS
	tracheobronchitis NOS

A term without an essential modifier is the unspecified form of the condition, though there are exceptions. Unqualified terms can be classified to a three-character category for a more specific type of condition. For example: Mitral stenosis is a common descriptor used as a diagnosis. ICD-10-CM assumes the cause to be rheumatic, whether or not "rheumatic" is included in the diagnosis.

I05	Rheumatic mitral valve diseases
Includes:	conditions classifiable to both I05.0 and I05.2-I05.9, whether specified as rheumatic or not
I05.0	Rheumatic mitral stenosis

} Braces

ICD-9-CM uses braces to enclose a series of terms, each of which is modified by the word(s) following the brace. This is not so in ICD-10-CM; no braces are used. For example:

ICD-9-CM

Code 560.9 includes obstruction, occlusion, stenosis, or stricture of intestine or colon.

560.9	Unspecified intestinal obstruction
	Enterostenosis
	Obstruction
	Occlusion ⎫
	Stenosis ⎬ of intestine or colon
	Stricture ⎭

ICD-10-CM

K56.69	Other intestinal obstruction
	Enterostenosis NOS
	Obstructive ileus NOS
	Occlusion of colon or intestine NOS
	Stenosis of colon or intestine NOS
	Stricture of colon or intestine NOS

Note that no braces were used to list the inclusion terms in K56.69.

KEY POINT

Code to the highest level of specificity allowed by the medical record documentation.

KEY POINT

Incorporating all common subclassifications and including full titles clarify a code's meaning even when the code contains six characters.

[ ] Brackets

Brackets enclose synonyms, alternative wordings, or explanatory phrases in ICD-9-CM and ICD-10-CM. For example: Crohn's disease is defined by the phrase in brackets as regional enteritis.

K50   Crohn's disease [regional enteritis]

In ICD-9-CM, brackets are also used to enclose the fifth digits available for the fourth-digit subcategory. Since ICD-10-CM presents the five- and six-character subclassifications in their natural sequence, this use of brackets is not necessary in ICD-10-CM.

: Colon

ICD-9-CM employs colons in the tabular list following an incomplete term that needs one or more modifiers to assign the term to the given code. The colon is used for the term that has more than one possible essential modifier. In ICD-10-CM, colons appear in the tabular list after includes and excludes notes or other coding instruction such as "Note." Colons may also appear following an incomplete term that requires one or more of the terms following the colon to be documented to support code assignment.

A68   Relapsing fevers
            Includes: recurrent fever
            Excludes2:   Lyme disease (A69.2-)
C22   Malignant neoplasm of liver and intrahepatic bile ducts
            Excludes1:   malignant neoplasm of biliary tract NOS (C24.9)
                        secondary malignant neoplasm of liver (C78.7)
            Use additional code to identify:
               alcohol abuse and dependence (F10.-)
               hepatitis B (B16.-, B18.0–B18.1)
               hepatitis C (B17.1-, B18.2)

, Comma

Commas are found in both ICD-10-CM and ICD-9-CM for the same reasons. Words following a comma are often essential modifiers. For example, the term "postpartum" is an essential modifier and must be present in the statement for deep-vein thrombosis or pelvic thrombophlebitis to assign code O87.1.

O87.1   Deep phlebothrombosis in the puerperium
            Deep-vein thrombosis, postpartum
            Pelvic thrombophlebitis, postpartum

Commas also appear in code descriptions as essential modifiers:

O88.011   Air embolism in pregnancy, first trimester

( ) Parentheses

In ICD-9-CM, parentheses enclose supplementary words that may be present or absent in the statement of a disease or procedure, but do not affect the code. Parentheses also enclose the categories included in a subchapter, and a code or code range listed in an excludes note. The same rules for parentheses apply to ICD-10-CM.

Nonessential modifiers usually appear in the three-character category that has been assigned the unspecified form of the disease modified. For example: The nonessential modifiers in the example below are: (acute), (chronic), (nonpuerperal), and (subacute).

 KEY POINT

Parentheses enclose terms that are called "nonessential modifiers." A patient's condition need not match the nonessential modifiers for that code to be selected.

N61   Inflammatory disorders of breast
            Includes: abscess (acute) (chronic) (nonpuerperal) of areola
                           abscess (acute) (chronic) (nonpuerperal) of breast
                           carbuncle of breast
                           infective mastitis (acute) (subacute) (nonpuerperal)
                           mastitis (acute) (subacute) (nonpuerperal) NOS

§ Section Mark

The section mark symbol in some versions of ICD-9-CM precedes a code to denote the placement of a footnote at the bottom of the page. The footnote applies to all subdivisions within that code. This symbol is not found in ICD-10-CM; rather, the subdivisions are listed in their natural sequence. For example:

ICD-9-CM

789   Other symptoms involving abdomen and pelvis
            The following fifth-digit subclassification is to be used for codes 789.0, 789.3, 789.4, and 789.6:
            0   unspecified site
            1   right upper quadrant
            2   left upper quadrant
            3   right lower quadrant
            4   right lower quadrant
            5   periumbilic
            6   epigastric
            7   generalized
            9   other specified site
                   multiple sites

    §789.0   Abdominal pain
                   § Requires fifth-digit. See above for codes and definitions.

ICD-10-CM

R10.1   Pain localized to upper abdomen
            R10.10   Upper abdominal pain, unspecified
            R10.11   Right upper quadrant pain
            R10.12   Left upper quadrant pain
            R10.13   Epigastric pain

Inclusion Term, Includes Note

Inclusion terms and includes notes carry the same meaning in ICD-10-CM as they do in ICD-9-CM.

Since titles are not always self-explanatory, the tabular list contains inclusion terms to clarify the content (intent) of the chapter, subchapter, category, or subdivision to which the terms apply. These "inclusion" terms are listed below the code title and describe other conditions classified to that code, such as synonyms of the condition listed in the code title, or an entirely different condition. For example:

R71.8   Other abnormality of red blood cells
            Abnormal red-cell morphology NOS
            Abnormal red-cell volume NOS
            Anisocytosis
            Poikilocytosis

Inclusion notes appearing under chapter and subchapter titles provide general definitions to the content of that section. These notes apply to each category within the chapter or subchapter. For example:

☞ **KEY POINT**

Many of the alternative names found in the alphabetic index are not listed as inclusion terms in the tabular list. To code accurately, consult the Index and then verify the code found in the tabular list.

Chapter 16 Certain Conditions Originating in the Perinatal Period (P00–P96)

Note: These codes are for use when the listed maternal conditions are specified as the cause of confirmed morbidity or potential morbidity which have their origin in the perinatal period (before birth through the first 28 days after birth). Codes from these categories are also for use for newborns who are suspected of having an abnormal condition resulting from exposure from the mother or the birth process, but without signs or symptoms, and, which after examination and observation, is found not to exist. These codes may be used even if treatment is begun for a suspected condition that is ruled out.

Infections Specific to the Perinatal Period (P35–P39)

        Includes: infections acquired in utero or during birth

Inclusion notes appearing under three-, four-, and five-character codes may define or provide a list of specific terms applicable to that category, and, if subdivided, to each subdivision.

The inclusion note appearing under the three-character category Q60 applies to all codes beneath it:

Q60   Renal agenesis and other reduction defects of kidney
          Includes: congenital absence of kidney
                         congenital atrophy of kidney
                         infantile atrophy of kidney
        Q60.0   Renal agenesis, unilateral
        Q60.1   Renal agenesis, bilateral
        Q60.2   Renal agenesis, unspecified
        Q60.3   Renal hypoplasia, unilateral
        Q60.4   Renal hypoplasia, bilateral
        Q60.5   Renal hypoplasia, unspecified
        Q60.6   Potter's syndrome

Notes

Throughout the Tabular List in ICD-9-CM, notes describe the general content of the succeeding categories and provide instructions for using the codes. The same holds true for ICD-10-CM. For example:

G09   Sequelae of inflammatory diseases of central nervous system

Note: This category is to be used to indicate conditions whose primary classification is to G00–G08 as the cause of sequelae, themselves classifiable elsewhere. The "sequelae" include conditions specified as residuals.

Code first condition resulting from (sequela) of inflammatory diseases of central nervous system

Excludes Notes

Exclusion notes always appear with the word "excludes."

The purpose of excludes notes is to guide readers to proper application of codes. In ICD-9-CM, there has been significant confusion regarding excludes notes. In ICD-9-CM, an excludes note may indicate that two codes are mutually exclusive, and are not to be reported together. For example, the excludes note with the code for male stress incontinence of urine excludes the code for female stress incontinence. These codes are mutually exclusive and would never be reported correctly together. However, the excludes note for 304.6 Other specified drug dependence has a different role. This excludes note excludes tobacco (305.1) from the drugs identified by 304.6. It would be appropriate and correct to report both codes for a patient with a tobacco habit and a glue-sniffing habit.

KEY POINT

The placement of instructional notes is important. Notes appearing at the beginning of chapters apply to all categories within the chapter. Notes appearing at the beginning of subchapters apply to all codes within the subchapter. Notes appearing at three-character categories apply to all four-, five-, six-, and seven-character codes within the various subdivisions.

KEY POINT

The excludes notes in ICD-10-CM are labeled as a type 1 or 2 excludes note:

An "Excludes1" note indicates codes listed elsewhere that would never be used together. The two conditions are not the same, and are, in fact, mutually exclusive.

An "Excludes2" note indicates codes that may be reported together with the listed codes, if appropriate. This excludes note is clarifying that the excluded condition is not considered part of the main code, and can be reported in addition to the main code.

The excludes notes have been expanded in ICD-10-CM so there is no confusion over the intent of the codes. The excludes notes in ICD-10-CM are labeled as a type 1 or 2 excludes note:

An Excludes1 note indicates codes listed elsewhere that would never be used together. The two conditions are not the same, and are, in fact, mutually exclusive. It may also be referred to as pure excludes note; meaning "not coded here." For example, Excludes1 is used when two conditions cannot occur together, such as a congenital form versus an acquired form of the same condition.

An Excludes2 note may be interpreted as "not included here." It indicates codes that may be reported together with the listed codes, if appropriate. This note is clarifying that the excluded condition is not considered part of the main code, and could be reported in addition to the main code.

General exclusions are found at the beginning of a chapter, block, or category title. For example:

Chapter 5 Mental and Behavioral Disorders (F01–F09)

Includes: disorders of psychological development
Excludes 2:   symptoms, signs and abnormal clinical laboratory findings, not
            elsewhere classified (R00–R99)

An excludes note is a warning that you may be in the wrong category, so read it carefully when checking a code listed in the tabular list. Some excludes notes are warning that the two conditions are not the same and do not occur together. For example, the excludes note for three-character category Q16 shows that this is not the code for congenital deafness. That code is found in category H90.

Q16   Congenital malformations of ear causing impairment of hearing
      Excludes 1:   congenital deafness (H90.-)

Some excludes notes are warning that the codes in that section do not include that particular condition and you will need to look elsewhere. The codes may or may not be appropriately used together. For example, the excludes note for three-character category T83 shows that this code does not include, or specify, the failure or rejection of a transplanted organ. The correct code can be found in category T86.

T83   Complications of genitourinary prosthetic devices, implants and grafts
      Includes: Normal wear and tear with regular use
                Worn out genitourinary prosthetic device, implant or graft
      Excludes 2:   failure and rejection of transplanted organs and tissues (T86.-)

Certain categories represent diseases in combination, or the specific manifestation in combination with the etiology. Exclusion notes in these cases instruct you not to use the code if the condition mentioned in the exclusion note is also present. Using both codes is inaccurate, redundant, and confusing. Examples: if the patient had cholecystitis and cholelithiasis, choose the appropriate code under category K80.

K81   Cholecystitis
      Excludes 1:   cholecystitis with cholelithiasis (K80.-)

If the patient has a mycobacterium infection of tuberculosis, choose the correct code from A15-A19 and not A31.

A31   Infection due to other mycobacteria
      Excludes 2:   leprosy (A30.-)
                tuberculosis (A15–19)

Exclusion notes may reference the condition excluded. Sometimes, however, a condition may be so general that coding instructions are provided instead of a code reference. The absence of a code reference or coding instruction tells you that this is a "normal" condition, not to be coded at all. For example, this excludes note directs you to the Alphabetic Index.

Z39.0 Encounter for care and examination immediately after delivery
Care and observation in uncomplicated cases when the delivery occurs outside a healthcare facility
Excludes 1: care for postpartum complication — see Alphabetic Index

'Code First' Note

The ICD-10-CM "code first" note tells you that two codes are necessary to describe the condition. The code first note appears within a category that describes the manifestation of a condition. The additional code, (i.e., the one used first), describes the etiology of the condition. Code first notes may identify the additional code or examples of the additional code required; a range of codes, or instructions to code the underlying disease, or identify the causative drug or substance. Review the medical record prior to coding the underlying disease.

K87 Disorders of gallbladder, biliary tract and pancreas in diseases classified elsewhere
Code first underlying disease
Excludes1: cytomegaloviral pancreatitis (B25.2)
mumps pancreatitis (B26.3)
syphilitic gallbladder (A52.74)
syphilitic pancreas (A52.74)
tuberculosis of gallbladder (A18.83)
tuberculosis of pancreas (A18.83)

G25.1 Drug-induced tremor
Code first (T36–T50) to identify drug

'Use' Note

"Use" notes common to both ICD-9-CM and ICD-10-CM carry the same meaning: a specific instruction to use an additional code to completely describe a condition. The additional code may identify the following:

- The cause of the disease:
  J02.8 Acute pharyngitis due to other specified organisms
  Use additional code (B95–B97) to identify infectious agent

- An associated condition:
  F94.1 Reactive attachment disorder of childhood
  Use additional code to identify any associated failure to thrive or growth retardation

- The nature of the condition:
  O91 Infections of breast associated with pregnancy, the puerperium and lactation
  Use additional code to identify infection

Depending on the nature of the diagnosis and associated conditions documented, additional codes may be required for accurate and complete reporting. A note may indicate or otherwise suggest one or more potential conditions that may warrant additional codes. The phrase "such as" may be used to direct the coder to identify and report any associated manifestations, as well as providing an example.

K50 Crohn's disease [regional enteritis]
Includes: granulomatous enteritis
Excludes1: ulcerative colitis (K51.-)

Use additional code to identify manifestations, such as:
pyoderma gangrenosum (L88)

 KEY POINT

Since general exclusion notes are not repeated, review the exclusion notes prior to final code selection.

 KEY POINT

The additional code requested by the "code first" note is never optional. The additional code requested must always precede, on any coding document, the code containing the code first note.

Typeface

Chapter and subchapter titles, three-digit categories, and all valid codes and their titles, including those requiring the alpha extension, are in bold typeface in the tabular list. Main terms in the alphabetic index are also in bold typeface.

Excludes, includes, use, and code first underlying notes, as well as all rubrics not used for primary tabulations of disease, are not bolded.

Terminology

The connective "and" can be interpreted to mean "and/or" in the tabular list and the alphabetic index. The connective "also" may indicate that the sites or conditions are included in the code (i.e., a combination code).

The preposition "with" in the alphabetic index references the code for diseases in combination. A "with" reference always follows the main term (or subterm) of reference (e.g., "with" appears as a subterm but not in strict alphabetical sequence).

.– Point Dash

A point dash (.–) replaces the list of options available at a level of specificity past the three-character category. It instructs you to turn to the category or subcategory referenced to review the subdivisions available for coding.

In ICD-10-CM, the following excludes note indicates the category J02 for a patient who has an acute sore throat. The point dash indicates the code is incomplete. An additional digit completes the code.

J03	Acute tonsillitis	
	Excludes1:	acute sore throat (J02.-)
		hypertrophy of tonsils (J35.1)
		peritonsillar abscess (J36)
		sore throat NOS (J02.9)
		streptococcal sore throat (J02.2)
	Excludes2:	chronic tonsillitis (J35.0)

ARRANGEMENT OF THE ALPHABETIC INDEX

The alphabetic index in ICD-10-CM is divided into three sections, similar to ICD-9-CM. It consists of the main alphabetic index to disease and injury, an external cause index, and a table of drugs and chemicals.

The main section in the alphabetic index of ICD-10-CM contains alphabetically sequenced terms pertaining to diseases, syndromes, pathological conditions, injuries, and signs and symptoms as reasons to contact the health care provider. The alphabetic index is organized by main terms, printed in bold type for easy reference. Main terms identify disease conditions. For example, chronic tonsillitis is found under the main term "tonsillitis."

Adjectives, such as "chronic" and "hereditary," and references to anatomic sites, such as "foot" and "kidney," appear as main terms with cross references to "see condition." For example, "Chronic — see condition; Kidney — see condition."

Neoplasms are listed in the alphabetic index in two ways: by anatomic site and morphology. The list of anatomic sites is found in a table under the main term entry "Neoplasm, neoplastic." The table contains six columns: "malignant primary," "malignant secondary," "malignant ca in situ," "benign, uncertain behavior," and "unspecified."

Histological terms for neoplasms, such as "Carcinoma," and "Adenoma," are listed as main terms in the alphabetic index with cross references to the neoplasm table. Each

KEY POINT

"Use" notes are not optional. Information requested by the use note must be coded if the associated condition or cause is present in the source document.

morphological term appears with its morphology code from ICD-Oncology (ICD-O). For example:

ICD-10-CM

Adenoma (M8140/0) — *see also* Neoplasm, benign

The alphabetically-listed terms in the external cause index describe the circumstances of an accident or act of violence (the underlying cause or means of injury). The main terms represent the type of accident or violent encounter (e.g., "assault," "collision"). The index includes terms for codes classified to V00–Y98, excluding drugs and chemicals.

The Table of Drugs and Chemicals is an extensive, but not exhaustive (new products are developed every day) resource containing a list of drugs, industrial solvents, corrosives, metals, gases, noxious plants, household cleaning products, pesticides, and other toxic agents that can be harmful. The table provides the diagnostic codes for poisoning by and adverse effect of these products—whether the poisoning is accidental (unintentional), an assault, self-inflicted, or undetermined whether accidental or intentional.

ALPHABETIC INDEX CONVENTIONS

The extensive amount of information in ICD-10-CM requires the complete understanding of the conventions and rules established to accurately assign a code.

The National Center for Health Statistics (NCHS) has clinically modified the ICD-10 index developed by the WHO. These modifications include adding entries for new fifth- and sixth-digit subclassifications, and deleting entries for codes that do not apply to the clinical modification.

Main Term

The alphabetic index is organized by main terms printed in bold typeface for easy reference. Main terms describe disease conditions. For example, acute bronchitis is found under the main term "Bronchitis," and congestive heart failure is found under "Failure."

There are exceptions to the rule. Obstetric conditions are found under "Delivery," "Pregnancy," and "Puerperal," and under main terms for specific conditions such as "Labor" and "Vomiting."

Complications of medical and surgical procedures are indexed under "complications" and under the terms relating to specific conditions, including "Dehiscence" and "Infection."

Late effects of certain conditions (e.g., cerebral infections, injuries, infectious diseases) are found under the main term "Sequelae" with a note to "see also condition."

The Z codes from chapter 21, "Factors Influencing Health Status and Contact with Health Services," are found under main terms such as "Examination," "History," "Observation," "Problem," "Screening," "Status," or "Vaccination."

MODIFIERS

Main terms in the alphabetic index may be followed by nouns or adjectives that further describe them. These descriptors are called modifiers, and there are two types: essential modifiers and nonessential modifiers.

Essential modifiers are descriptors that affect code selection for a given diagnosis, due to the axis of classification. For coding purposes, these modifiers describe essential differences in

KEY POINT

If a term describing a condition can be expressed in more than one form, all forms will appear in the main term entry. For example, "excess," "excessive," and "excessively" are listed together in the Alphabetic Index.

KEY POINT

An essential modifier that is the sole essential modifier for a main term appears in the Alphabetic Index on the same line as the main term, separated by a comma. For example: Insufflation, fallopian Z31.41. "Fallopian" is an essential modifier, and the only essential modifier of the main term "insufflation."

the site, etiology, or clinical type of disease. All terms must be present in the diagnosis to code according to the category modified.

ICD-10-CM

In the ICD-10-CM index, the axis of classification for pneumonia is etiology or cause. "Aspiration," "pneumococcal," and "viral" are essential modifiers of pneumonia. Each term describes a different cause that requires a different code. As such, separate subterm entries exist for each subclassification code. The modifiers must be present in the diagnosis to assign these codes. For example:

Pneumonia J18.9
Aspiration pneumonia J69.0
Pneumococcal pneumonia J13
Viral pneumonia J12.9

Main terms with multiple essential modifiers present each modifier on a separate line in a list indented below the main term. These multiple essential modifiers are called "subterms." For example, "allergic," "cluster," and "drug-induced" are essential modifiers for the main term "Headache." Each appears as a subterm under "Headache."

Headache R51
    allergic NEC G44.8
    cluster (chronic) (episodic) G44.0
    drug-induced NEC G44.4

Subterms may also be modified by other essential modifiers. In the alphabetic index they are further indented. For example, "visual" is an essential modifier of the main term "Disorder." "Cortex" is an essential modifier of the subterm "visual," and "blindness" is an essential modifier of the main term "Disorder" and subterms "visual" and "cortex."

Disorder
    visual
        cortex
            blindness H47.619
            left brain H47.612
            right brain H47.611

Nonessential modifiers do not affect code selection for a given diagnosis, due to the axis of classification. Nonessential modifiers appear as parenthetical terms following the words they modify. For example: Etiology is the axis of classification for pneumonia. The terms "acute," "double," and "septic" are nonessential modifiers since they describe conditions other than the cause of pneumonia. The code for "pneumonia" is J18.9 despite the absence or presence of any of the nonessential modifiers.

Pneumonia (acute) (Alpenstich) (benign) (bilateral) (brain) (cerebral) (circumscribed) (congestive) (creeping) (delayed resolution) (double) (epidemic) (fever) (flash) (fulminant) (fungoid) (granulomatous) (hemorrhagic) (incipient) (infantile) (infectious) (infiltration) (insular) (intermittent) (latent) (migratory) (organized) (overwhelming) (primary (atypical)) (progressive) (pseudolobar) (purulent) (resolved) (secondary) (senile) (septic) (suppurative) (terminal) (true) (unresolved) (vesicular) J18.9

Nonessential modifiers may follow subterms in the alphabetic index. For example:

Murmur (cardiac) (heart) (organic) R01.1
    aortic (valve) — *see* Endocarditis, aortic

KEY POINT

Nonessential modifiers may be present or absent for the diagnosis to be coded. Either way, the code remains the same.

Abbreviations

In the alphabetic index the abbreviation NEC, "not elsewhere classified," serves as a warning with ill-defined terms. The code is assigned only if a review of the code choices does not yield an appropriate code for the condition.

NEC following "Granuloma, foreign body (in soft tissue)" indicates that M60.20 may not be the correct code or subcategory for classifying a foreign body granuloma. Before assigning the NEC code for a given diagnosis, you must first scan all the available subterms to determine whether there is another entry that is more specific. This ensures that the most appropriate code is assigned.

In this case, NEC references the residual category for a condition, e.g., the category for "other specified" forms of soft tissue foreign body granulomas. As you scan the subterms in the index, you may be directed to a specified subcategory, such as for skin or subcutaneous tissue, L92.3, or to a more appropriate code within the NEC subcategory.

An index entry may also appear as "specified NEC." This convention ensures that the correct code will be chosen although the term to be coded does not appear in the index.

Granuloma
    foreign body (in soft tissue) NEC M60.20
        shoulder region M60.219
        skin L92.3
        specified site NEC M60.28
        subcutaneous tissue L92.3

Cross References

Cross references in the alphabetic index point to all the possible information for a term or its synonyms.

There are two types of cross references: "— see" and "— see also."

In ICD-10-CM, "see" directs you to another term in the index that provides more complete information. It is also used with anatomical site main entries to remind you that the index is organized by condition. For example, the cross reference "see" indicates that the term "hardening of arteries" is coded to "arteriosclerosis."

Hardening
    artery — *see* Arteriosclerosis

Or, you are directed to the condition affecting the heart.

Heart — *see* condition

The cross reference "see also" directs you to another main term if you need more information than what is listed under the first term selected. For example:

Necrosis, necrotic (ischemic) — *see also* Gangrene

Modifiers under "necrosis" are not definitive. Modifiers applying to "necrosis" may be the same as those for "gangrene." If the modifier cannot be found under "necrosis," the cross reference instructs you to "— see also Gangrene."

Notes

New to the ICD-10-CM index is the omission of the notes that were common in ICD-9-CM. Because the information in the notes section of the ICD-9-CM index is repeated in the tabular section of ICD-9-CM, it may have been considered redundant. Editors may also have felt that to retain the notes in the index encouraged coders to code from the index—a practice considered taboo by experienced coders.

CODING AXIOM

In ICD-10-CM, as in ICD-9-CM, you should always seek your code first in the index and then verify your selection in the tabular section.

KEY POINT

Review the alphabetic index for cross references and notes prior to referring to the tabular list. Notes at the beginning of main terms may not be repeated.

Etiology and Manifestation of Disease

You must code both the etiology and the manifestation of the disease for certain conditions.

Myasthenia G70.9
  in
      diabetes mellitus—see E09–E13 with .44
      pernicious anemia D51.0 [G73.3]
      thyrotoxicosis E05.90 [G73.3]
          with thyroid storm E05.91 [G73.3]

DISCUSSION QUESTIONS

1.   What do we mean by "axis of classification?" Please give examples of some axes.

_____

_____

_____

2.   Explain the rules surrounding use of parentheses in the tabular section and index to diseases.

_____

_____

_____

3.   Why should you use caution in coding with a code designated as NEC or NOS?

_____

_____

_____

4.   What are alpha extensions and how are they used?

_____

_____

_____

5.   Discuss the two types of excludes notes and how each is different.

_____

_____

_____

Chapter 3: ICD-10-CM Code Families

This chapter provides a detailed review and analysis of the changes to individual chapters and the code "families," i.e., the block of three-character categories the chapters contain. While not every single revision has been identified in every chapter, the highlights given here should help you feel assured that coding correctly with ICD-10-CM, even though it is not the way you are accustomed to under ICD-9-CM, is not so drastically different in most cases.

With any revision to a classification, changes are made for specific reasons. Overall, as mentioned in chapter 1, conditions have been grouped in a way that is most appropriate for general epidemiological purposes and the evaluation of healthcare.

Specific reasons for changes to the contents of the chapters include the desire to do the following:

- Increase clinical detail about a specific disorder
- Reclassify diseases because of recent scientific information
- Identify recently discovered diseases, (i.e., since the last revision)
- Accommodate the required detail of a group of diseases
- Make effective use of available space

In general, conditions were moved as a group or individual conditions were reclassified. For example, certain disorders of the immune mechanism was expanded and the category group was moved to "Diseases of the Blood and Blood-forming Organs." In ICD-9-CM, these disorders are included with "Endocrine, Nutritional, and Metabolic Diseases."

OBJECTIVES

In this chapter, you will learn:

- How to identify each code family
- About the structural changes to ICD-10-CM at the three-character category level
- The organizational adjustments that have occurred to certain individual diseases

CHAPTER 1

Chapter 1, Certain Infectious and Parasitic Diseases, contains 22 code families depicted by the code's first character of "A" and "B." They are:

A00–A09	Intestinal infectious diseases
A15–A19	Tuberculosis
A20–A28	Certain zoonotic bacterial diseases
A30–A49	Other bacterial diseases
A50–A64	Infections with a predominantly sexual mode of transmission
A65–A69	Other spirochetal diseases
A70–A74	Other diseases caused by chlamydiae
A75–A79	Rickettsioses
A80–A89	Viral infections of the central nervous system
A90–A99	Arthropod-borne viral fevers and viral hemorrhagic fevers
B00–B09	Viral infections characterized by skin and mucous membrane lesions
B10	Other human herpesviruses
B15–B19	Viral hepatitis
B20	Human immunodeficiency virus [HIV] disease
B25–B34	Other viral diseases
B35–B49	Mycoses
B50–B64	Protozoal diseases
B65–B83	Helminthiases

B85–B89	Pediculosis, acariasis and other infestations
B90–B94	Sequelae of infectious and parasitic diseases
B95–B97	Bacterial, viral and other infectious agents
B99	Other infectious diseases

ICD-10-CM Subchapter Restructuring

After reviewing different disease categories, the developers of ICD-10 restructured some of their groupings to bring together those groups that were related by cause. For example, the ICD-9-CM subchapter "Syphilis and Other Venereal Diseases" has been rearranged, and the subchapter "Rickettsioses and Other Arthropod-borne Diseases" has been split into two separate subchapters in ICD-10-CM.

ICD-9-CM

Rickettsioses and Other Arthropod-borne Diseases (080–088)

Syphilis and Other Venereal Diseases (090–099)

Other Spirochetal Diseases (100–104)

ICD-10-CM

Infections with a Predominantly Sexual Mode of Transmission (A50–A64)

Other Spirochetal Diseases (A65–A69)

Rickettsioses (A75–A79)

Arthropod-borne Viral Fevers and Hemorrhagic Fevers (A90–A99)

Category Title Changes

As the examples above illustrate, a number of category and subchapter titles have been revised in chapter 1. Titles were changed to better reflect the content, which was often necessary when specific types of diseases were given their own block, a new category was created, or an existing category was redefined.

ICD-9-CM

| 046 | Slow virus infections and prion diseases of central nervous system |

ICD-10-CM

| A81 | Atypical virus infections of central nervous systems |

Organizational Adjustments

When comparing ICD-9-CM to ICD-10-CM, some codes have been added, deleted, combined, and moved.

The code for human immunodeficiency virus disease followed the subchapter, "Other Bacterial Diseases" in ICD-9-CM. The code for human immunodeficiency virus disease has been moved in ICD-10-CM to follow the subchapter for viral hepatitis.

ICD-9-CM

| 042 | Human immunodeficiency virus [HIV] disease |

ICD-10-CM

| B20 | Human immunodeficiency virus [HIV] disease |

The ICD-10 code for opportunistic mycoses, B48.7, has been deleted in ICD-10-CM. The conditions that would have been classified to this code have been moved to B48.8.

 KEY POINT

In some cases, the codes in ICD-10 and ICD-10-CM closely resemble those in ICD-9-CM. For example:

ICD-9-CM
021.2   Pulmonary tularemia

ICD-10-CM
A21.2   Pulmonary tularemia

In other cases, the codes and nomenclature are quite different:

ICD-9-CM
233.0   Carcinoma in situ of breast

ICD-10-CM
There are 24 codes for carcinoma in situ of breast, including:

D05.12   Intraductal carcinoma in situ of left female breast

KEY POINT

The term "certain" has been added to the title of chapter 1, "Infectious and Parasitic Diseases," to stress the fact that localized infections are classified with the diseases of the pertinent body system.

ICD-9-CM
118   Opportunistic mycoses

ICD-10-CM
B48.8   Other specified mycoses
        Adiaspiromycosis
        Infection of tissue and organs by alternaria
        Infection of tissue and organs by dreschlera
        Infection of tissue and organs by fusarium
        Infection of tissue and organs by saprophytic fungi NEC

There was no specific code in ICD-9-CM for septicemia due to enterococcus. A code has been added to the ICD-10-CM to classify this disorder.

ICD-10-CM
A41.81   Sepsis due to enterococcus

CHAPTER 2

Chapter 2, "Neoplasms," contains 19 code families depicted by the code's first character of "C" and "D." The letter D is also shared with the next chapter, "Diseases of the Blood and Blood-Forming Organs and Certain Disorders Involving the Immune System." C and D code families for this chapter are:

C00–C75	Malignant neoplasms, stated or presumed to be primary, of specified sites, except of lymphoid, hematopoietic and related tissue
C00–C14	Malignant neoplasms of lip, oral cavity and pharynx
C15–C26	Malignant neoplasms of digestive organs
C30–C39	Malignant neoplasms of respiratory and intrathoracic organs
C40–C41	Malignant neoplasms of bone and articular cartilage
C43–C44	Malignant neoplasms of skin
C45–C49	Malignant neoplasms of mesothelial and soft tissue
C50	Malignant neoplasms of breast
C51–C58	Malignant neoplasms of female genital organs
C60–C63	Malignant neoplasms of male genital organs
C64–C68	Malignant neoplasms of urinary tract
C69–C72	Malignant neoplasms of eye, brain and other parts of central nervous system
C73–C75	Malignant neoplasms of thyroid and other endocrine glands
C76–C80	Malignant neoplasms of ill-defined, secondary and unspecified sites
C81–C96	Malignant neoplasms, stated or presumed to be primary, of lymphoid, hematopoietic and related tissue
D00–D09	In situ neoplasms
D10–D36	Benign neoplasms
D37–D48	Neoplasms of uncertain behavior
D49	Neoplasms of unspecified behavior

Category Title Changes
A number of category titles have been revised in chapter 2. Titles were changed to better reflect the category's content, which was often necessary when specific types of diseases were given their own block, a new category was created, or an existing category was redefined.

ICD-9-CM

141   Malignant neoplasm of tongue

ICD-10-CM

C01   Malignant neoplasm of base of tongue
C02   Malignant neoplasm of other and unspecified parts of tongue

Organizational Adjustments

When comparing ICD-9-CM to ICD-10-CM, some codes have been added, deleted, combined, and moved.

The codes for malignant neoplasm of retroperitoneum and peritoneum were in the subchapter, "Malignant Neoplasm of the Digestive Organs and Peritoneum" in ICD-9-CM. These codes have been moved in ICD-10-CM to the subchapter, "Malignant neoplasms of mesothelial and soft tissue."

ICD-9-CM

Malignant Neoplasm of Digestive Organs and Peritoneum (150–159)

150   Malignant neoplasm of esophagus
151   Malignant neoplasm of stomach
152   Malignant neoplasm of small intestine, including duodenum
153   Malignant neoplasm of colon
154   Malignant neoplasm of rectum, rectosigmoid junction, and anus
155   Malignant neoplasm of liver and intrahepatic bile ducts
156   Malignant neoplasm of gallbladder and extrahepatic bile ducts
157   Malignant neoplasm of pancreas
158   Malignant neoplasm of retroperitoneum and peritoneum
159   Malignant neoplasm of other and ill-defined sites within the digestive organs and peritoneum

ICD-10-CM

Malignant Neoplasms of Mesothelial and Soft Tissue (C45–C49)

C45   Mesothelioma
C46   Kaposi's sarcoma
C47   Malignant neoplasm of peripheral nerves and autonomic nervous system
C48   Malignant neoplasm of retroperitoneum and peritoneum
C49   Malignant neoplasm of other connective and soft tissue

The codes for the cervical, thoracic, and abdominal sites for malignant neoplasm of the esophagus have been revised in ICD-10-CM. Codes and descriptions have been reclassified as follows:

ICD-9-CM

150   Malignant neoplasm of esophagus
     150.0   Cervical esophagus
     150.1   Thoracic esophagus
     150.2   Abdominal esophagus
     150.3   Upper third of esophagus
     150.4   Middle third of esophagus
     150.5   Lower third of esophagus
     150.8   Other specified part
     150.9   Esophagus, unspecified

ICD-10-CM

C15   Malignant neoplasm of esophagus
     C15.3   Malignant neoplasm of upper third of esophagus
     C15.4   Malignant neoplasm of middle third of esophagus

CODING AXIOM

One of ICD's specialty-based adaptations is the International Classification of Diseases for Oncology (ICD-O). This dual-axis classification is used in cancer registries and in pathology and other departments specializing in cancer.

KEY POINT

While all codes beginning with C report neoplasms, codes beginning with D are divided between neoplasms and diseases of the blood-forming organs and immune disorders.

C15.5   Malignant neoplasm of lower third of esophagus
C15.8   Malignant neoplasm of overlapping sites of esophagus
C15.9   Malignant neoplasm of esophagus, unspecified

In ICD-9-CM, 199.1 was used to classify a malignant neoplasm without specification as to site for either a primary or secondary site. In ICD-10-CM, category C80 reports malignancy without a site specification.

ICD-10-CM

C80   Malignant neoplasm without specification of site
         Excludes1:   malignant neoplasm of specified multiple sites- code to each site
         C80.0   Disseminated malignant neoplasm, unspecified
                       Carcinomatosis NOS
                       Generalized cancer, unspecified site (primary) (secondary)
                       Generalized malignancy, unspecified site (primary) (secondary)
         C80.1   Malignant neoplasm, unspecified
                       Cancer unspecified site (primary) (secondary)
                       Carcinoma unspecified site (primary) (secondary)
                       Malignancy unspecified site (primary) (secondary)

CHAPTER 3

Chapter 3, "Diseases of the Blood and Blood-forming Organs and Certain Disorders Involving the Immune Mechanism," contains seven code families depicted by the code's first character of "D," which is also shared with the previous chapter, "Neoplasms." The coding families in this chapter are:

D50–D53   Nutritional anemias
D55–D59   Hemolytic anemias
D60–D64   Aplastic and other anemias and other bone marrow failure syndromes
D65–D69   Coagulation defects, purpura and other hemorrhagic conditions
D70–D77   Other disorders of blood and blood-forming organs
D78   Intraoperative and postprocedural complications of spleen
D80–D89   Certain disorders involving the immune mechanism

ICD-10-CM Category Restructuring

In ICD-9-CM, there were no subchapters in the chapter for diseases of blood and blood-forming organs. Blocks have been added to this restructured chapter for ICD-10-CM. The arrangement of the various disorders, given the addition of these new blocks, has resulted in restructuring of the categories.

ICD-9-CM

280   Iron deficiency anemias
281   Other deficiency anemias
282   Hereditary hemolytic anemias
283   Acquired hemolytic anemias
284   Aplastic anemia and other bone marrow failure syndromes
285   Other and unspecified anemias
286   Coagulation defects
287   Purpura and other hemorrhagic conditions
288   Diseases of white blood cells
289   Other diseases of blood and blood-forming organs

 KEY POINT

In ICD-10-CM, the contents of chapter 3 and chapter 4 are different than in ICD-9-CM. First, the number of categories for disorders of the immune mechanism was expanded. Then, they were put with diseases of the blood and blood-forming organs. Finally, this combination of disorders was moved before the chapter on endocrine, nutritional and metabolic diseases.

ICD-10-CM

Nutritional Anemias (D50–D53)

D50	Iron deficiency anemia
D51	Vitamin B12 deficiency anemia
D52	Folate deficiency anemia
D53	Other nutritional anemias

Category Title Changes

A number of category title revisions were made in chapter 3. Titles were changed to better reflect the category's content. This was often necessary when specific types of diseases were given their own block, a new category was created, or an existing category was redefined.

ICD-9-CM

281	Other deficiency anemias	
	281.0	Pernicious anemia
	281.1	Other vitamin B12 deficiency anemia
	281.2	Folate-deficiency anemia
	281.3	Other specified megaloblastic anemias not elsewhere classified
	281.4	Protein-deficiency anemia
	281.8	Anemia associated with other specified nutritional deficiency
	281.9	Unspecified deficiency anemia

ICD-10-CM

D50	Iron deficiency anemia	
D51	Vitamin B12 deficiency anemia	
D52	Folate deficiency anemia	
D53	Other nutritional anemias	
	D53.0	Protein deficiency anemia
	D53.1	Other megaloblastic anemias, not elsewhere classified
	D53.2	Scorbutic anemia
	D53.8	Other specified nutritional anemias

Organizational Adjustments

When comparing ICD-9-CM to ICD-10-CM, some codes have been added, deleted, combined, and moved.

The code for chronic lymphadenitis, nonspecific mesenteric lymphadenitis, and unspecified lymphadenitis in ICD-9-CM were classified to the chapter on diseases of the blood and blood-forming organs. These conditions have been moved in ICD-10 to the chapter for diseases of the circulatory system where they are best classified with other disorders of the lymphatic vessels and lymph nodes.

ICD-9-CM

289	Other diseases of blood and blood-forming organs	
	289.1	Chronic lymphadenitis
	289.2	Nonspecific mesenteric lymphadenitis
	289.3	Lymphadenitis, unspecified, except mesenteric

ICD-10-CM

I88	Nonspecific lymphadenitis	
	I88.0	Nonspecific mesenteric lymphadenitis
	I88.1	Chronic lymphadenitis, except mesenteric
	I88.8	Other nonspecific lymphadenitis
	I88.9	Nonspecific lymphadenitis, unspecified

The specific code for iron deficiency anemia secondary to inadequate dietary iron intake that was available in ICD-9-CM is deleted in ICD-10. The condition that would have been classified to this code will now be coded to the residual subcategory.

ICD-9-CM

280.1   Iron deficiency anemia secondary to inadequate dietary iron intake

ICD-10-CM

D50.8   Other iron deficiency anemias
           Iron deficiency anemia due to inadequate dietary iron intake

There was no specific code in ICD-9-CM for agranulocytosis secondary to cancer chemotherapy. A new code has been added to the ICD-10-CM to classify this disorder.

ICD-10-CM

D70.1   Agranulocytosis secondary to cancer chemotherapy

CHAPTER 4

Chapter 4, "Endocrine, Nutritional and Metabolic Diseases," contains 10 code families depicted by the code's first character of "E." They are:

E00–E07	Disorders of thyroid gland
E08–E13	Diabetes mellitus
E15–E16	Other disorders of glucose regulation and pancreatic internal secretion
E20–E35	Disorders of other endocrine glands
E36	Intraoperative complications of endocrine system
E40–E46	Malnutrition
E50–E64	Other nutritional deficiencies
E65–E68	Overweight, obesity and other hyperalimentation
E70–E90	Metabolic disorders
E89	Postprocedural endocrine and metabolic complications and disorders, not elsewhere classified

ICD-10-CM Category Restructuring

The review of the different disease categories resulted in the restructuring of some of them by the developers of ICD-10. This was done to separate out certain disorders and to give them a specific three-character category range. For example, in ICD-9-CM there is a subchapter for nutritional deficiencies (260–269), which includes malnutrition and other nutritional deficiencies. In ICD-10-CM, malnutrition has been given its own separate subchapter (E40–E46) and so has other nutritional deficiencies (E50–E64).

ICD-9-CM

Nutritional Deficiencies (260–269)

260   Kwashiorkor
261   Nutritional marasmus
262   Other severe, protein-calorie malnutrition
263   Other and unspecified protein-calorie malnutrition
264   Vitamin A deficiency
265   Thiamin and niacin deficiency states
266   Deficiency of B-complex components
267   Ascorbic acid deficiency
268   Vitamin D deficiency
269   Other nutritional deficiencies

ICD-10-CM

Malnutrition (E40–E46)

E40   Kwashiorkor
E41   Nutritional marasmus

E42	Marasmic kwashiorkor
E43	Unspecified severe protein-calorie malnutrition
E45	Retarded development following protein-calorie malnutrition
E46	Unspcified protein-calorie malnutrition

Other Nutritional Deficiencies (E50–E64)

E50	Vitamin A deficiency
E51	Thiamine deficiency
E52	Niacin deficiency [pellagra]
E53	Deficiency of other B group vitamins
E54	Ascorbic acid deficiency
E55	Vitamin D deficiency
E56	Other vitamin deficiencies

✓ QUICK TIP

Although their alpha placement is purely coincidental, it may help you remember code families to consider the following:

- Most neoplasm codes begin with "C," as in cancer.
- Diabetes and other endocrine disorders begin with "E," as in endocrinology.
- Nephrology codes can be found under "N."
- Obstetrical codes begin with the letter "O."
- Perinatal codes begin with the letter "P."

Category Title Changes

A number of category title revisions were made in chapter 4. Titles were changed to better reflect the category's content, which was often necessary when specific types of diseases were given their own block, a new category was created, or an existing category was redefined.

ICD-9-CM

265	Thiamin and niacin deficiency states
266	Deficiency of B-complex components

ICD-10-CM

E51	Thiamine deficiency
E52	Niacin deficiency [pellagra]
E53	Deficiency of other B group vitamins

Organizational Adjustments

When comparing ICD-9-CM to ICD-10-CM, some codes have been added, deleted, combined, or moved.

A code for certain types of adult osteomalacia was a subcategory code of vitamin D deficiency in ICD-9-CM. These conditions were moved in ICD-10-CM to a separate three-digit category for adult osteomalacia in the musculoskeletal and connective tissue disease chapter.

ICD-9-CM

268		Vitamin D deficiency
	268.2	Osteomalacia, unspecified

ICD-10-CM

M83		Adult osteomalacia
	M83.0	Puerperal osteomalacia
	M83.1	Senile osteomalacia
	M83.2	Adult osteomalacia due to malabsorption
	M83.3	Adult osteomalacia due to malnutrition
	M83.4	Aluminum bone disease
	M83.5	Other drug-induced osteomalacia in adults
	M83.8	Other adult osteomalacia
	M83.9	Adult osteomalacia, unspecified

☞ KEY POINT

There are many reasons for changes to the contents of the chapters, including the need for increased clinical detail about a specific disorder, and the reclassification of diseases due to increased knowledge of their causes.

CHAPTER 5

Chapter 5, "Mental and Behavioral Disorders," contains 11 code families depicted by the code's first character of "F." They are:

F01–F09	Mental disorders due to known physiological conditions
F10–F19	Mental and behavioral disorders due to psychoactive substance use
F20–F29	Schizophrenia, schizotypal and delusional, and other non-mood psychotic disorders
F30–F39	Mood [affective] disorders
F40–F48	Anxiety, dissociative, stress-related, somatoform and other nonpsychotic mental disorders
F50–F59	Behavioral syndromes associated with physiological disturbances and physical factors
F60–F69	Disorders of adult personality and behavior
F70–F79	Mental retardation
F80–F89	Pervasive and specific developmental disorders
F90–F98	Behavioral and emotional disorders with onset usually occurring in childhood and adolescence
F99	Unspecified mental disorder

ICD-10-CM Subchapter Restructuring

Chapter 5 underwent a number of revisions, including the expansion of the number of subchapters from three to eleven. With this increase, ICD-10 arranges specific disorders differently than they are in ICD-9-CM and broadens the clinical detail. Based on the ICD-10 arrangement of chapter 5, ICD-10-CM has made further modifications to these expanded subchapter divisions and titles. Titles were changed to better reflect the block's content, which was often necessary when specific types of diseases were given their own block or defined differently.

ICD-9-CM

Chapter 5—Mental Disorders (290–319)

Psychoses (290–299)
Organic Psychotic Conditions (290–294)
Other Psychoses (295–299)
Neurotic Disorders, Personality Disorders, and Other Nonpsychotic Mental Disorders (300–316)
Mental Retardation (317–319)

Organizational Adjustments

When comparing ICD-9-CM to ICD-10-CM, some codes have been added, deleted, combined, or moved. The code for tension headache was found in ICD-9-CM chapter 5 under the subchapter "Neurotic Disorders, Personality Disorders, and Other Nonpsychotic Mental Disorders." The code for this condition has been moved in ICD-10-CM and is found in chapter 6, "Diseases of the Nervous System." These changes were made to maintain consistency between ICD-9-CM and ICD-10-CM classification systems. Specific codes that classify tension headache by type and severity were added to ICD-9-CM effective October 1, 2009.

 KEY POINT

Three chapters in ICD-10 underwent substantial review and revision: chapters 5, 19, and 20. Be sure you understand the changes made to these chapters so that you can code correctly from them.

ICD-9-CM

307   Special symptoms or syndromes, not elsewhere classified

       307.8   Pain disorders related to psychological factors

              307.81   Tension headache

                   Excludes: headache:

                              NOS (784.0)

                                  migraine (346.0-346.9)

                                  syndromes (339.00-339.89)

                                  tension type (339.10-339.12)

ICD-10-CM

G44   Other headache syndromes

       G44.2   Tension-type headache

              G44.20   Tension-type headache, unspecified

                      G44.201   Tension-type headache, unspecified, intractable

                      G44.209   Tension-type headache, unspecified, not intractable

                                  Tension headache NOS

              G44.21   Episodic tension-type headache

                      G44.211   Episodic tension-type headache, intractable

                      G44.219   Episodic tension-type headache, not intractable

                                  Episodic tension-type headache NOS

              G44.22   Chronic tension-type headache

                      G44.221   Chronic tension-type headache, intractable

                      G44.229   Chronic tension-type headache, not intractable

                                  Chronic tension-type headache NOS

The specific code for psychogenic dysmenorrhea has been deleted in ICD-10-CM. This condition that is currently classified to code 306.52 will now be coded to the residual subcategory.

ICD-9-CM

306.52   Psychogenic dysmenorrhea

ICD-10-CM

F45.8   Other somatoform disorders

          Psychogenic dysmenorrhea

          Psychogenic dysphagia, including "globus hystericus"

          Psychogenic pruritus

          Psychogenic torticollis

          Somatoform autonomic dysfunction

          Teeth-grinding

There were no codes in ICD-9-CM for denoting specific types of anorexia nervosa. New codes have been added to ICD-10-CM to classify the two types.

ICD-10-CM

F50.0   Anorexia nervosa

       F50.00   Anorexia nervosa, unspecified

       F50.01   Anorexia nervosa, restricting type

       F50.02   Anorexia nervosa, binge eating/purging type

CHAPTER 6

Chapter 6, "Diseases of the Nervous System," contains 11 code families depicted by the code's first character of "G." They are:

G00–G09	Inflammatory diseases of the central nervous system
G10–G13	Systemic atrophies primarily affecting the central nervous system
G20–G26	Extrapyramidal and movement disorders
G30–G32	Other degenerative diseases of the nervous system
G35–G37	Demyelinating diseases of the central nervous system
G40–G47	Episodic and paroxysmal disorders
G50–G59	Nerve, nerve root and plexus disorders
G60–G64	Polyneuropathies and other disorders of the peripheral nervous system
G70–G73	Diseases of myoneural junction and muscle
G80–G83	Cerebral palsy and other paralytic syndromes
G89–G99	Other disorders of the nervous system

ICD-10-CM Category Restructuring

After reviewing the different disease categories, the developers of ICD-10 restructured some of them to bring together those groups that are somehow related. For example, toward the end of chapter 6, new categories for intraoperative complications and postprocedural disorders specific to the nervous system were created.

ICD-9-CM

349.0 Reaction to spinal or lumbar puncture
349.1 Nervous system complications from surgically implanted device
997.0 Nervous system complications
    997.00 Nervous system complication, unspecified
    997.01 Central nervous system complication
    997.02 Iatrogenic cerebrovascular infarction or hemorrhage
    997.09 Other nervous system complications

998.1 Hemorrhage or hematoma or seroma complicating a procedure
    998.11 Hemorrhage complicating a procedure
    998.12 Hematoma complicating a procedure
    998.13 Seroma complicating a procedure
998.2 Accidental puncture or laceration during a procedure

ICD-10-CM

G97 Intraoperative and postprocedural complications and disorders of nervous system, not elsewhere classified
    G97.0 Cerebrospinal fluid leak from spinal puncture
    G97.1 Other reaction to spinal and lumbar puncture
    G97.2 Intracranial hypotension following ventricular shunting
    G97.3 Intraoperative and postprocedural hemorrhage or hematoma complicating a nervous system procedure
        G97.31 Intraoperative hemorrhage of a nervous system organ during a nervous system procedure
        G97.32 Intraoperative hemorrhage of other organ during a nervous system procedure
    G97.4 Accidental puncture and laceration of a nervous system organ or structure during a procedure
        G97.41 Accidental puncture and laceration of a nervous system organ or structure during a nervous system procedure

 DEFINITIONSS

Somatoform disorder. A chronic, but fluctuating, neurotic disorder that begins early in life and is characterized by recurrent and multiple somatic complaints for which medical attention is sought but which are not apparently due to any physical illness.

 KEY POINT

No change was made to the classification of those situations where postprocedural conditions are not specific to a particular body system. They can be found in ICD-10-CM in chapter 19, "Injury, Poisoning and Certain Other Consequences of External Causes," compatible with where you would find them in ICD-9-CM.

	G97.42	Accidental puncture and laceration of a nervous system organ or structure during other procedure
G97.5		Postprocedural hemorrhage and hematoma of a nervous system organ or structure following a procedure
	G97.51	Postprocedural hemorrhage and hematoma of a nervous system organ or structure following a nervous system procedure
	G97.52	Postprocedural hemorrhage and hematoma of a nervous system organ or structure following other procedure
G97.8		Other intraoperative and postprocedural complications and disorders of nervous system Use additional code to further specify disorder
	G97.81	Other intraoperative complications of nervous system
	G97.82	Other postprocedural complications and disorders of nervous system

Category Title Changes

A number of category title revisions were made in chapter 6. Titles were changed to better reflect the category's content, which was often necessary when specific types of diseases were given their own block, a new category was created, or an existing category was redefined.

ICD-9-CM

354   Mononeuritis of upper limb and mononeuritis multiplex

ICD-10-CM

G56   Mononeuropathies of upper limb

Organizational Adjustments

When comparing ICD-9-CM to ICD-10-CM, some codes have been added, deleted, combined, and moved.

The code for Tay-Sachs disease, which includes gangliosidosis, found in the nervous system and sense organs chapter in ICD-9-CM, has been moved in ICD-10-CM. Specific codes were created for Tay-Sachs and the different types of gangliosidosis in ICD-10-CM and are found in chapter 4, "Endocrine, Nutritional and Metabolic Disorders."

ICD-9-CM

330.1   Cerebral lipidoses
        Amaurotic (familial) idiocy
        Disease:
            Batten
            Jansky-Bielschowsky
            Kufs'
            Spielmeyer-Vogt
            Tay-Sachs
        Gangliosidosis

ICD-10-CM

E75.0		GM2 gangliosidosis
	E75.00	GM2 gangliosidosis, unspecified
	E75.01	Sandhoff disease
	E75.02	Tay-Sachs disease
	E75.09	Other GM2 gangliosidosis
E75.1		Other and unspecified gangliosidosis
	E75.10	Unspecified gangliosidosis
	E75.11	Mucolipidosis IV
	E75.19	Other gangliosidosis

The code for eosinophilic meningitis has been deleted in ICD-10-CM and is now coded to the residual code.

ICD-9-CM
322.1   Eosinophilic meningitis

ICD-10-CM
G03.8   Meningitis due to other specified causes

While ICD-9-CM does have code 331.0 Alzheimer's disease, it provides no further detail about the disorder. Alzheimer's has been assigned its own category in ICD-10-CM, with four new valid four-digit codes to classify this disorder based on onset.

ICD-10-CM
G30   Alzheimer's disease
 Includes: Alzheimer's dementia senile and presenile forms
 Use additional code for any associated:
  delirium, if applicable (F05)
  with behavioral disturbance (F02.81)
  without behavioral disturbance (F02.80)
 Excludes1: senile degeneration of brain NEC (G31.1)
   senile dementia NOS (F03)
   senility NOS (R54)
 G30.0 Alzheimer's disease with early onset
 G30.1 Alzheimer's disease with late onset
 G30.8 Other Alzheimer's disease
 G30.9 Alzheimer's disease, unspecified

CHAPTER 7

Chapter 7, "Diseases of the Eye and Adnexa," contains 11 code families depicted by the code's first character of "H," which is also shared with the next chapter, "Diseases of the Ear and Mastoid Process." The coding families in this chapter are:

Diseases of the Eye and Adnexa (H00–H59)

H00–H05	Disorders of eyelid, lacrimal system and orbit
H10–H11	Disorders of conjunctiva
H15–H21	Disorders of sclera, cornea, iris and ciliary body
H25–H28	Disorders of lens
H30–H36	Disorders of choroid and retina
H40–H42	Glaucoma
H43–H44	Disorders of vitreous body and globe
H46–H47	Disorders of optic nerve and visual pathways
H49–H52	Disorders of ocular muscles, binocular movement, accommodation and refraction
H53–H54	Visual disturbances and blindness
H55–H57	Other disorders of eye and adnexa
H59	Intraoperative and postprocedural complications and disorders of eye and adnexa, not elsewhere classified

ICD-10-CM Category Restructuring

The ICD-9-CM has only one subchapter for disorders of the eye and adnexa under the chapter for diseases of the nervous system. ICD-10-CM has reclassified these diseases into their own chapter, according to the blocks described above. For example, diseases of the eyelids fall into the middle in ICD-9-CM's subchapter. In ICD-10-CM, it is the first block.

 KEY POINT

Diseases of the eye and ear are no longer grouped with nervous system diseases. In ICD-10-CM, eye and ear diseases are found in two chapters, sharing the letter "H."

 KEY POINT

Some codes specific to certain disorders are being further subclassified in ICD-10-CM, to specify which side of the body is affected by that condition in a single code.

For example:

ICD-9-CM
371.70	Corneal deformity, unspecified
371.71	Corneal ectasia
371.72	Descemetocele
371.73	Corneal staphyloma

ICD-10-CM
H18.70	Unspecified corneal deformity
H18.71	Corneal ectasia
H18.711	Corneal ectasia, right eye
H18.712	Corneal ectasia, left eye
H18.713	Corneal ectasia, bilateral
H18.719	Corneal ectasia, unspecified eye
H18.72	Corneal staphyloma
H18.721	Corneal staphyloma, right eye
H18.722	Corneal staphyloma, left eye
H18.723	Corneal staphyloma, bilateral
H18.729	Corneal staphyloma, uspecified eye
H18.73	Descemetocele
H18.731	Descemetocele, right eye
H18.732	Descemetocele, left eye
H18.733	Descemetocele, bilateral

Category Title Changes

A number of category title revisions were made in chapter 7. Titles were changed to better reflect the category's content, which was often necessary when specific types of diseases were given their own block, a new category was created, or an existing category was redefined.

ICD-9-CM

366.0	Infantile, juvenile, and presenile cataract
366.1	Senile cataract

ICD-10-CM

H25	Age-related cataract	
H26	Other cataract	
	H26.0	Infantile and juvenile cataract

Organizational Adjustments

When comparing ICD-9-CM to ICD-10-CM, some codes have been added, deleted, combined, or moved.

In ICD-9-CM, the code for amaurosis fugax is an inclusion term under code 362.34. The code for this disease has been moved in ICD-10-CM. It now has its own code and is found in the chapter for diseases of the nervous system.

ICD-9-CM

362.34	Transient arterial occlusion
	Amaurosis fugax

ICD-10-CM

G45.3	Amaurosis fugax

A new set of codes has been added to ICD-10-CM to classify code 365.83 Aqueous misdirection (malignant glaucoma) by the affected eye(s).

ICD-9-CM

365.83	Aqueous misdirection
	Malignant glaucoma

ICD-10-CM

H40.83	Aqueous misdirection
	Malignant glaucoma
H40.831	Aqueous misdirection, right eye
H40.832	Aqueous misdirection, left eye
H40.833	Aqueous misdirection, bilateral
H40.839	Aqueous misdirection, unspecified eye

CHAPTER 8

Chapter 8, "Diseases of the Ear and Mastoid Process," contains five code families depicted by the code's first character of "H," which is also shared with the previous chapter, "Diseases of the Eye and Adnexa." These are the coding families:

H60–H62	Diseases of external ear
H65–H75	Diseases of middle ear and mastoid
H80–H83	Diseases of inner ear
H90–H94	Other disorders of ear
H95	Intraoperative and postprocedural complications and disorders of ear and mastoid process, not elsewhere classified

---

> **☞ KEY POINT**
>
> "Diseases of the Eye and Adnexa" is a new chapter, as is "Diseases of the Ear and Mastoid Process." In ICD-9-CM, the codes for these diseases were included within chapter 6, "Diseases of the Nervous System and Sense Organs."

ICD-10-CM Category Restructuring

"Diseases of the Ear and Mastoid Process" is a new chapter. In ICD-9-CM, the codes for these diseases were included within chapter 6, "Diseases of the Nervous System and Sense Organs." In addition, the ICD-9-CM has only one subchapter for disorders of the ear and mastoid process. ICD-10-CM reclassified these diseases according to the blocks described above.

Category Title Changes

A number of category title revisions were made in chapter 8. Titles were changed to better reflect the category's content, which was often necessary when specific types of diseases were given their own block, a new category was created, or an existing category was redefined.

ICD-9-CM
381	Nonsuppurative otitis media and Eustachian tube disorders
382	Suppurative and unspecified otitis media

ICD-10-CM
H65	Nonsuppurative otitis media
H66	Suppurative and unspecified otitis media
H67	Otitis media in diseases classified elsewhere
H68	Eustachian salpingitis and obstruction
H69	Other and unspecified disorders of the Eustachian tube

Organizational Adjustments

When comparing ICD-9-CM to ICD-10-CM, some codes have been added, deleted, combined, or moved.

The code for cerebrospinal fluid otorrhea, found under the subchapter for diseases of the ear and mastoid process in the nervous system and sense organs chapter in ICD-9-CM, has not been included in the new chapter for diseases of the ear and mastoid process in ICD-10-CM, but is found in chapter 6, "Diseases of the Nervous System."

ICD-9-CM
388.61	Cerebrospinal fluid otorrhea

ICD-10-CM
G96.0	Cerebrospinal fluid leak

The codes for acoustic nerve disorder have not been completely developed in ICD-10-CM. The condition classified to this code in ICD-9-CM is now under a grouping of codes, with the reserved fifth digit for future expansion.

ICD-9-CM
388.5	Disorders of acoustic nerve

ICD-10-CM
H93.3x	Disorders of acoustic nerve
H93.3x1	Disorders of right acoustic nerve
H93.3x2	Disorders of left acoustic nerve
H93.3x3	Disorders of bilateral acoustic nerves
H93.3x9	Disorders of unspecified acoustic nerve

There is no specific code in ICD-9-CM for acute recurrent otitis media. There are several codes available under two subcategories in ICD-10-CM to code this condition by type and laterality in ICD-10-CM.

H65.04	Acute serous otitis media, recurrent, right ear

KEY POINT

Some codes specific to certain disorders are being further subclassified in ICD-10-CM, to specify which side of the body is affected by that condition in a single code. For Instance:

380.31	Hematoma of auricle or pinna

This disorder is reported using one of four codes in ICD-10-CM:

H61.12	Hematoma of pinna
	Hematoma of auricle
H61.121	Hematoma of pinna, right ear
H61.122	Hematoma of pinna, left ear
H61.123	Hematoma of pinna, bilateral
H61.129	Hematoma of pinna, unspecified ear

DEFINITIONS

Cerebrospinal fluid otorrhea.
Discharge of cerebrospinal fluid escaping from the external ear canal as a result of fracture or disease of the temporal bone.

H65.05	Acute serous otitis media, recurrent, left ear
H65.06	Acute serous otitis media, recurrent, bilateral
H65.07	Acute serous otitis media, recurrent, unspecified ear

and

H65.114	Acute and subacute allergic otitis media (mucoid) (sanguinous) (serous), recurrent, right ear
H65.115	Acute and subacute allergic otitis media (mucoid) (sanguinous) (serous), recurrent, left ear
H65.116	Acute and subacute allergic otitis media (mucoid) (sanguinous) (serous), recurrent, bilateral
H65.117	Acute and subacute allergic otitis media (mucoid) (sanguinous) (serous), recurrent, unspecified ear

 KEY POINT

The codes in this chapter, I00-I99, and those in the chapter on pregnancy, childbirth and the puerperium O00-O99, represent a challenge in accurate reporting as the alpha character I and O can be recorded incorrectly as 1 and 0 if great care is not taken.

CHAPTER 9

Chapter 9, "Diseases of the Circulatory System," contains 10 code families, depicted by the code's first character of "I." They are:

I00–I02	Acute rheumatic fever
I05–I09	Chronic rheumatic heart diseases
I10–I15	Hypertensive diseases
I20–I25	Ischemic heart diseases
I26–I28	Pulmonary heart disease and diseases of pulmonary circulation
I30–I52	Other forms of heart disease
I60–I69	Cerebrovascular diseases
I70–I79	Diseases of arteries, arterioles and capillaries
I80–I89	Diseases of veins, lymphatic vessels and lymph nodes, not elsewhere classified
I95–I99	Other and unspecified disorders of the circulatory system

ICD-10-CM Category Restructuring

After reviewing the different disease categories, developers of ICD-10 restructured some of them to bring together those groups that are related in some way. For example, in ICD-10-CM, the final block includes the following: gangrene, not elsewhere classified, intraoperative and postprocedural complications and disorders of the circulatory system, not elsewhere classified, and other and unspecified disorders of the circulatory system.

Category Title Changes

A number of category title revisions were made in chapter 9. Titles were changed to better reflect the category's content, which was often necessary when specific types of diseases were given their own block, a new category was created, or an existing category was redefined.

ICD-9-CM

394	Diseases of mitral valve
395	Diseases of aortic valve
396	Diseases of mitral and aortic valves
397	Diseases of other endocardial structures

ICD-10-CM

I05	Rheumatic mitral valve diseases
I06	Rheumatic aortic valve diseases
I07	Rheumatic tricuspid valve diseases
I08	Multiple valve diseases

Organizational Adjustments

When comparing ICD-9-CM to ICD-10-CM, some codes have been added, deleted, combined, or moved.

The codes for transient cerebral ischemia are included in ICD-9-CM's "Disease of the Circulatory System" chapter. These codes have been moved in ICD-10-CM. They are now classified under "Diseases of the Nervous System."

ICD-9-CM

435		Transient cerebral ischemia
	435.0	Basilar artery syndrome
	435.1	Vertebral artery syndrome
	435.2	Subclavial steal syndrome
	435.3	Vertebrobasilar artery syndrome
	435.8	Other specified transient cerebral ischemias
	435.9	Unspecified transient cerebral ischemia

ICD-10-CM

G45		Transient cerebral ischemic attacks and related syndromes
	G45.0	Vertebro-basilar artery syndrome
	G45.1	Carotid artery syndrome (hemispheric)
	G45.2	Multiple and bilateral precerebral artery syndromes
	G45.3	Amaurosis fugax
	G45.4	Transient global amnesia
	G45.8	Other transient cerebral ischemic attacks and related syndromes
	G45.9	Transient cerebral ischemic attack, unspecified

The codes that specified the type of hypertension—malignant, benign, or unspecified—have been deleted in ICD-10-CM. Hypertension no longer uses type as an axis of classification.

ICD-9-CM

401.0	Essential hypertension, malignant
401.1	Essential hypertension, benign
401.9	Essential hypertension, unspecified

ICD-10-CM

I10	Essential (primary) hypertension	
	Includes:	high blood pressure
		hypertension (arterial) (benign) (essential) (malignant) (primary) (systemic)
	Excludes1:	hypertensive disease complicating pregnancy, childbirth and the puerperium (O10-O11, O13-O160)
	Excludes2:	essential (primary) hypertension involving vessels of brain (I60-I69)
		essential (primary) hypertension involving vessels of eye (H35.0)

There is no single code in ICD-9-CM for arteriosclerotic heart disease with angina. Codes have been added to the ICD-10-CM to classify the combination of the underlying disease and the symptom.

ICD-10-CM

I25.10	Atherosclerotic heart disease of native coronary artery without angina pectoris	
	Atherosclerotic heart disease NOS	
I25.11	Atherosclerotic heart disease of native coronary artery with angina pectoris	
	I25.110	Atherosclerotic heart disease of native coronary artery with unstable angina pectoris
		Excludes1: unstable angina without atherosclerotic heart disease (I20.0)

✓ QUICK TIP

Documentation requirements for circulatory disorders are greater with ICD-10-CM than under ICD-9-CM. For instance, in subdermal hemorrhage, ICD-10-CM codes available for this condition specify acute, subacute, or chronic.

I25.111   Atherosclerotic heart disease of native coronary artery with angina pectoris with documented spasm
           Excludes1:   angina pectoris with documented spasm without atherosclerotic heart disease (I20.1)

I25.118   Atherosclerotic heart disease of native coronary artery with other forms of angina pectoris
           Excludes1:   other forms of angina pectoris without atherosclerotic heart disease (I20.8)

I25.119   Atherosclerotic heart disease of native coronary artery with unspecified angina pectoris
           Atherosclerotic heart disease with angina NOS
           Atherosclerotic heart disease with ischemic chest pain
           Excludes1:   unspecified angina pectoris without atherosclerotic heart disease (I20.9)

 KEY POINT

Some common symptoms and complications were added as fifth-digit extensions to certain diagnosis codes in ICD-10-CM, resulting in an increased number of combination code classifications. A combination code is a single code used to classify two diagnoses, or a diagnosis with an associated manifestation or complication.

CHAPTER 10

Chapter 10, "Diseases of the Respiratory System," contains 11 code families depicted by the code's first character of "J." They are:

J00–J06	Acute upper respiratory infections
J09–J18	Influenza and pneumonia
J20–J22	Other acute lower respiratory infections
J30–J39	Other diseases of upper respiratory tract
J40–J47	Chronic lower respiratory diseases
J60–J70	Lung diseases due to external agents
J80–J84	Other respiratory diseases principally affecting the interstitium
J85–J86	Suppurative and necrotic conditions of the lower respiratory tract
J90–J94	Other diseases of the pleura
J95–J99	Other diseases of the respiratory system
J95	Intraoperative and postprocedural complications and disorders of respiratory system, not elsewhere classified
J96–J99	Other diseases of the respiratory system

ICD-10-CM Category Restructuring

After reviewing the different disease categories, developers of ICD-10 restructured some of them to bring together those groups that are related in some way. For example, in ICD-9-CM, "Pneumonia and influenza" falls directly after "Acute respiratory infections" and "Other diseases of the upper respiratory tract." In ICD-10-CM, "Influenza and pneumonia" is followed by a new family for other acute lower respiratory infections.

ICD-9-CM

460–466 Acute respiratory infections
470–478 Other diseases of the upper respiratory tract
480–488 Pneumonia and influenza
490–496 Chronic obstructive pulmonary disease and allied conditions

ICD-10-CM

J00–J06 Acute upper respiratory infections
J09–J18 Influenza and pneumonia
J20–J22 Other acute lower respiratory infections
J30–J39 Other diseases of upper respiratory tract
J40–J47 Chronic lower respiratory diseases

Category Title Changes

A number of category title revisions were made in chapter 10. Titles were changed to better reflect the category's content, which was often necessary when specific types of diseases were given their own block, a new category was created, or an existing category was redefined.

ICD-9-CM

490	Bronchitis, not specified as acute or chronic
491	Chronic bronchitis
492	Emphysema
493	Asthma
494	Bronchiectasis
495	Extrinsic allergic alveolitis
496	Chronic airway obstruction, not elsewhere classified

ICD-10-CM

J40	Bronchitis, not specified as acute or chronic
J41	Simple and mucopurulent chronic bronchitis
J42	Unspecified chronic bronchitis
J43	Emphysema
J44	Other chronic obstructive pulmonary disease
J45	Asthma
J47	Bronchiectasis

Organizational Adjustments

When comparing ICD-9-CM to ICD-10-CM, some codes have been added, deleted, combined, or moved.

Lobar pneumonia is listed as an inclusion term under code 481. This condition has been moved in ICD-10-CM and is now classified in the three-character category J18 Pneumonia, unspecified organism.

ICD-9-CM

481	Pneumococcal pneumonia [Streptococcus pneumoniae pneumonia]
	Lobar pneumonia, organism unspecified

ICD-10-CM

J18.1	Lobar pneumonia, unspecified organism

The code for "pneumonia due to gram-negative anaerobes" has been deleted in ICD-10-CM. This condition is now classified to the residual subcategory for bacterial pneumonia.

ICD-9-CM

482.81	Pneumonia due to other specified bacteria, anaerobes

ICD-10-CM

J15.8	Pneumonia due to other specified bacteria

There is no specific code in ICD-9-CM for acute recurrent sinusitis. Seven codes have been added to the ICD-10-CM to classify this disorder by type.

ICD-10-CM

J01.01	Acute recurrent maxillary sinusitis
J01.11	Acute recurrent frontal sinusitis
J01.21	Acute recurrent ethmoidal sinusitis
J01.31	Acute recurrent sphenoidal sinusitis
J01.41	Acute recurrent pansinusitis
J01.81	Other acute recurrent sinusitis
J01.91	Acute recurrent sinusitis, unspecified

 KEY POINT

While many conditions are getting their own specific code in ICD-10-CM, some codes specific to certain disorders are being classified to the residual subcategory in ICD-10-CM.

For example:

519.2	Mediastinitis

In ICD-10-CM, this disorder is reported as:

J98.5	Diseases of mediastinum, not elsewhere classified
	Fibrosis of mediastinum
	Hernia of mediastinum
	Retraction of mediastinum
	Mediastinitis

The asthma codes in ICD-9-CM are classified as extrinsic, intrinsic, chronic obstructive, other, and unspecified. In ICD-10-CM, this organizational method of classifying asthma has been totally restructured.

ICD-9-CM

493.0   Extrinsic asthma
> Asthma:
>> allergic with stated cause
>> atopic
>> childhood
>> hay
>> platinum
>> hay fever with asthma

493.1   Intrinsic asthma
> Late-onset asthma

493.2   Chronic obstructive asthma
> Asthma with COPD
> Chronic asthmatic bronchitis

493.8   Other forms of asthma
> 493.81   Exercise induced bronchospasm
> 493.82   Cough variant asthma

493.9   Asthma, unspecified
> Asthma (bronchial) (allergic NOS)
> Bronchitis:
>> allergic
>> asthmatic

ICD-10-CM

J45   Asthma
> Includes: Allergic (predominantly) asthma
>> Allergic bronchitis NOS
>> Allergic rhinitis with asthma
>> Atopic asthma
>> Extrinsic allergic asthma
>> Hay fever with asthma
>> Idiosyncratic asthma
>> Intrinsic nonallergic asthma
>> Nonallergic asthma
>
> Use additional code to identify:
>> exposure to environmental tobacco smoke (Z58.87)
>> exposure to tobacco smoke in the perinatal period (P96.81)
>> history of tobacco use (Z87.82)
>> occupational exposure to environmental tobacco smoke (Z57.31)
>> tobacco dependence (F17.-)
>> tobacco use (Z72.0)
>
> Excludes1:   detergent asthma (J69.8)
>> eosinophilic asthma (J82)
>> lung diseases due to external agents (J60–J70)
>> miner's asthma (J60)
>> wheezing NOS (R06.2)
>> wood asthma (J67.8)
>
> Excludes2:   asthma with chronic obstructive pulmonary disease
>> chronic asthmatic (obstructive) bronchitis
>> chronic obstructive asthma

> J45.2   Mild intermittent asthma
>> J45.20   Mild intermittent asthma, uncomplicated
>>> Mild intermittent asthma, NOS
>> J45.21   Mild intermittent asthma with (acute) exacerbation
>> J45.22   Mild intermittent asthma with status asthmaticus
> J45.3   Mild persistent asthma
>> J45.30   Mild persistent asthma, uncomplicated
>>> Mild persistent asthma, NOS

	J45.31	Mild persistent asthma with (acute) exacerbation
	J45.32	Mild persistent asthma with status asthmaticus
J45.4	Moderate persistent	
	J45.40	Moderate persistent, uncomplicated
		Moderate persistent asthma NOS
	J45.41	Moderate persistent with (acute) exacerbation
	J45.42	Moderate persistent with status asthmaticus
J45.5	Severe persistent	
	J45.50	Severe persistent, uncomplicated
		Severe persistent asthma NOS
	J45.51	Severe persistent with (acute) exacerbation
	J45.52	Severe persistent with status asthmaticus
J45.9	Other and unspecified asthma	
	J45.90	Unspecified asthma

Asthmatic bronchitis NOS
Childhood asthma NOS
Late onset asthma

		J45.901	Unspecified asthma with (acute) exacerbation
		J45.902	Unspecified asthma with status asthmaticus
		J45.909	Unspecified asthma, uncomplicated

Asthma NOS

	J45.99	Other asthma
		J45.990	Exercise induced bronchospasm
		J45.991	Cough variant asthma
		J45.998	Other asthma

CHAPTER 11

Chapter 11, "Diseases of the Digestive System," contains 10 code families, depicted by the code's first character of "K." They are:

K00–K14	Diseases of oral cavity and salivary glands
K20–K31	Diseases of esophagus, stomach and duodenum
K35–K38	Diseases of appendix
K40–K46	Hernia
K50–K52	Noninfective enteritis and colitis
K55–K63	Other diseases of intestines
K65–K68	Diseases of peritoneum and retroperitoneum
K70–K77	Diseases of liver
K80–K87	Disorders of gallbladder, biliary tract and pancreas
K90–K94	Other diseases of the digestive system

ICD-10-CM Category Restructuring

After reviewing the different disease categories, developers of ICD-10 restructured some of them to bring together those groups that are related in some way. In chapter 11, the new blocks are K70–K77, "Diseases of liver," and K80–K87, "Disorders of gallbladder, biliary tract and pancreas."

Category Title Changes

A number of category title revisions were made in chapter 11. Titles were changed to better reflect the category's content, which was often necessary when specific types of diseases were given their own block, a new category was created, or an existing category was redefined.

ICD-9-CM

565	Anal fissure and fistula

QUICK TIP

In ICD-9-CM, two codes were required for acute bronchitis and its cause. In ICD-10-CM, only one code will be necessary. For example, "acute bronchitis due to streptococcus" is coded J20.2.

ICD-10-CM

K60   Fissure and fistula of anal and rectal regions

Organizational Adjustments

When comparing ICD-9-CM to ICD-10-CM, some codes have been added, deleted, combined, or moved.

Jaw disorders were deleted from the chapter, "Diseases of the Digestive System" and added to the chapter, "Musculoskeletal and Connective Tissue Disorders" in ICD-10-CM.

ICD-9-CM

Diseases of the Digestive System

524   Dentofacial anomalies, including malocclusion
526   Diseases of jaws

ICD-10-CM

Diseases of the Musculoskeletal System and Connective Tissue

M26   Dentofacial anomalies [including malocclusion]
M27   Other diseases of jaws

The codes that specified whether obstruction was mentioned in conjunction with a gastric, duodenal, peptic, or gastrojejunal ulcer have been deleted in ICD-10-CM. Obstruction is no longer an axis of classification for ulcers. For example:

ICD-9-CM

531.00   Acute gastric ulcer with hemorrhage without mention of obstruction
531.01   Acute gastric ulcer with hemorrhage with obstruction

ICD-10-CM

K25.0   Acute gastric ulcer with hemorrhage

There was no single code in ICD-9-CM for alcoholic hepatitis with ascites. A new code has been added to the ICD-10-CM to classify this disorder.

ICD-10-CM

K70.10   Alcoholic hepatitis without ascites
K70.11   Alcoholic hepatitis with ascites

CHAPTER 12

Chapter 12, "Diseases of the Skin and Subcutaneous Tissue," contains nine code families, depicted by the code's first character of "L." They are:

L00–L08	Infections of the skin and subcutaneous tissue
L10–L14	Bullous disorders
L20–L30	Dermatitis and eczema
L40–L45	Papulosquamous disorders
L50–L54	Urticaria and erythema
L55–L59	Radiation-related disorders of the skin and subcutaneous tissue
L60–L75	Disorders of skin appendages
L76	Intraoperative and postprocedural complications of dermatologic procedures
L80–L99	Other disorders of the skin and subcutaneous tissue

ICD-10-CM Category Restructuring

After reviewing the different disease categories, developers of ICD-10 restructured some of them to bring together those groups that are related in some way. In ICD-9-CM, there are only three subchapters for diseases of the skin and subcutaneous tissue. They are, "Infections of Skin and Subcutaneous Tissue," "Other Inflammatory Conditions of Skin and Subcutaneous Tissue," and "Other Diseases of Skin and Subcutaneous Tissue." In ICD-10-CM, these disorders have been rearranged to fit into the new blocks shown above.

Category Title Changes

A number of category title revisions were made in chapter 12. Titles were changed to better reflect the category's content, which was often necessary when specific types of diseases were given their own block, a new category was created, or an existing category was redefined.

ICD-9-CM

681	Cellulitis and abscess of finger and toe
682	Other cellulitis and abscess

ICD-10-CM

L03	Cellulitis and acute lymphangitis

Organizational Adjustments

When comparing ICD-9-CM to ICD-10-CM, some codes have been added, deleted, combined, or moved.

The code for carbuncle and furuncle of the breast is listed as an inclusion site under code 680.2 in ICD-9-CM. The code for this condition has been moved in ICD-10-CM and is found in the chapter, "Diseases of the Genitourinary System."

ICD-9-CM

680.2	Carbuncle and furuncle, trunk

ICD-10-CM

N61	Inflammatory disorders of breast

Classifications for seborrhea have been revised and expanded in ICD-10-CM. Category L21 Seborrheic dermatitis includes four separate subclassifications for seborrhea, with exclusions for the conditions specified as infective dermatitis (L30.3) or seborrheic keratosis (L82.-).

 KEY POINT

Many conditions have been assigned their own codes in ICD-10-CM, and then are further subclassified to specify which side of the body is affected by that condition in a single code.

For example:

680.3	Carbuncle and furuncle of upper arm and forearm
680.4	Carbuncle and furuncle of hand
680.6	Carbuncle and furuncle of leg, except foot
680.7	Carbuncle and furuncle of foot

Carbuncle and furuncle each have their own subclassifications by body area with laterality included:

L02.423	Furuncle of right upper limb
L02.424	Furuncle of left upper limb
L02.435	Carbuncle of right lower limb
L02.436	Carbuncle of left lower limb
L02.521	Furuncle of right hand
L02.522	Furuncle of left hand
L02.631	Carbuncle of right foot

 KEY POINT

Another condition that has moved from chapter 12 is clubbing of fingers. This condition is found in the chapter, "Symptoms, Signs and Abnormal Clinical and Laboratory Findings, Not Elsewhere Classified" in ICD-10-CM.

ICD-9-CM
706.3   Seborrhea

ICD-10-CM
L21   Seborrheic dermatitis
> Excludes2: infective dermatitis (L30.3) seborrheic keratosis (L82.-)

    L21.0   Seborrhea capitis
> Cradle cap

    L21.1   Seborrheic infantile derm

    L21.9   Seborrheic dermatitis, unspecified
> Seborrhea NOS

In ICD-9-CM, codes 707.00–707.09 report pressure ulcer by anatomical site.

ICD-10-CM
L89   Pressure ulcer
    L89.1   Pressure ulcer of the back

Separate classifications (707.20–707.25) identify the severity of pressure ulcers by stage. ICD-10-CM includes specific subclassification codes which specify anatomic site and severity, by stage.

    L89.14   Pressure ulcer of left lower back

        L89.141   Pressure ulcer of left lower back, stage I
> Pressure area of left lower back
> Pressure ulcer of left lower back limited to erythema only

        L89.142   Pressure ulcer of left lower back, stage II
> Pressure ulcer of left lower back with abrasion, blister, partial thickness skin loss involving epidermis and dermis
> Pressure ulcer of left lower back with skin loss NOS

        L89.143   Pressure ulcer of left lower back, stage III
> Pressure ulcer of left lower back with full thickness skin loss involving damage or necrosis of subcutaneous tissue extending to underlying fascia

        L89.144   Pressure ulcer of left lower back, stage IV
> Pressure ulcer of left lower back with necrosis of muscle, bone, and supporting structures (i.e., tendon or joint capsule)

        L89.149   Pressure ulcer of left lower back, unspecified stage

CHAPTER 13

Chapter 13, "Diseases of the Musculoskeletal System and Connective Tissue," contains 18 code families, depicted by the code's first character of "M." They are:

M00–M02	Infectious arthropathies
M05–M14	Inflammatory polyarthropathies
M15–M19	Osteoarthritis
M20–M25	Other joint disorders
M26–M27	Dentofacial anomalies [including malocclusion] and other disorders of jaw
M30–M36	Systemic connective tissue disorders
M40–M43	Deforming dorsopathies
M45–M49	Spondylopathies
M50–M54	Other dorsopathies
M60–M63	Disorders of muscles
M65–M67	Disorders of synovium and tendon
M70–M79	Other soft tissue disorders
M80–M85	Disorders of bone density and structure

M86–M90	Other osteopathies
M91–M94	Chondropathies
M95	Other disorders of the musculoskeletal system and connective tissue
M96	Intraoperative and postprocedural complications and disorders of musculoskeletal system, not elsewhere classified
M99	Biomechanical lesions, not elsewhere classified

ICD-10-CM Category Restructuring

After reviewing the different disease categories, developers of ICD-10 restructured some of them to bring together those groups that are related in some way. For example, in ICD-9-CM, the category for arthropathy associated with infections is included in the first subchapter, "Arthropathies and Related Disorders." In ICD-10-CM, "Infectious arthropathies" is an entire block containing separate three-character categories based on: the type of etiological relationship, whether it is a direct or indirect infection, and whether it is reactive and postinfective.

Category Title Changes

A number of category title revisions were made in chapter 13. Titles were changed to better reflect the category's content, which was often necessary when specific types of diseases were given their own block, a new category was created, or an existing category was redefined.

ICD-9-CM

| 714 | Rheumatoid arthritis and other inflammatory polyarthropathies |

ICD-10-CM

M05	Rheumatoid arthritis with rheumatoid factor
M06	Other rheumatoid arthritis
M07	Enteropathic arthropathies
M08	Juvenile arthritis

Organizational Adjustments

When comparing ICD-9-CM to ICD-10-CM, some codes have been added, deleted, combined, or moved.

In ICD-9-CM, gout is classified to chapter 3, "Endocrine, Nutritional, and Metabolic Diseases and Immunity Disorders," and in ICD-10-CM, to chapter 13, "Diseases of the Musculoskeletal System and Connective Tissue."

ICD-9-CM

| 274 | Gout |

ICD-10-CM

| M10 | Gout |

The code for swelling of limb has been deleted in ICD-10-CM. This condition is now classified to the residual three-character category for other soft tissue disorders not elsewhere classified. The ICD-10-CM Index provides direction to "see Disorder, soft tissue, specified type NEC."

ICD-9-CM

| 729.81 | Swelling of limb |

ICD-10-CM

| M79.8 | Other specified soft tissue disorders |

There was no single code in ICD-9-CM for osteoporosis with pathological fracture. Codes have been added to the ICD-10-CM to classify the combination of these two conditions and to further describe additional types of osteoporosis (anatomic site of fracture, laterality and seventh character extensions to identify the circumstances of the encounter).

ICD-10-CM

M80   Osteoporosis with current pathological fracture

The appropriate 7th character is to be added to each code from category M80:

A   initial encounter for fracture
D   subsequent encounter for fracture with routine healing
G   subsequent encounter for fracture with delayed healing
K   subsequent encounter for fracture with nonunion
P   subsequent encounter for fracture with malunion
S   sequela

M80.0   Age-related osteoporosis with current pathological fracture
　　　　Involutional osteoporosis with current pathological fracture
　　　　Osteoporosis NOS with current pathological fracture
　　　　Postmenopausal osteoporosis with current pathological fracture
　　　　Senile osteoporosis with current pathological fracture

　　M80.00   Age-related osteoporosis with current pathological fracture, unspecified site
　　M80.01   Age-related osteoporosis with current pathological fracture, shoulder
　　　　M80.011   Age-related osteoporosis with current pathological fracture, right shoulder
　　　　M80.012   Age-related osteoporosis with current pathological fracture, left shoulder
　　　　M80.019   Age-related osteoporosis with current pathological fracture, unspecified shoulder

CHAPTER 14

Chapter 14, "Diseases of the Genitourinary System," contains 11 code families, depicted by the code's first character of "N." They are:

N00–N08   Glomerular diseases
N10–N16   Renal tubulo-interstitial diseases
N17–N19   Acute renal failure and chronic kidney disease
N20–N23   Urolithiasis
N25–N29   Other disorders of kidney and ureter
N30–N39   Other diseases of the urinary system
N40–N51   Diseases of male genital organs
N60–N64   Disorders of breast
N70–N77   Inflammatory diseases of female pelvic organs
N80–N98   Noninflammatory disorders of female genital tract
N99   Other disorders of genitourinary system

ICD-10-CM Category Restructuring

After reviewing the different disease categories, developers of ICD-10 restructured some of them to bring together those groups that are related by cause. For example, in ICD-9-CM, there is no separate subchapter for urolithiasis, and the various sites where a calculus may occur are not grouped together. In ICD-10-CM, this condition has its own block and sites as listed below:

DEFINITIONS

Direct infection of a joint. Occurs when organisms invade synovial tissue and microbial antigen is present in the joint.

ICD-9-CM

Other Diseases of Urinary System (590–599)

592   Calculus of kidney and ureter
593   Other disorders of kidney and ureter
594   Calculus of lower urinary tract

ICD-10-CM

Urolithiasis (N20–N23)

N20   Calculus of kidney and ureter
N21   Calculus of lower urinary tract
N22   Calculus of urinary tract in diseases classified elsewhere

Category Title Changes

A number of category title revisions were made chapter 14. Titles were changed to better reflect the category's content, which was often necessary when specific types of diseases were given their own block, a new category was created, or an existing category was redefined.

ICD-9-CM

599   Other disorders of urethra and urinary tract

ICD-10-CM

N39   Other disorders of urinary system

Organizational Adjustments

When comparing ICD-9-CM to ICD-10-CM, some codes have been added, deleted, combined, or moved.

The code for galactocele has been deleted in ICD-10-CM. This condition is coded in the residual three-character category for other disorders of breast.

ICD-9-CM

611.5   Galactocele

ICD-10-CM

N64.8   Other specified disorders of breast
              Galactocele

CHAPTER 15

Chapter 15, "Pregnancy, Childbirth, and the Puerperium," contains nine code families, depicted by the code's first character of "O." They are:

O00–O08	Pregnancy with abortive outcome
O09	Supervision of high-risk pregnancy
O10–O16	Edema, proteinuria and hypertensive disorders in pregnancy, childbirth and the puerperium
O20–O29	Other maternal disorders predominantly related to pregnancy
O30–O48	Maternal care related to the fetus and amniotic cavity and possible delivery problems
O60–O77	Complications of labor and delivery
O80, 082	Encounter for delivery
O85–O92	Complications predominantly related to the puerperium
O94–O9A	Other obstetric conditions, not elsewhere classified

KEY POINT

While many conditions are getting their own specific code in ICD-10-CM, some codes specific to certain disorders are being classified to the residual subcategory in ICD-10-CM.

For example:

602.2   Atrophy of prostate

This disorder is reported with one code in ICD-10-CM:

N42.89   Other specified disorders of the prostate

KEY POINT

The codes in chapter 15 should only be used on the mother's record and not on the newborn's record.

ICD-10-CM Category Restructuring

After reviewing the different disease categories, developers of ICD-10 restructured some of them to bring together those groups that are related in some way. For example, in ICD-9-CM, the codes for encounter for supervision of high-risk pregnancy are found in the V codes. These codes have been moved to ICD-10-CM chapter for pregnancy, childbirth and the puerperium, category O09 Supervision of high-risk pregnancy. Subclassifications have been expanded to include the etiology of the high risk status and (current) trimester of pregnancy.

Category Title Changes

A number of category title revisions were made in chapter 15. Titles were changed to better reflect the category's content, which was often necessary when specific types of diseases are given their own block, a new category was created, or an existing category was redefined.

ICD-9-CM
652   Malposition and malpresentation of fetus

ICD-10-CM
O32   Maternal care for malpresentation of fetus

Organizational Adjustments

When comparing ICD-9-CM to ICD-10-CM, some codes have been added, deleted, combined, or moved.

The codes for complete legally and illegally induced abortions without complications are classified with the abortion codes in ICD-9-CM. These have been moved to chapter 21 in ICD-10-CM under "Elective termination of pregnancy."

ICD-9-CM
635.92   Legally induced abortion without mention of complication, complete
636.92   Illegally induced abortion without mention of complication, complete

ICD-10-CM
Z33.2   Encounter for elective termination of pregnancy

The code for breech or other malpresentation successfully converted to cephalic presentation has been deleted in ICD-10-CM. This condition is now classified to the residual category under three-character rubric O32.

ICD-9-CM
652.1   Breech or other malpresentation successfully converted to cephalic presentation

ICD-10-CM
O32   Maternal care for malpresentation of fetus

There is no specific code in ICD-9-CM for a malignant neoplasm complicating pregnancy, childbirth, and the puerperium. A new category has been added to the ICD-10-CM to classify maternal malignant neoplasms and other harm or injury, confirmed or suspected, that affects any trimester, delivery, or the puerperium.

ICD-10-CM
O9A   Maternal malignant neoplasms, traumatic injuries and abuse classifiable elsewhere but complicating pregnancy, childbirth and the puerperium

CHAPTER 16

Chapter 16, "Certain Conditions Originating in the Perinatal Period," contains 11 code families, depicted by the code's first character of "P." They are:

P00–P04	Newborn affected by maternal factors and by complications of pregnancy, labor, and delivery
P05–P08	Disorders related to length of gestation and fetal growth
P09	Abnormal findings on neonatal screening
P10–P15	Birth trauma
P19–P29	Respiratory and cardiovascular disorders specific to the perinatal period
P35–P39	Infections specific to the perinatal period
P50–P61	Hemorrhagic and hematological disorders of newborn
P70–P74	Transitory endocrine and metabolic disorders specific to newborn
P76–P78	Digestive system disorders of newborn
P80–P83	Conditions involving the integument and temperature regulation of newborn
P84	Other problems with newborn
P90–P96	Other disorders originating in the perinatal period

ICD-10-CM Category Restructuring

After reviewing the different disease categories, developers of ICD-10 restructured some of them to bring together those groups that are related by type of condition. For example, in ICD-9-CM, there are only two subchapters, "Maternal Causes of Perinatal Morbidity and Mortality," and "Other Conditions Originating in the Perinatal Period." In ICD-10-CM, the conditions have been reorganized into the blocks described above.

Category Title Changes

A number of category title revisions were made in chapter 16. Titles were changed to better reflect the category's content, which was often necessary when specific types of diseases were given their own block, a new category was created, or an existing category was redefined.

ICD-9-CM

769	Respiratory distress syndrome
770	Other respiratory conditions of fetus and newborn

ICD-10-CM

Respiratory and Cardiovascular Disorders Specific to the Perinatal Period (P19–P29)

P19	Metabolic academia in newborn
P22	Respiratory distress of newborn
P23	Congenital pneumonia
P24	Neonatal aspiration
P25	Interstitial emphysema and related conditions originating in the perinatal period
P26	Pulmonary hemorrhage originating in the perinatal period
P27	Chronic respiratory disease originating in the perinatal period
P28	Other respiratory conditions originating in the perinatal period

Organizational Adjustments

When comparing ICD-9-CM to ICD-10-CM, some codes have been added, deleted, combined, or moved.

 KEY POINT

The fifth digits for maternity codes in ICD-9-CM were not adopted for ICD-10-CM. Instead, the last character in the code represents the patient's trimester. Because certain obstetric conditions or complications occur at only one point in the obstetric period, not all codes include all three trimesters or a character to describe the trimester at all.

The code for fetal alcohol syndrome is found in the chapter, "Certain Conditions Originating in the Perinatal Period" in ICD-9-CM. This code has been moved to the chapter, "Congenital Malformations, Deformations and Chromosomal Abnormalities" in ICD-10-CM.

ICD-9-CM

760.71   Noxious influences affecting fetus or newborn via placenta or breast milk, alcohol

ICD-10-CM

Q86.0   Fetal alcohol syndrome (dysmorphic)

There is no specific code in ICD-9-CM for exposure to tobacco smoke in the perinatal period. A new code has been added to the ICD-10-CM to classify this disorder.

ICD-10-CM

P96.81   Exposure to (parental)(environmental) tobacco smoke in the perinatal period

CHAPTER 17

Chapter 17, "Congenital Malformations, Deformations and Chromosomal Abnormalities," contains 11 code families, depicted by the code's first character of "Q." They are:

Q00–Q07	Congenital malformations of the nervous system
Q10–Q18	Congenital malformations of eye, ear, face and neck
Q20–Q28	Congenital malformations of the circulatory system
Q30–Q34	Congenital malformations of the respiratory system
Q35–Q37	Cleft lip and cleft palate
Q38–Q45	Other congenital malformations of the digestive system
Q50–Q56	Congenital malformations of genital organs
Q60–Q64	Congenital malformations of the urinary system
Q65–Q79	Congenital malformations and deformations of the musculoskeletal system
Q80–Q89	Other congenital malformations
Q90–Q99	Chromosomal abnormalities, not elsewhere classified

ICD-10-CM Category Restructuring

After reviewing the different disease categories, developers of ICD-10 restructured some of them to bring together those groups that are related in some way. For example, ICD-9-CM has no subchapters for the above conditions. In ICD-10-CM, 11 blocks have been created.

Category Title Changes

A number of category title revisions were made in chapter 17. Titles were changed to better reflect the category's content, which was often necessary when specific types of diseases were given their own block, a new category was created, or an existing category was redefined.

ICD-9-CM

741   Spina bifida
742   Other congenital anomalies of nervous system

ICD-10-CM

Congenital Malformations of the Nervous System (Q00–Q07)

Q00   Anencephaly and similar malformations
Q01   Encephalocele
Q02   Microcephaly
Q03   Congenital hydrocephalus

KEY POINT

The chapters, "Diseases of the Genitourinary System," "Pregnancy, Childbirth and the Puerperium," "Certain Conditions Originating in the Perinatal Period," and "Congenital Malformations, Deformations and Chromosomal Abnormalities" are placed sequentially in ICD-10-CM.

CODING AXIOM

The title of the ICD-9-CM chapter, "Congenital Anomalies," has been expanded to include "Deformations and Chromosomal Abnormalities."

Q04	Other congenital malformations of brain
Q05	Spina bifida
Q06	Other congenital malformations of spinal cord
Q07	Other congenital malformations of nervous system

Organizational Adjustments

When comparing ICD-9-CM to ICD-10-CM, some codes have been added, deleted, combined, or moved.

The code for persistent fetal circulation is classified to code 747.83 in ICD-9-CM. This condition has been moved in ICD-10-CM to the chapter, "Certain Conditions Originating in the Perinatal Period."

ICD-9-CM

747.83   Persistent fetal circulation

ICD-10-CM

P29.3   Persistent fetal circulation

The code for congenital chorioretinal degeneration has a similar classification structure in ICD-9-CM as it does in ICD-10-CM.

ICD-9-CM

743.53   Chorioretinal degeneration, congenital

ICD-10-CM

Q14.3   Congenital malformation of choroid

Certain congenital anomalies of limbs, such as indeterminate sex and pseudohermaphroditism, have been given revised or expanded classifications in ICD-10-CM.

ICD-9-CM

752.7   Indeterminate sex and pseudohermaphroditism
      Gynandrism
      Hermaphroditism
      Ovotestis
      Pseudohermaphroditism (male) (female)
      Pure gonadal dysgenesis
      Exludes: androgen insensitivity (259.50-259.52)
                pseudohermaphroditism:
                    female, with adrenocortical disorder (255.2)
                    male, with gonadal disorder (257.8)
                    with specified chromosomal anomaly (758.0-758.9)
                testicular feminization syndrome (259.50-259.52)

ICD-10-CM

Q56   Indeterminate sex and pseudohermaphroditism
      Excludes1:   46,XX true hermaphrodite (Q99.1)
               androgen insensitivity syndrome(E34.5)
               chimera 46,XX/46,XY
               true hermaphrodite (Q99.0)
               female pseudohermaphroditism with adrenocortical disorder (E25.-)
               pseudohermaphroditism with specified chromosomal anomaly
                   (Q96–Q99)
               pure gonadal dysgenesis (Q99.1)
Q56.0   Hermaphroditism, not elsewhere classified
      Ovotestis
Q56.1   Male pseudohermaphroditism, not elsewhere classified
      46, XY with streak gonads
      Male pseudohermaphroditism NOS

 KEY POINT

The arrangement of the conditions classified to chapter 17, "Congenital Malformations, Deformations and Chromosomal Abnormalities," is, for the most part, by body system.

Q56.2   Female pseudohermaphroditism, not elsewhere classified
         Female pseudohermaphroditism NOS
Q56.3   Pseudohermaphroditism, unspecified
Q56.4   Indeterminate sex, unspecified
         Ambiguous genitalia

CHAPTER 18

Chapter 18, "Symptoms, Signs and Abnormal Clinical and Laboratory Findings, Not Elsewhere Classified," contains 14 code families, depicted by the code's first character of "R." They are:

R00–R09	Symptoms and signs involving the circulatory and respiratory systems
R10–R19	Symptoms and signs involving the digestive system and abdomen
R20–R23	Symptoms and signs involving the skin and subcutaneous tissue
R25–R29	Symptoms and signs involving the nervous and musculoskeletal systems
R30–R39	Symptoms and signs involving the urinary system
R40–R46	Symptoms and signs involving cognition, perception, emotional state and behavior
R47–R49	Symptoms and signs involving speech and voice
R50–R69	General symptoms and signs
R70–R79	Abnormal findings on examination of blood, without diagnosis
R80–R82	Abnormal findings on examination of urine, without diagnosis
R83–R89	Abnormal findings on examination of other body fluids, substances and tissues, without diagnosis
R90–R94	Abnormal findings on diagnostic imaging and in function studies, without diagnosis
R97	Abnormal tumor markers
R99	Ill-defined and unknown cause of mortality

ICD-10-CM Category Restructuring

After reviewing the different disease categories, developers of ICD-10 restructured some of them to bring together those groups that are related in some way. For example, in ICD-9-CM, all symptoms are grouped together under one subchapter. In ICD-10-CM, separate blocks have been created (similar to the separate code categories within ICD-9-CM) and the disorders placed, for the most part, according to body system.

Category Title Changes

A number of category title revisions were made in chapter 18. Titles were changed to better reflect the category's content, which was often necessary when specific types of diseases were given their own block, a new category was created, or an existing category was redefined.

ICD-9-CM

786   Symptoms involving respiratory system and other chest symptoms

ICD-10-CM

R05   Cough
R06   Abnormalities of breathing
R07   Pain in throat and chest
R09   Other symptoms and signs involving the circulatory and respiratory system

Organizational Adjustments

When comparing ICD-9-CM to ICD-10-CM, some codes have been added, deleted, combined, or moved.

The code for gangrene is listed in the chapter for symptoms in ICD-9-CM. This condition has been moved in ICD-10-CM to the chapter, "Diseases of the Circulatory System."

ICD-9-CM

785.4   Gangrene

ICD-10-CM

I96   Gangrene, not elsewhere classified

The code for elevated prostate specific antigen (PSA) has been moved in ICD-10-CM. This condition is now classified to the category for other abnormal tumor markers (R97).

ICD-9-CM

790.93   Elevated prostate specific antigen (PSA)

ICD-10-CM

R97.2   Elevated prostate specific antigen (PSA)

Code classifications for coma have been expanded to reflect clinical severity in accordance with clinical coma scaling used in assessing trauma. Instructional notations have been included to direct the coder to sequence first the associated trauma or fracture. Seventh-character extensions describe the circumstances of coma at the time of encounter for health care services.

ICD-9-CM

780.01   Coma

ICD-10-CM

R40.2   Coma
        Coma NOS
        Unconsciousness NOS
        Codes first any associated:
           coma in fracture of skull (S02.-)
           coma in intracranial injury (S06.-)
        The appropriate 7th character is to be added to each code from subcategory R40.21-, R40.22-, R40.23-:
         0   unspecified time
         1   in the field [EMT or ambulance]
         2   at arrival to emergency department
         3   at hospital admission
         4   24 hours or more after hospital admission
        A code from each subcategory is required to complete the coma scale
        Note: These codes are intended primarily for trauma registry and research use but may be utilized by all users of the classification who wish to collect this information
    R40.20   Unspecified coma
    R40.21   Coma scale, eyes open
        R40.211   Coma scale, eyes open, never
        R40.212   Coma scale, eyes open, to pain
        R40.213   Coma scale, eyes open, to sound
        R40.214   Coma scale, eyes open, spontaneous
    R40.22   Coma scale, best verbal response
        R40.221   Coma scale, best verbal response, none
        R40.222   Coma scale, best verbal response, incomprehensible words
        R40.223   Coma scale, best verbal response, inappropriate words
        R40.224   Coma scale, best verbal response, confused conversation

KEY POINT

Not all signs and symptoms are classified to this chapter. Those that point rather definitely to a given diagnosis have been assigned to a category in other chapters of the classification. For example, a mass or lump in the breast is coded to the chapter, "Diseases of the Genitourinary System."

	R40.225	Coma scale, best verbal response, oriented
R40.23		Coma scale, best motor response
	R40.231	Coma scale, best motor response, none
	R40.232	Coma scale, best motor response, extension
	R40.233	Coma scale, best motor response, abnormal
	R40.234	Coma scale, best motor response, flexion withdrawal
	R40.235	Coma scale, best motor response, localizes pain
	R40.236	Coma scale, best motor response, obeys commands

CHAPTER 19

Chapter 19, "Injury, Poisoning and Certain Other Consequences of External Causes," contains 20 code families, depicted by the code's first character of either "S" or "T." The S section includes classifications for different types of injuries related to single body regions. The T section classifies injuries to unspecified body regions as well as poisoning and certain other consequences of external causes. The code families are:

S00–S09	Injuries to the head
S10–S19	Injuries to the neck
S20–S29	Injuries to the thorax
S30–S39	Injuries to the abdomen, lower back, lumbar spine, pelvis, and external genitals
S40–S49	Injuries to the shoulder and upper arm
S50–S59	Injuries to the elbow and forearm
S60–S69	Injuries to the wrist and hand
S70–S79	Injuries to the hip and thigh
S80–S89	Injuries to the knee and lower leg
S90–S99	Injuries to the ankle and foot
T07	Unspecified multiple injuries
T14	Injury of unspecified body region
T15–T19	Effects of foreign body entering through natural orifice
T20–T32	Burns and corrosions
T33–T34	Frostbite
T36–T50	Poisoning by adverse effects of drugs and underdosing of medicaments and biological substances
T51–T65	Toxic effects of substances chiefly nonmedicinal as to source
T66–T78	Other and unspecified effects of external causes
T79	Certain early complications of trauma
T80–T88	Complications of surgical and medical care, not elsewhere classified

ICD-10-CM Category Restructuring

The axis of classification for chapter 19, "Injury, Poisoning and Certain Other Consequences of External Causes" (chapter 17, "Injury and Poisoning," in ICD-9-CM), has been changed from type of injury and then site of injury in ICD-9-CM to body region and then to type of injury in ICD-10. ICD-10-CM further enhances this restructuring by adding codes for laterality and alpha extensor characters for sequelae and status of the encounter. For example, "Fractures" is the first subchapter in the injury and poisoning chapter of ICD-9-CM. The breakdown is then by site, e.g., vault of skull, base of skull. For ICD-10, the first subchapter in "Injury, Poisoning and Certain Other Consequences of External Causes" describes injuries to the head (the body region), and then a breakdown by type of injury, e.g., superficial injury of head, open wound of head.

ICD-9-CM

Chapter 17 Injury and Poisoning

Fractures (800–829)

Fracture of Skull (800–804)

800	Fracture of vault of skull
801	Fracture of base of skull
802	Fracture of face bones
803	Other and unqualified skull fractures
804	Multiple fractures involving skull or face with other bones

ICD-10-CM

Chapter 19 Injury, Poisoning and Certain Other Consequences of External Causes

Injuries to the Head (S00–S09)

S00	Superficial injury of head
S01	Open wound of head
S02	Fracture of skull and facial bones
S03	Dislocation and sprain of joints and ligaments of head
S04	Injury of cranial nerve
S05	Injury of eye and orbit
S06	Intracranial injury
S07	Crushing injury of head
S08	Avulsion and traumatic amputation of part of head
S09	Other and unspecified injuries of head

Category Title Changes

A number of category title revisions were made in chapter 19 due to the restructuring described above. Titles were changed to better reflect the category's content, which was often necessary when specific types of diseases were given their own block, a new category was created, or an existing category was redefined. For example, frostbite has its own block of three-character categories, T33–T34.

Organizational Adjustments

When comparing ICD-9-CM to ICD-10-CM, some codes have been added, deleted, combined, or moved.

The code for cataract fragments in the eye following cataract surgery is found in the chapter for injury and poisoning in ICD-9-CM. The condition has been moved to the chapter, "Diseases of the Eye and Adnexa" in ICD-10-CM.

ICD-9-CM

998.82   Cataract fragments in eye following cataract surgery

ICD-10-CM

H59.02	Cataract (lens) fragments in eye following cataract surgery	
	H59.021	Cataract (lens) fragments in eye following cataract surgery, right eye
	H59.022	Cataract (lens) fragments in eye following cataract surgery, left eye
	H59.023	Cataract (lens) fragments in eye following cataract surgery, bilateral
	H59.029	Cataract (lens) fragments in eye following cataract surgery, unspecified eye

The code for non-healing surgical wound has been deleted in ICD-10-CM. This condition is now classified to the residual subcategory for other complications of procedures not elsewhere classified.

 KEY POINT

Chapter 19 uses the S-section for coding different types of injuries related to single body regions, and the T-section to cover injuries to unspecified and multiple body regions, as well as poisoning, burns, and certain other consequences of external causes.

ICD-9-CM

998.83   Non-healing surgical wound

ICD-10-CM

T81.89xA Other complications of procedures, not elsewhere classified, initial encounter

CHAPTER 20

Chapter 20, "External Causes of Morbidity," contains 30 code families depicted by the code's first character of "V," "W," and "X." They are:

V00–X58	Accidents
V00–V99	Transport accidents
V00–V09	Pedestrian injured in transport accident
V10–V19	Pedal cyclist injured in transport accident
V20–V29	Motorcycle rider injured in transport accident
V30–V39	Occupant of three-wheeled motor vehicle injured in transport accident
V40–V49	Car occupant injured in transport accident
V50–V59	Occupant of pick-up truck or van injured in transport accident
V60–V69	Occupant of heavy transport vehicle injured in transport accident
V70–V79	Bus occupant injured in transport accident
V80–V89	Other land transport accidents
V90–V94	Water transport accidents
V95–V97	Air and space transport accidents
V98–V99	Other and unspecified transport accidents
W00–X58	Other external causes of accidental injury
W00–W19	Falls
W20–W49	Exposure to inanimate mechanical forces
W50–W64	Exposure to animate mechanical forces
W65–W74	Accidental drowning and submersion
W85–W99	Exposure to electric current, radiation and extreme ambient air temperature and pressure
X00–X08	Exposure to smoke, fire and flames
X10–X19	Contact with heat and hot substances
X30–X39	Exposure to forces of nature
X52, X58	Accidental exposure to other specified factors
X71–X83	Intentional self-harm
X92–Y08	Assault
Y21–Y33	Event of undetermined intent
Y35–Y38	Legal intervention, operations of war, military operation, and terrorism
Y62–Y84	Complications of medical surgical care
Y62–Y69	Misadventures to patients during surgical and medical
Y70–Y82	Medical devices associated with adverse incidents in diagnostic and therapeutic use
Y83–Y84	Surgical and other medical procedures as the cause of abnormal reaction of the patient, or of later complication, without mention of misadventure at the time of the procedure
Y90-Y98	Supplementary factors related to causes of morbidity classified elsewhere

 KEY POINT

Where multiple sites of injury are specified in the titles, the word "with" indicates involvement of both sites, and the word "and" indicates involvement of either or both sites.

ICD-10-CM Category Restructuring

After reviewing the different disease categories, developers of ICD-10 restructured some of them to bring together those groups that are related in some way. For example, in ICD-9-CM, the supplementary classification of external causes of injury and poisoning (E codes) is found at the end of the tabular list. In ICD-10-CM, these codes follow chapter 19, "Injury, Poisoning and Certain Other Consequences of External Causes." In addition, the transport accident section has been completely revised and extended, with blocks of categories identifying the victim's mode of transport.

It is also important to note that after the events of September 11, 2001, the National Center for Health Statistics (NCHS) recognized a definite need for accurate statistical classifications to characterize deaths and illnesses related to acts of terrorism. The NCHS has developed a new set of codes within the framework of ICD-10, the classification presently used for mortality reporting, and ICD-9-CM, used for morbidity, to allow these identifications to be reported.

The new codes for terrorism were implemented into ICD-9-CM for 2002 within the existing chapter for external causes.

Since the ICD-10 classification system is not under U.S. maintenance, implementing new codes into ICD-10 requires international deliberation under the World Health Organization's (WHO's) sanction and can take much longer. The codes have been presented and will be placed in the "U" chapter, reserved for future additions and changes. Although not adopted by WHO at the time of publication of this book, these U.S. codes will be distinguished by an asterisk to separate them from official WHO ICD-10 codes.

ICD-9-CM

In ICD-9-CM, the main axis is whether the event is a traffic or non-traffic accident.

Supplementary Classification of External Causes of Injury and Poisoning (E800–E999)

E800–E807	Railway Accidents
E810–E819	Motor Vehicle Traffic Accidents
E820–E825	Motor Vehicle Nontraffic Accidents
E826–E829	Other Road Vehicle Accidents

ICD-10-CM

In ICD-10, the main axis is the injured person's mode of transport. For land transpor accidents, categories V01–V89, the vehicle of which the injured person is an occupant is identified in the first two characters since it is perceived as the essential issue for prevention purposes.

External Causes of Morbidity (V00–Y98)

V00–X58	Accidents
V00–V99	Transport accidents
V00–V09	Pedestrian injured in transport accident
V10–V19	Pedal cyclist injured in transport accident
V20–V29	Motorcycle rider injured in transport accident
V30–V39	Occupant of three-wheeled motor vehicle injured in transportt accident
V40–V49	Car occupant injured in transport accident
V50–V59	Occupant of pick-up truck or van injured in transport accident
V60–V69	Occupant of heavy transport vehicle injured in transport accident
V70–V79	Bus occupant injured in transport accident

 KEY POINT

The late effect codes are scattered throughout this chapter in ICD-9-CM. In ICD-10-CM, sequalae of external cause is indicated by using the seventh-character extension "s":

V95.01xs	Helicopter crash injuring occupant, sequelae
W23.0xxs	Caught, crushed, jammed, or pinched between moving objects, sequelae
X15.0xxs	Contact with hot stove (kitchen), sequelae
X76.xxxs	Intentional self-harm by smoke, fire and flames, sequelae
Y28.0xxs	Contact with sharp glass, undetermined intent, sequelae

 CODING AXIOM

ICD-10-CM uses a placeholder character "X" as a fifth or sixth character placeholder in certain codes to allow for future expansion. Where a placeholder exists, the X must be used for the code to be considered a valid code.

V80–V89	Other land transport accidents
V90–V94	Water transport accidents
V95–V97	Air and space transport accidents
V98–V99	Other and unspecified transport accidents

Category Title Changes

A number of category title revisions were made in chapter 20. Titles were changed to better reflect the category's content, which was often necessary when specific types of diseases were given their own block, a new category was created, or an existing category was redefined.

ICD-9-CM

E917	Striking against or struck accidentally by objects or persons

ICD-10-CM

W21	Striking against or struck by sports equipment
W22	Striking against or struck by other objects
W50	Accidental hit, strick, kick, twist, bite or scratch by another person
W51	Accidental striking against or bumped into by another person
W52	Crushed, pushed or stepped on by crowd or human stampede

Organizational Adjustments

When comparing ICD-9-CM to ICD-10-CM, some codes have been added, deleted, combined, or moved.

The late effect codes for external causes are located in various subchapters throughout the supplementary classification in ICD-9-CM. In ICD-10-CM, all late effects for each intent, i.e., accidents, suicide, etc., can be denoted by adding the sequela extension (s) to the code itself, where appropriately identified.

ICD-9-CM

E929	Late effects of accidental injury
E959	Late effects of self-inflicted injury
E969	Late effects of injury purposely inflicted by other person
E977	Late effects of injuries due to legal intervention
E989	Late effects of injury, undetermined whether accidentally or purposely inflicted
E999	Late effect of injury due to war operations and terrorism

ICD-10-CM

V00.02xs	Pedestrian on foot injured in collision with skateboarder, sequelae
W50.4xxs	Accidental scratch by another person, sequelae
X71.0xxs	Intentional self-harm by drowning and submersion while in bathtub, sequelae
Y02.8xxs	Assault by pushing or placing victim before other moving object, sequelae
Y24.8xxs	Other firearm discharge, undetermined intent, sequelae

The codes for accidental poisoning by drugs, medicinal substances, and biologicals (E850–E858) and by other solid and liquid substances, gases, and vapors (E860–E869) have been moved in ICD-10-CM. The specific substance is identified with a code from the T36–T50 range for poisoning by and adverse effects of drugs, medicaments, and biological substances, or the T51–T65 range for toxic effects of substances chiefly nonmedicinal, using the code identified as accidental (unintentional).

ICD-9-CM

E856	Accidental poisoning by antibiotics
E860.4	Accidental poisoning by fusel oil

KEY POINT

Contents of this chapter were often referred to as the "E codes" chapter in ICD-9-CM supplementary classification. With ICD-10-CM, there are four alphabetic characters, V, W, X, and Y, that make up the next-to-last chapter of the classification.

ICD-10-CM

T36.0x1A Poisoning by penicillins, accidental (unintentional), initial encounter
T51.3x1A Toxic effect of fusel oil, accidental (unintentional), initial encounter

There is no specific code in ICD-9-CM for exposure to radon. A new code has been added to ICD-10-CM to classify this health risk factor, used with seventh-character extensions to identify initial encounter, subsequent encounter, and sequelae.

ICD-10-CM

X39.01xA Exposure to radon, initial encounter
X39.01xD Exposure to radon, subsequent encounter
X39.01xS Exposure to radon, sequelae

Chapter 21

Chapter 21, "Factors Influencing Health Status and Contact with Health Services," contains 13 code families, depicted by the code's first character of "Z." They are:

Z00–Z13	Persons encountering health services for examination and investigation
Z14–Z15	Genetic carrier and genetic susceptibility to disease
Z16	Infection with drug resistant microorganisms
Z17	Estrogen receptor status
Z20–Z28	Persons with potential health hazards related to communicable diseases
Z30–Z39	Persons encountering health services in circumstances related to reproduction
Z40–Z53	Persons encountering health services for specific procedures and health care
Z55–Z65	Persons with potential health hazards related to socioeconomic and psychosocial circumstances
Z66	Do not resuscitate [DNR] status
Z67	Blood type
Z69–Z76	Persons encountering health services in other circumstances
Z79–Z99	Persons with potential health hazards related to family and personal history and certain conditions influencing health status

 KEY POINT

This chapter, which in previous revisions of ICD constituted a supplementary classification, permits the classification of environmental events and circumstances as the cause of injury, poisoning, and other adverse effects. Where a code from this section is applicable, it is intended that it shall be used in addition to a code from another chapter of the classification indicating the nature of the condition.

ICD-10-CM Category Restructuring

After reviewing the different disease categories, developers of ICD-10 restructured some of them to bring together those groups that are related in some way. For example, in ICD-9-CM, the categories for problems related to household, economic, family, and other psychosocial circumstances are classified under the subchapter for persons encountering health services in other circumstances. The categories for these types of problems have been moved to their own subchapter for persons with potential health hazards related to socioeconomic and psychosocial circumstances in ICD-10-CM. There is also a new, stand-alone category to denote a DNR order.

Category Title Changes

A number of category title revisions were made in chapter 21. Titles were changed to better reflect the category's content, which was often necessary when specific types of diseases were given their own block, a new category was created, or an existing category was redefined.

DEFINITIONS

Z codes. Used to report reasons for encounters. A corresponding procedure code should accompany a Z code if a procedure is performed.

ICD-9-CM

V60	Housing, household, and economic circumstances
V61	Other family circumstances
V62	Other psychosocial circumstances

ICD-10-CM

Z59	Problems related to housing and economic circumstance
Z60	Problems related to social environment
Z61	Problems related to negative life events in childhood
Z62	Other problems related to upbringing
Z63	Other problems related to primary support group, including family circumstances
Z64	Problems related to certain psychosocial circumstances
Z65	Problems related to other psychosocial circumstances

When comparing ICD-9-CM to ICD-10-CM, some codes have been added, deleted, combined, or moved.

The codes for supervision of high-risk pregnancy, category V23, are found in the V code chapter in ICD-9-CM. These situations have been moved in ICD-10-CM to a new category in the chapter, "Pregnancy, Childbirth and the Puerperium." For example:

ICD-9-CM

V23.0	Pregnancy with a history of infertility

ICD-10-CM

O09.00	Supervision of pregnancy with history of infertility, unspecified trimester
O09.01	Supervision of pregnancy with history of infertility, first trimester
O09.02	Supervision of pregnancy with history of infertility, second trimester
O09.03	Supervision of pregnancy with history of infertility, third trimester

The codes for orthopaedic aftercare, V54.0–V54.9, have been changed to category Z47 in ICD-10-CM. Aftercare for healing fracture has been eliminated from this category. Fracture codes now have seventh-character extensions to indicate subsequent encounter or sequela. Healing fracture aftercare encounters should be reported with the appropriate fracture code with the extension "d."

ICD-9-CM

V54.0	Aftercare involving internal fixation device
V54.1	Aftercare for healing traumatic fracture
V54.2	Aftercare for healing pathologic fracture
V54.8	Other orthopedic aftercare
V54.9	Unspecified orthopedic aftercare

ICD-10-CM

Z47.1	Aftercare following joint replacement surgery
Z47.2	Encounter for removal of internal fixation device

There is no specific code in ICD-9-CM for an encounter for paternity testing. A new code has been added to ICD-10-CM to classify encounters for this purpose.

ICD-10-CM

Z02.81	Encounter for paternity testing

DISCUSSION QUESTIONS

1. Why was the term, "certain" added to the title of chapter 1, "Certain Infectious and Parasitic Diseases?" Give examples.

_____

_____

_____

2. How has the classification of conditions as sequelae changed in ICD-10-CM? Give examples.

_____

_____

_____

3. Can you think of any reasons for some changes that render ICD-10-CM less specific than ICD-9-CM?

_____

_____

_____

4. Where can codes for signs and symptoms be found in ICD-10-CM?

_____

_____

_____

5. Identify the chapter(s) where codes for external causes relative to the E codes are found in ICD-10-CM.

_____

_____

_____

Chapter 4: Introduction to ICD-10-PCS

Parallel procedure coding systems have been in place for many years in the United States to report health care data and facilitate reimbursement for services. In general, hospitals report ICD-9-CM codes for diagnoses and inpatient procedures, but they also use the American Medical Association's CPT codes to report outpatient procedures and other services. On the other hand, physicians use ICD-9-CM to report diagnostic and encounter information only, and CPT codes to report their associated procedures and services. The CPT book, first published in 1966, may be used to report outpatient (office) services, and inpatient (hospital) procedures and other services performed and billed by the physician.

The 1990s, however, ushered in several changes in the way we deliver health care, which fueled discussions of a single system for procedural coding. For example, the advent of ambulatory surgical centers and physician office surgical suites allows once exclusively inpatient services to be performed as either outpatient or inpatient services. The administrative simplification provisions of the Health Insurance Portability and Accountability Act (HIPAA) of 1996 brought a clear demand to the issue of a single procedure coding system, which has since been the task of the Department of Health and Human Services (HHS) Coding and Classification Implementation Team.

CURRENT CODING SYSTEMS

Volume 3 of ICD-9-CM and CPT codes are summarized in the following two sections.

ICD-9-CM Volume 3

In 1979, when the ninth version of ICD was published, a separate and third volume of ICD-9-CM was created to house procedure classifications. The Centers for Medicare and Medicaid Services (CMS, formerly HCFA) maintains the volume 3 codes, which include operative, diagnostic, and therapeutic procedures. Code revisions are addressed at the ICD-9-CM Coordination and Maintenance Committee meetings, held twice annually.

Volume 3 procedures are classified into two-digit category code sections (or, rubrics), which are arranged mainly by body system, within 18 chapters. The codes are organized hierarchically, whereby the two-digit code category shares a common anatomical system or type of service. Three- and four-digit subcategory codes further differentiate the procedures into specific types, techniques, or operative sites.

Within this section, code category 37 specifically classifies certain other operations on the heart and pericardium. Some of those codes are listed hierarchically below. For example:

37	Other operations on heart and pericardium	
	37.2	Diagnostic procedures on heart and pericardium
		37.21 Right heart cardiac catheterization
		37.22 Left heart cardiac catheterization
	37.7	Insertion, revision, replacement, and removal of pacemaker leads; insertion of temporary pacemaker system; or revision of cardiac device pocket
		37.73 Initial insertion of transvenous lead [electrode] into atrium
		37.74 Insertion or replacement of epicardial lead (electrode) into epicardium

The ICD-9-CM procedure classification system faces many challenges, including the following:

- Contains overlapping and duplicate codes
- Includes inconsistent and outdated terminology
- Lacks codes for certain types of services
- Lacks sufficient specificity and detail

It has been recognized that ICD-9-CM, including the volume 3 procedure classification, does not have sufficient available space to continue to provide adequate coding options. As technology advances and procedure services continue to evolve, ICD-9-CM is unable to accommodate those changes with clinical codes.

ICD-10-PCS

ICD-10-PCS is a procedure coding system that will be used to report inpatient procedures effective October 1, 2013. This system will be used to collect data, facilitate reimbursement, and support electronic health record initiatives.

The Centers for Medicare and Medicaid Services (CMS) maintains the inpatient procedure classification, currently ICD-9-CM, volume 3. In 1993, CMS contracted with 3M Health Information Systems to design and develop a procedure classification system to replace ICD-9-CM, volume 3. The resulting system, ICD-10-PCS, was released in 1998 after an independent contractor tested and evaluated it. It has been updated regularly since that time. As new codes have been added and codes revised in ICD-9-CM, ICD-10-PCS has been updated accordingly to maintain congruency between the classifications.

ICD-10-PCS was created with a multiaxial, seven-character, alphanumeric structure. This structure provides ease of revision and update to accommodate the rapid and ongoing changes in medical and surgical technologies, and can accommodate a vast number of codes for distinct procedural services. As such, it provides a more comprehensive and complete listing of procedural services with exponentially greater capacity for expandability. Additional improvements incorporated into ICD-10-PCS include:

- Standardized terminology
- Diagnostic information excluded from procedure classifications
- Reduced and restricted NEC (other specified) and NOS (unspecified) coding options
- Increased level of specificity; promoting greater data granularity

A major goal in developing ICD-10-PCS was to require less effort on the coder's part to construct accurate codes. Since the release of the initial draft in 1998, the system has evolved based on extensive input from multiple segments of the health care industry. After intensive testing and revision, the consensus is that ICD-10-PCS will provide the precision and expandable multiaxial structure necessary to enhance and support the health care data initiatives of medical research, epidemiology, and statistical analysis, as well as to meet the needs of the coding and reimbursement community.

CPT

The current CPT provides a listing of services and procedures and their individual codes within specific sections of CPT. There are eight sections: evaluation and management, anesthesia, surgery, radiology, pathology and laboratory, medicine, category II, and category III codes. Each section is assigned a block of codes and is further broken into subsections. For example, the radiology subsections are diagnostic radiology, diagnostic ultrasound, radiation oncology, and nuclear medicine. Several appendixes follow the eight sections. These may include an appendix on modifiers; summary of additions, deletions, and revisions; clinical examples; summary of CPT add-on codes; and many more. Guidelines within each section provide definitions, explanations of terms, and factors relevant to the

FOR THE RECORD

The advent of the prospective payment system (PPS) has resulted in a steady increase in outpatient visits with an associated decline in the number of hospital admissions.

FOR MORE INFO

The draft ICD-10-PCS reference manual is available on the CMS website at:

http://www.cms.hhs.gov/ICD10/01m_200 9_ICD10PCS.asp.

section. Parenthetical information found throughout the sections highlight the coding guidelines, designate coding changes such as deletions, and provide directions for finding the correct code.

The AMA is working to improve the structure and process of CPT. According to the AMA, health practitioners should anticipate changes to the editorial process of developing new and revised codes, while coders should expect structural modifications to simplify procedure coding (inpatient and outpatient) while also meeting the requirements of HIPAA. The AMA is developing a system to meet several objectives, including the following:

- Maintain CPT's position as the standard for procedural coding for the health care community, and ensure that CPT is the national and international procedural coding nomenclature that facilitates reimbursement and analysis of health care information
- Enhance the use of CPT by practicing physicians
- Improve CPT to address the needs of various non-physician health care professionals, including nurses, social workers, psychologists, optometrists, physician assistants and nurse practitioners, chiropractors, and therapists (occupational, speech, physical)
- Improve CPT to address the needs of hospitals, managed care organizations, long term care, ambulatory care professional and trade associations, clinical specialty societies, and researchers
- Develop comprehensive information regarding the correct use of CPT, including guidelines, policies, and procedures
- Develop a process to reflect changing practice patterns and new technologies
- Explore issues related to the reliability of CPT coding, i.e. that different users arrive at the same code for the same service

ICD-10-PCS was developed to complement ICD-10-CM in the inpatient arena, but is vastly different from CPT in terms of its design, intent, structure, and maintenance.

In the August 22, 2008, proposed rule, CMS explained that the CPT coding system was not considered a viable alternative to ICD-10-CM and ICD-10-PCS code sets because the CPT codes do not adequately capture facility-based, nonphysician services. In the August 17, 2000, final rule (65 CMS-0013-F23 FR 50312), CMS adopted the HCPCS and CPT codes as the official procedure coding systems for outpatient reporting. ICD-9-CM procedure codes are not a HIPAA standard for coding in these settings, and while some hospitals may elect to double code their outpatient records using both HCPCS and CPT, as well as ICD-9-CM procedure codes for internal purposes, it is not a requirement. It was further explained in the January 15, 2009, final rule (45 CFR Part 162 CMS-0013-F) that, although the required implementation date for ICD-10-CM for diagnoses is effective October 1, 2013, ICD-10-PCS will be required reporting only for inpatient hospital procedures. A second HIPAA transaction standards rule—X12 version 5010 and NCPDP version D.0—establishes earlier effective dates, the latest being January 1, 2013. The HIPAA transactions software must be updated accordingly to accommodate both ICD-10-CM and ICD-10-PCS.

ICD-10-PCS is a procedure coding system that will be used to report inpatient procedures effective October 1, 2013. This system will be used to collect data, facilitate reimbursement, and support electronic health record initiatives.

The Centers for Medicare and Medicaid Services (CMS) maintains the inpatient procedure classification, currently ICD-9-CM, volume 3. In 1993, CMS contracted with 3M Health Information Systems to design and develop a procedure classification system to replace ICD-9-CM, volume 3. The resulting system, ICD-10-PCS, was released in 1998 after an independent contractor tested and evaluated it. It has been updated regularly since that time. As new codes have been added and codes revised in ICD-9-CM, ICD-10-PCS has been updated accordingly to maintain congruency between the classifications.

ICD-10-PCS was created with a multiaxial, seven-character, alphanumeric structure. This structure provides ease of revision and update to accommodate the rapid and ongoing changes in medical and surgical technologies, and can accommodate a vast number of codes for distinct procedural services. As such, it provides a more comprehensive and complete listing of procedural services with exponentially greater capacity for expandability. Additional improvements incorporated into ICD-10-PCS include:

- Standardized terminology
- Diagnostic information excluded from procedure classifications
- Reduced and restricted NEC (other specified) and NOS (unspecified) coding options
- Increased level of specificity; promoting greater data granularity

A major goal in developing ICD-10-PCS was to require less effort on the coder's part to construct accurate codes. Since the release of the initial draft in 1998, the system has evolved based on extensive input from multiple segments of the health care industry. After intensive testing and revision, the consensus is that ICD-10-PCS will provide the precision and expandable multiaxial structure necessary to enhance and support the health care data initiatives of medical research, epidemiology, and statistical analysis, as well as to meet the needs of the coding and reimbursement community.

ICD-10-PCS OBJECTIVES

An early draft of the 3M project described objectives derived from the inadequacies in the present procedural coding system. Among these objectives that were subsequently incorporated in ICD-10-PCS are the following:

- Completeness—A unique code for all substantially different procedures
- Expandability—Easy incorporation of unique codes for new procedures
- Uniformly structured—Consistent meaning of individual characters in the codes
- Standardized terminology—No multiple definitions for the same terms, and each term assigned a specific meaning (found in an accompanying glossary)

Additional attributes in the procedural coding system include the following:

- The "not elsewhere classified" option was eliminated, except for newly approved radiopharmaceuticals and new devices. The NEC option can be used prior to the addition of the radiopharmaceuticals and devices to the coding system. In every other case, ICD-10-PCS should contain all possible operations, body parts, and approaches.
- Diagnostic information is excluded from the procedure description to enhance data collection. There are no codes for specific diagnoses (e.g., aneurysm, hernia, cleft lip, enterocele).
- There are no eponyms. For example, the Bardenheurer operation is identified as ligation and suturing of an arterial fistula, rather than by the eponym.
- There is no Latin terminology. Everything is reduced to simple anatomical and procedural terms.

KEY POINT

ICD-10-PCS Draft Coding Guidelines are located in the ICD-10-PCS Reference Manual and can be downloaded at the following URL:

http://www.cms.hhs.gov/ICD10/01m_200 9_ICD10PCS.asp.

See appendix B for the complete draft guidelines.

ICD-10-PCS Draft Coding Guidelines and Resources

ICD-10-PCS Draft Coding Guidelines are located in ICD-10-PCS Reference Manual and can be downloaded at the following URL: http://www.cms.hhs.gov/ICD10/01m_2009_ICD10PCS.asp.

Multiple resources are available on the CMS website, including code tables, indexes, code descriptions, mapping files, resource tables, a reference manual, historical information, and current code updates.

The guidelines are organized into sections covering general instruction, medical and procedure coding, and a section for other coding instruction. Coding guidelines for ICD-10-PCS need to be carefully reviewed as part of orientation and training. Coders will need to be as well versed in application of guidelines for the ICD-10-PCS as they are with coding guidelines for ICD-9-CM and CPT. Ingenix regularly publishes updated versions of the complete text, with additional forthcoming publications to help in the transition between code sets.

ICD-10-PCS coding guidelines follow a similar philosophy as do some ICD-9-CM coding guidelines and conventions in that the purpose of the classification of procedures and services performed is the same. However, due to the drastic difference between the structure, organization, and granularity of systems, a comparison of the two sets of guidelines would be an apple-to-orange comparison.

It will be necessary to continue to keep current with the guidelines as they are updated. New ICD-9-CM procedures will be added to the PCS structure as they are approved by CMS until such time as ICD-9-CM becomes obsolete and ICD-10-PCS replaces it for coding and reporting purposes. Coders need to thoroughly review the guidelines to understand all of the rules and instructions for proper coding. There are no codes for diagnoses in ICD-10-PCS; diagnoses are coded using ICD-9-CM or ICD-10-CM, as appropriate, for the encounter or setting.

ICD-10-PCS Organization

The developers of ICD-10-PCS resolved problems inherent in the existing procedural coding systems by rewriting the system's salient features. Codes in ICD-10-PCS contain seven alphanumeric characters, and although there are thousands of possible codes, PCS distills all medical services into approximately 59 global root operations distributed among the 16 sections (0-H).

Multiple additional resources are available on the CMS website, including code tables, indexes, code descriptions, mapping files, resource tables, a reference manual, historical information, and current code updates.

ICD-10-PCS Index

The index allows codes to be located alphabetically. It is arranged by root operations with subentries by body system, body part, operation, and device. The index also may be consulted for a specific operation term such as hysterectomy, where a cross-reference advises the coder to see "Resection, Female Reproductive System, 0VT." Following is an example of entries in the index:

Fasciectomy
—*see* Resection, Bursa, Ligaments, 0MB.
—*see* Excision, Bursae and Ligaments 0MB
—*see* Resection, Bursae and Ligaments 0MT
Fasciectomy —*see* Excision, Bursa, Ligaments, 0MT
Fascioplasty —*see* Repair, Bursa, Ligaments, 0MQ
Formation
—*see* Bypass
—*see* Creation

 FOR MORE INFO

An ICD-9-CM to ICD-10-PCS general equivalence mapping (GEM) crosswalk is available on the CMS website. Select 2009 Mapping:

http://www.cms.hhs.gov/ICD10/01m_2009_ICD10PCS.asp

Fragmentation
    by Body System
        Anatomical Regions, General 0WF
        Central Nervous System 00F
        Eye 08F
        Female Reproductive System 0UF
        Gastrointestinal System 0DF
        Heart & Great Vessels 02F
        Hepatobiliary Sytem & Pancreas 0FF
        Mouth & Throat 0CF
        Respiratory System 0BF
        Urinary Sytem 0TF
    by Body Part
        Ampulla of Vater 0FFC
        Anus 0DFQ
        Appendix 0DFJ
        Ascending Colon 0DFK
        Bladder 0TFB
        Bladder Neck 0TFC
        Bronchus
            Lower Lobe, Left 0BF1
            Segmental, Lingula 0BF9
        Canal, Spinal 00F3
        Carina 0BF2
        Cavity, Pelvic 0WF1

The index lists only the first three to four characters (values) of the code. Therefore, it is not possible to construct a procedure code exclusively from the alphabetic index. The purpose of the index is to locate the appropriate table from which the coder can construct a procedure code.

The most recent version of the ICD-10-PCS index provides meticulous cross references from previously used ICD-9-CM index terms. Some coders may find that they will often be referred to a different main term in ICD-10, than they are used to using in ICD-9-CM when indexing a procedure. It is highly likely that most encoders will include this cross-referencing logic in the product's programming. However, because main terms are not always congruent between the coding systems, it may initially take more time to code a procedure—even with the assistance of an encoder—because of the need for terminology translation between certain procedure classifications.

The following table gives abbreviated examples of how main terms for indexing procedures have changed from ICD-9-CM to ICD-10-PCS. This table is not an all-inclusive comparison but should give coders and coding managers a good idea of the nature and scope of the disparity between systems.

ICD-9-CM Index Terms	ICD-10-PCS Index Terms
Nephrectomy, lobectomy	Excision, Resection
Stripping, dilation & curettage	Extraction, Resection
Fulguration, cautery	Destruction
Amputation, disarticulation	Detachment
Reduction	Reposition
Thoracentesis	Drainage
Thrombectomy, choledocholithotomy	Extirpation
Lithotripsy	Fragmentation
Arthroscopy, laparotomy	Inspection
Angioplasty	Dilation, Repair, Replacement
Ligation	Occlusion

Fundoplication, cerclage	Restriction
Graft	Replacement, Supplement
Adjustment	Revision
Ostotomy, cordotomy	Division
Adhesiolysis	Release
Herniorrhaphy, suture	Repair
Lift, augmentation	Alteration
Arthrodesis	Fusion

Table of Codes

Code tables are organized in a series by section and body system. All seven characters must contain valid values as specified in the code tables to construct a valid procedure code. For example, the medical and surgical section (section 0), is organized by 31 body system values. Within this section, the first character represents the section, the second character represents the body system, and the third character represents the type of procedure (root operation). The values for characters 1–3 are provided at the top of each table. Each body system subdivision contains a table that lists possible values for the remaining character (characters 4–7). These tables provide valid choices of values that are required to construct a complete code.

A table may be separated into rows to specify the valid choices of values in characters 4–7. The columns in the tables contain the valid values for characters 4–7. The rows indicate the valid combinations of values to construct a code. Any combination of values not contained in a single row of the tables will result in an invalid code.

Medical and Surgical Related Sections

0	Medical and surgical
1	Obstetrics
2	Placement
3	Administration
4	Measurement and monitoring
5	Extracorporeal assistance and performance
6	Extracorporeal therapies
7	Osteopathic
8	Other procedures
9	Chiropractic

Ancillary Sections

B	Imaging
C	Nuclear medicine
D	Radiation oncology
F	Physical rehabilitation and diagnostic audiology
G	Mental health
H	Substance abuse treatment

Each subsequent place in the code has a specific function. The meaning of each place in a code may differ from one section to another. Thus, the fifth character in the imaging section (B) identifies the contrast material used, while the fifth character in the medical and surgical section (0) identifies the surgical approach.

For example, the seven characters for the "Medical and Surgical" section are organized as follows:

1	2	3	4	5	6	7
Section	Body System	Root Operation	Body Part	Approach	Device	Qualifier

KEY POINT

The letters I and O are not used in ICD-10-PCS, so that confusion with numbers 1 and 0 can be eliminated. Therefore, each place in a seven-character ICD-10-PCS code could have any of 34 values (numbers 0–9, or any of 24 letters). This is an enormous advantage over any code systems that are strictly numeric.

KEY POINT

The third character identifies the root operation, except in "Radiation Oncology," "Rehabilitation," and "Mental Health." In many sections, only a few root operations are performed and these operations are defined for use in that section (i.e., irrigation in the section, "Administration"). The section, "Medical and Surgical," however, uses an extensive list of root operations. The sections, "Obstetrics" and "Placement" also use some of these root operations in addition to section-specific root operations.

Medical and Surgical Section

The key to the second character in the section, "Medical and Surgical" is as follows:

0	Central nervous system
1	Peripheral nervous system
2	Heart and great vessels
3	Upper arteries
4	Lower arteries
5	Upper veins
6	Lower veins
7	Lymphatic and hemic system
8	Eye
9	Ear, nose, sinus
B	Respiratory system
C	Mouth and throat
D	Gastrointestinal system
F	Hepatobiliary system and pancreas
G	Endocrine system
H	Skin and breast
J	Subcutaneous tissue and fascia
K	Muscles
L	Tendons
M	Bursa, ligaments
N	Head and facial bones
P	Upper bones
Q	Lower bones
R	Upper joints
S	Lower joints
T	Urinary system
U	Female reproductive system
V	Male reproductive system
W	Anatomical regions, general
X	Anatomical regions, upper extremities
Y	Anatomical regions, lower extremities

The third character in the section, "Medical Surgical" represents the root operation, which specifies the underlying objective of the procedure (e.g., bypass). There are 31 root operations in the medical and surgical section. Each root operation is given a precise definition. The root operation characters are consistent through all body systems.

The fourth character indicates the specific part of the body system on which the procedure was performed (e.g., appendix). Body parts are not to be equated with organs. For example, the upper, middle, and lower esophagus are three body parts, and each can be excised or resected. The body part includes lesions, polyps, etc. found in/on the body part.

The fifth character indicates the approach used to perform the procedure (e.g., open). The approach characters are consistent through all body systems. There are seven different approaches.

The sixth character indicates whether any device was used in the procedure (e.g., synthetic substitute). This character is used to specify only devices that remain after the procedure is completed.

The seventh character is a qualifier that has a unique meaning for individual procedures. Examples of qualifiers include:

- Type of transplant
- Second site for a transplant
- Second site for a bypass
- Original procedure in a revision
- Type of fluid taken out during a drainage

Medical and Surgical Root Procedures

The following is the key to procedures reported as the third character in the medical and surgical section of ICD-10-PCS. The official description for ICD-10-PCS follows, along with some examples in parentheses of appropriate services reported under each defined procedure.

1. Alteration: Modifying the anatomical structure of a body part without affecting the function of the body part (facelift or breast augmentation)

2. Bypass: Altering the route of passage of the contents of a tubular body part (gastrojejunal bypass or coronary artery bypass)

3. Change: Taking out or off a device from a body part and putting back an identical or similar device in or on the same body part without cutting or puncturing the skin or a mucous membrane (recasting a fracture or replacing an ostomy tube)

4. Control: Stopping, or attempting to stop, postprocedural bleeding (control of bleeding following tonsillectomy)

5. Creation: Making a new genital structure that does not take over the function of a body part (sex change operation)

6. Destruction: Physical eradication of a portion or all of a body part by the direct use of destructive agent, force, or energy (crush fallopian tube or fulgurate rectal polyps)

7. Detachment: Cutting off all or a portion of the upper or lower extremities (amputation of foot or partial penectomy)

8. Dilation: Expanding an orifice or the lumen of a tubular body part (tracheal or urethral dilation)

9. Division: Cutting into a body part without draining fluids and/or gases from the body part in order to separate or transect a body part. (nerve division)

10. Drainage: Taking or letting out fluids and/or gases from a body part (I&D of abscess, arthrocentesis, or\ thoracentesis)

11. Excision: Cutting out or off, without replacement, a portion of a body part (wedge ostectomy, partial nephrectomy, pulmonary segmentectomy)

12. Extirpation: Taking or cutting out solid matter from a body part (sequestrectomy or cholelithotomy)

13. Extraction: Pulling or stripping out or off all or a portion of a body part by the use of force (vein stripping, tooth extraction, phrenic nerve avulsion, or dermabrasion)

14. Fragmentation: Breaking solid matter in a body part into pieces (lithotripsy)

15. Fusion: Joining together portions of an articular body part rendering the articular body part immobile (spinal fusion, ankle arthrodesis)

16. Insertion: Putting in a nonbiological appliance that monitors, assists, performs, or prevents a physiological function, but does not physically take the place of a body part (pacemaker insertion)

17. Inspection: Visually and/or manually exploring a body part (diagnostic arthroscopy or exploratory laparotomy)

18. Map: Locating the route of passage of electrical impulses and/or locating functional areas in a body part (mapping cardiac conduction pathways, local cortical areas)

19. Occlusion: Completely closing the orifice or lumen of a tubular body part (ligation of vas deferens or ligation of fallopian tube)

20. Reattachment: Putting back in or on all or a portion of a body part to its normal location or other suitable location (replant parathyroid, reattach amputated finger, or reattach severed kidney)

21. Release: Freeing a body part from an abnormal physical constraint (lysis of peritoneal adhesions or freeing the median nerve)

22. Removal: Taking out or off a device from a body part (pacemaker removal or stent removal)

23. Repair: Restoring to the extent possible, a body part to its normal anatomic structure and function (tracheoplasty, suture laceration, herniorrhaphy or repair of episiotomy)

24. Replacement: Putting in or on a biological or synthetic material that physically takes the place and/or function of all or a portion of a body part (total knee replacement, intraocular lens insertion)

25. Reposition: Moving to its normal location or other suitable location all or a portion of a body part (position undescended testicle or reposition aberrant kidney)

26. Resection: Cutting out or off, without replacement, all of a body part (cholecystectomy or total gastrectomy)

27. Restriction: Partially closing the orifice or lumen of a tubular body part (fundoplication or cervical cerclage)

28. Revision: Correcting to the extent possible a malfunctioning or displaced device (revision of hip replacement, strabismus surgery, or gastroenterostomy)

29. Supplement: Putting in or on biological or synthetic material that physically reinforces and/or augments the function of a body part

30. Transfer: Moving, without taking out, all or a portion of a body part to another location to take over the function of all or a portion of a body part (nerve transfer or tendon transfer)

31. Transplantation: Putting in or on all or a portion of a living body part taken from another individual or animal to physically take the place and/or function of all or a portion of a similar body part (lung, kidney, or heart transplant)

It's important to note that the definitions in ICD-10-PCS do not always mirror the language of the medical record. There is no use of Latin terminology or eponyms. This poses some challenges for coders, and will demand a much higher level of anatomic literacy and understanding of procedural terminology from coders, along with a resolve to be more concise and detailed in documentation by physicians.

Variances Between Sections

Certain procedural services require capture of specific data elements. Therefore, the ICD-10-PCS character definitions may vary somewhat between the sections. This variance is necessary to facilitate specific relevant data capture as it relates to the type of procedure or intervention. The seven characters for "Imaging" codes are organized as follows:

DEFINITIONS

Eponyms. Namesakes for certain diseases or syndromes. They are listed as main terms in alphabetic sequence.

QUICK TIP

In CPT coding and common medical documentation practices, the term "excision" is used to describe the removal of all or part of a body organ or structure. However, ICD-10-PCS defines "excision" as the cutting out or off (without replacement) a portion of a body part. ICD-10-PCS differentiates excision from "resection"; resection reports the cutting out or off (without replacement) of an entire body part. Therefore, while the medical record may document the "excision" of an appendix, the appropriate root procedure term used to classify the removal of the entire organ in ICD-10-PCS would be "resection."

1	2	3	4	5	6	7
Section	Body System	Root Types	Body Part	Contrast Qualifier	Contrast	Qualifier

The root procedure and definitions for imaging are represented by the third character.

0   Plain radiography
1   Fluoroscopy
2   Computerized tomography (CT scan)
3   Magnetic resonance imaging (MRI)
4   Ultrasonography

Character 2 denotes the body system (e.g., central nervous system), while character 4 identifies the specific body part (e.g., brain).

The fifth character specifies the type of contrast material used in the imaging procedures. Contrast is differentiated by the concentration of the contrast material (high or low osmolar).

The sixth character provides further detail about the procedure, such as enhanced or unenhanced imaging or the use of laser technology.

The seventh character is a qualifier that has a unique meaning for individual imaging procedures, such as those that specify intraoperative (0) and densitometry (1) examinations.

Each section of ICD-10-PCS has certain characteristics and coding conventions that set it apart, for example:

Obstetrics codes are structured similarly to medical surgery codes, and each character has the same meaning.

1	2	3	4	5	6	7
Section	Body System	Root Operation	Body Part	Approach	Device	Qualifier

However, the philosophy behind codes and their application may present some unique coding challenges due to their departure from ICD-9-CM procedure coding, such as:

- Multiple root operations exist, such as Inspection, Insertion, Change and Extraction. The root operations Abortion (A) and Delivery (E) are unique to the obstetrics section.
- The obstetrics section includes only those procedures performed on the products of conception. Procedures performed on the pregnant female (e.g., episiotomy) are coded to a separate root operation in the medical and surgical section.
- The obstetrics section includes only those procedures performed on the "products of conception": the fetus, amnion, umbilical cord, or placenta.
- A cesarean section, however, is coded to the obstetrical section, because it is considered an extraction.

Abortion procedures are classified according to whether the procedure was performed mechanically or by the insertion of a device. If a laminaria or abortifacient is used, the appropriate approach is classified as Via natural or artificial opening. Abortion procedures performed by mechanical means using instrumentation are classified to device value No device (Z).

QUICK TIP

Root operation Delivery applies only to manually assisted, vaginal delivery. It is defined as assisting the passage of the products of conception (fetus) from the genital canal. Cesarean deliveries are classified in the obstetrics section to the root operation Extraction.

ICD-10-PCS Tabular List

In ICD-10-PCS, a separate table is created for each possible combination of the first three characters of a code. For each body system, the tabular list begins with a listing of the operations performed (i.e., the root operations). When a procedure involves distinct parts, multiple codes are may be required to report the entire scope of the procedure. Multiple procedures may be required during an operative episode if:

- The root operation is performed on different body parts defined by distinct body part characters
- The root operation is repeated at different body sites defined by the same body part value
- Multiple procedures are performed on the same body part with separate objectives
- The intended operative approach is converted to a different approach

The tabular list for each body system also includes a listing of the body parts, approaches, devices, and qualifiers for that system. Each root operation in the body system follows these listings. At the top of each of the tables is the name of the section, body system, and root operation, as well as the definition of the root operation. The list is formatted as a grid with rows and columns. The four columns in the grid represent the last four characters of the code (which are labeled, "Body Part," "Approach," "Device," and "Qualifier" for the obstetrics and medical surgical sections). Each row in the grid specifies the allowable combinations of the last four characters. For example, following is the table that would be referenced to determine the correct code for transorifice intraluminal endoscopic fragmentation of calculus in the left renal pelvis.

OTF Rubric

0: Medical and surgical		T: Urinary system		F: Fragmentation			
Body Part Character 4		Approach Character 5		Device Character 6		Qualifier Character 7	
3	Kidney pelvis, right	0	Open	Z	No device	Z	No qualifier
4	Kidney pelvis, left	3	Percutaneous				
6	Ureter, right	4	Percutaneous endo-scopic				
7	Ureter, left	7	Via natural or artificial opening				
8	Bladder	8	Via natural or artificial opening, endoscopic				
9	Bladder neck	X	External				
B	Urethra						

The ICD-10-PCS code for this procedure would be built as follows:

1	2	3	4	5	6	7
Section	Body System	Root Operation	Body Part	Approach	Device	Qualifier
Medical and Surgical	Urinary	Fragmentation	Kidney Pelvis, Left	Via Natural or Artificial Opening, Endoscopic	No Device	No Qualifier
O	T	F	4	8	Z	Z

0TF48ZZ   Transorifice intraluminal endoscopic fragmentation of calculus of left renal pelvis

Let's look at a few more examples of how a code would be built utilizing this grid concept in ICD-10-PCS.

Bilateral, open intraluminal endoscopic occlusion of fallopian tubes with insertion of intraluminal occlusion device:

1	2	3	4	5	6	7
Section	Body System	Root Operation	Body Part	Approach	Device	Qualifier
Medical and Surgical	Female Reproductive	Occlusion	Fallopian Tube, Bilateral	Via Natural or Artificial Opening, Endoscopic	Intraluminal Device	None
0	U	L	7	8	D	Z

0UL78DZ Bilateral, open intraluminal endoscopic occlusion of fallopian tubes with insertion of intraluminal occlusion device

Incision and drainage of subcutaneous tissue, anterior neck:

1	2	3	4	5	6	7
Section	Body System	Root Operation	Body Part	Approach	Device	Qualifier
Medical and Surgical	Subcutaneous Tissue	Drainage	Anterior Neck	Percutaneous	No Device	No Qualifier
0	J	9	4	3	Z	Z

0J943ZZ Drainage, subcutaneous tissue, anterior neck, percutaneous

Percutaneous intraluminal transfusion of autologous whole blood through the peripheral vein:

1	2	3	4	5	6	7
Section	Body System	Root Operation	Body Part	Approach	Device	Qualifier
Administration	Circulatory	Transfusion	Peripheral Vein	Percutaneous	Whole Blood	Autologous
3	0	2	3	3	H	0

30233H0 Percutaneous transfusion of autologous whole blood through the peripheral vein

LDR Brachytherapy, 1-125 implant, frontal lobe of brain:

1	2	3	4	5	6	7
Section	Body System	Modality	Body Part	Modality Qualifier	Isotope	Qualifier
Radiation Oncology	Central Nervous System	Brachytherapy	Brain	LDR	Iodine I25 (I125)	None
D	0	1	0	B	9	Z

D010B9Z LDR Brachytherapy, 1-125 implant, frontal lobe of brain

Let's take a look at a couple of examples of coding scenarios, coded both in ICD-9-CM and ICD-10-PCS:

Example 1:

Thoracentesis for treatment of pleural effusion

A 73-year-old male presents to the hospital for treatment of left pleural effusion. PMH is significant for congestive heart failure and chronic obstructive pulmonary disease. He has been hospitalized for community-acquired pneumonia twice within the last four years. PMSH is significant for long-term tobacco abuse. The patient continues to smoke 1–2 cigarettes per day.

Hospital course: The patient was admitted to the medical surgical unit. Diagnostic chest x-ray and ultrasound confirmed presence of left pleural effusion and mild, chronic congestive heart failure. The patient was placed on gentle diuresis and taken to the interventional radiology suite for ultrasound-guided thoracentesis. The procedure was successful and follow-up chest x-ray confirmed it to be without incident. The patient tolerated the procedure well and was discharged two days post-procedure.

ICD-9-CM Procedure:

Thoracentesis 34.91

ICD-10-PCS Procedure:

Drainage, pleural cavity, left, percutaneous 0W9B3ZZ

This table illustrates how the procedure code is constructed:

1	2	3	4	5	6	7
Section	Body System	Root Operation	Body Part	Approach	Device	Qualifier
Medical and Surgical	Anatomical Regions, General	Drainage	Pleural Cavity, Left	Percutaneous	No Device	No Qualifier
0	W	9	B	3	Z	Z

Rationale:

To code a thoracentesis procedure in ICD-10-PCS, it is essential to know the nature of the procedure. Thoracentesis is a method of draining fluid from the pleural cavity—the space between the membrane covering the lung (the pleura) and the lung. This space is normally filled with a certain amount of fluid. When too much fluid accumulates, due to disease or infection, a thoracentesis procedure may be indicated to normalize the fluid levels within this space. The accumulation of excess fluid is often diagnosed by the physician as pleural effusion.

Code 0W9B3ZZ Drainage, pleural cavity, left, percutaneous without drainage device, was assigned instead of code 0W9B3ZX Drainage, pleural cavity, left, percutaneous, diagnostic, since the procedure was therapeutic in nature and performed to treat a pleural effusion and normalize the fluid levels within the pleural cavity. Code 0W9B3ZX (diagnostic) would be assigned for diagnostic thoracentesis procedures, in which the fluid needs to be analyzed to diagnose and determine treatment options for infections or malignancies.

Example 2:

Removal of Intranasal Foreign Body

A 3-year-old female presents to the emergency department (ED) for removal of small object wedged in left nostril. PMH: Noncontributory; routine childhood illnesses. Immunizations are up to date. PMSH: The patient has two older siblings; both school age.

She attends preschool. HPI: At preschool today, the patient approached her teacher after craft time, crying and pulling on her nose. The teacher noticed obvious deformity of an object stuck in the left nostril, but was unable to remove the object, and subsequently called her parents. The patient is accompanied to the ED today by her mother. Exam: Obvious deformity of left nostril. Upon exam, what appears to be a pink, plastic round shaped object is wedged into the cavity.

Procedure: The patient is combative and crying. Her mother consented to restraints to facilitate removal of the object. Once the patient was adequately restrained, the object (what appears to be a bead) was removed with forceps, resulting in a minor abrasion of the left nostril. Bleeding was controlled adequately with direct pressure. The patient tolerated the procedure well and was discharged with instructions.

ICD-9-CM Procedure:
Removal of intraluminal foreign body from nose without incision 98.12

ICD-10-PCS Procedure:
Extirpation, matter from nose, external approach 09CKXZZ

This table illustrates how the procedure code is constructed:

1	2	3	4	5	6	7
Section	Body System	Root Operation	Body Part	Approach	Device	Qualifier
Medical and Surgical	Ear, Nose and Sinus	Extirpation	Nose	External	No Device	No Qualifier
0	9	C	K	X	Z	Z

Rationale:
The use of terminology may be one of the most notable distinctions between the two coding and classification systems. The language of ICD-10-PCS differs significantly from that of ICD-9-CM. When coding this procedure, the removal of a foreign body is classified as an "extirpation" in ICD-10-PCS. The nostril is equivalent to the "nose" body part value. Removal of the foreign body by forceps is classified as an external approach in ICD-10-PCS, being not otherwise classifiable as open or percutaneous approach. The foreign body itself is referred to as "matter" in the ICD-10-PCS long description.

DISCUSSION QUESTIONS

1.   Describe the procedure classifications currently in use in the inpatient and outpatient health care delivery settings.

_____

_____

_____

2.   Which health care providers will report ICD-10-PCS codes? When will this occur?

_____

_____

_____

3.   What parties were responsible for the creation of ICD-10-PCS? What were their primary goals? For which primary reason was ICD-10-PCS created?

_____

_____

_____

4.   Describe the primary characteristics of the ICD-10-PCS coding system.

_____

_____

_____

5.   How does terminology differ between coding systems? How will coders best deal with these discrepancies? How will medical documentation accommodate these demands?

_____

_____

_____

6.   Describe how an ICD-10-PCS code is constructed using the code tables.

_____

_____

_____

Chapter 5:
General Equivalence Mappings

General equivalence mappings (GEM) are relationships established between corresponding code sets in which the most likely code linkages are provided for the user. In certain circumstances, the relationships and linkages between code sets are fairly close; at times a 1:1 ratio. However, in many cases, this direct linkage is not always possible.

Both ICD-10-CM and ICD-10-PCS are advanced coding and classification systems. They have been developed to accommodate the ever-changing needs of the health care industry. As a result, the limitations of the preceding systems have been considered, and improvements have been incorporated into the new replacement systems. ICD-10-CM is a further evolution of ICD-9-CM that incorporates the changes in medical technology during the past 30 years. As such, the inherent classification and terminology revisions, coupled with the increased detail, have resulted in code classifications that are exponentially more specific. ICD-10-CM contains extensive, updated clinical concepts, patient encounter information, and anatomic designations from which the new alphanumeric codes are built.

ICD-10-PCS, on the other hand, even though it is an entirely new, separate coding system, is mapped similar to the diagnosis coding systems. The GEM files for the procedure coding systems (ICD-9-CM volume 3 and ICD-10-PCS) follow the same conventions, using the same "flags" as the diagnosis coding GEM files.

ICD-10-CM DIAGNOSIS CODE MAPPINGS

The 2009 version GEM files for ICD-10-CM and ICD-9-CM (volumes 1 and 2) are posted on the National Center for Health Statistics (NCHS) website, along with a user's guide that provides the user with essential information necessary to apply the mappings correctly. GEMS are differentiated from "crosswalks" in that their purpose is to help the user navigate between systems and translating code meanings. These tools are intended to help compare and analyze data. From these mappings, users may derive their own mappings suited to their individual needs.

Due to the fact that both systems are revisions of the International Classification of Disease (ICD), both code sets often share a high degree of commonality. The organization, formatting, and conventions of the systems are very similar. As a result, many mappings are straightforward. However, due to the increased data granularity (specificity) of the 10th revision, a series of possible code choices are often presented during linkages between certain codes. ICD-10-CM contains certain severity and anatomic specificity data elements, for example, that ICD-9-CM does not provide. In such cases, a seamless linkage is not possible.

Reconciliation methods between the two systems may vary, according to the intended use of the data. Data needs for claims adjudication may not be the same as those for research or statistical analysis. For example:

- One-to-one mapping: Provides a direct code-to code linkage, which offers the most likely code choice or "best compromise" between codes (e.g., claims analysis)

- One-to-many mapping: Provides a comparison of all possible code linkages (e.g., statistical analysis, data "trending," epidemiology)
- Forward mapping: Translation of existing ICD-9-CM coding data into ICD-10-CM equivalents
- Backward mapping: Translation of ICD-10-CM information back to the previous code set (ICD-9-CM) for comparison

ICD-10-CM contains a greater number of codes with a higher level of specificity than ICD-9-CM. Therefore, in most cases, one ICD-9-CM code is often mapped to multiple ICD-10-CM codes. For example:

ICD-9-CM
354.0   Carpal tunnel syndrome
        Median nerve entrapment
        Partial thenar atrophy

ICD-10-CM
G56.00   Carpal tunnel syndrome, unspecified side
G56.01   Carpal tunnel syndrome, right side
G56.02   Carpal tunnel syndrome, left side

In the example above, the inclusion of laterality into ICD-10-CM for classifying carpal tunnel syndrome provides a one-to-many code linkage from ICD-9-CM to ICD-10-CM. Similar mappings exist where certain variables such as severity indicators, axis refinements and anatomic specificity have been built into the ICD-10-CM system.

There are exceptions, however. Certain clinical concepts and code axes in ICD-9-CM have since been deemed nonessential, no longer clinically accurate or pertinent. In these cases, code descriptions or classifications have been either eliminated or reassigned in ICD-10-CM. For example, state of control is no longer a factor in code assignment for diabetes mellitus. ICD-10-CM diabetes mellitus codes are combination codes that report the type (type 1 or 2), the body system affected, and the presence and nature of certain complications.

Diagnosis:	Type 2 diabetes mellitus with neurological manifestation, uncontrolled	
ICD-9-CM:	250.62	Diabetes neurological manifestations, type 2 or unspecified type, uncontrolled
ICD-10-CM:	E11.40	Type 2 diabetes mellitus with diabetic neuropathy, unspecified

In ICD-10-CM, code classifications for diabetes mellitus no longer include code assignments for "controlled" or "uncontrolled" disease.

Combination Codes
ICD-10-CM uses combination code conventions similar to those in ICD-9-CM, whereby a combination code is a single code used to classify two diagnoses, or a diagnosis with an associated manifestation, complication, or cause. Codes in either system may be linked to more than one code, depending on the nature of the classification changes. For example:

ICD-9-CM:	250.40	Diabetes with renal manifestations, type II or unspecified type not stated as uncontrolled
ICD-10-CM:	E11.21	Type 2 diabetes mellitus with diabetic nephropathy

In the example above, type 2 diabetes mellitus with diabetic nephropathy may be linked directly with one-to-one mapping between each system. In the following example, changes to the ICD-10-CM structure result in multiple code linkage.

ICD-9-CM:	414.01	Coronary atherosclerosis of native artery
	413.9	Other and unspecified angina pectoris
ICD-10-CM:	I25.119	Atherosclerotic heart disease of native coronary artery with unspecified angina pectoris

In the example above, diagnoses that required multiple codes in ICD-9-CM are linked to reclassified combinations of codes in ICD-10-CM. Conversely, single combination codes in ICD-9-CM may be linked to multiple codes in ICD-10-CM.

How to Use the Diagnosis Code GEM Files

The GEM files are formatted as text files that can be downloaded and used to create specific mapping applications. These files contain a list of ICD-9-CM and ICD-10-CM code pairs. The first column lists the source system codes. The second column lists the target system codes. The I-9 map is listed by ICD-9-CM codes in sequential ascending order. Similarly, the I-10 map is listed by ICD-10-CM codes in sequential ascending order. The direction in which a code is mapped (to or from which code system) determines the "source" or "target" system. For example, if the user is mapping an ICD-9-CM code to an ICD-10-CM code, then the ICD-9-CM code is her "source" system, and the ICD-10-CM code is her "target" system.

In the GEM files, a code may be repeated more than once if there is more than one possible code equivalent in the other system. In this manner, the GEMs may provide a many-to-many code reference in which several possible translations may be presented, with new alternatives on each row, formatted as a code pair.

In the diagnosis code mappings, the term "entry" describes all the rows in the GEM file having the same first-listed code. The word "row" describes a single line within the file that contains a code pair of codes (e.g., I-9 and the equivalent I-10). The term "single entry" describes a one-to-one code linkage, whereas the term "multiple entry" describes a one-to-many or many-to-many code linkage. Multiple entry code linkages may be made in association with combination codes used in either system. The GEM files contain conventions (i.e., "flags") that assist in code linkage. These coded conventions appear as single-digit units contained in the third column directly to the left of the code pairing for the source and target systems. For a detailed description of these conventions and their applications, consult the GEM user's guide posted on the NCHS website at: http://www.cdc.gov/nchs/about/otheract/icd9/icd10cm.htm.

For a single-code GEM entry, the first flag in the third column may appear as a 1 (approximate) or a zero. The other flags are not applicable and have a value of zero. However, these conventions become of increased importance in mapping combinations of codes and codes with multiple possible equivalents.

The following example illustrates how the GEM conventions in the third column associate code linkage. The E11.35 code rubric is mapped to the ICD-9-CM equivalents.

E11.35	Type 2 diabetes mellitus with proliferative diabetic retinopathy
E11.351	Type 2 diabetes mellitus with proliferative diabetic retinopathy with macular edema
E11.359	Type 2 diabetes mellitus with proliferative diabetic retinopathy without macular edema

 KEY POINT

For a detailed description of these conventions, consult the GEM Users Guide posted on the NCHS website at: http://www.cdc.gov/nchs/about/otheract/icd9/icd10cm.html

The I-10 source GEM files for rubric E11.35 are listed as follows:

E11351 25050 10111
E11351 36202 10112
E11351 36207 10113
E11359 25050 10111
E11359 36202 10112

From left to right, the digits in the third column indicate the following GEM conventions. The following table is a magnified version of column three of the GEM files as listed above. Each digit is illustrated in greater detail:

Approximate Flag	No Map Flag	Combination Flag	Scenario	Choice List
1	0	1	1	1
1	0	1	1	2
1	0	1	1	3
1	0	1	1	1
1	0	1	1	2

The column headers in the table above describe the content of each digit of the third column of the GEM mapping files. Each digit represents the following:

Digit 1: Approximate flag—When populated with a "1," indicates that the code entry is not considered a direct equivalent clinical translation, but an approximate linkage

Digit 2: No map flag—When populated with a "1," indicates that a code in the source system is not linked to any code in the target system. Therefore, there is no mapping available.

Digit 3: Combination flag—When populated with a "1," indicates that more than one code in the target system is required to satisfy the full equivalent meaning of a code in the source system.

Digit 4: Scenario—In a combination code entry, a collection of codes from the target system contains the necessary codes that when combined as directed, will satisfy the equivalent meaning of a code in the source system. This digit also indicates the number of variations of diagnosis combinations included in the source system code.

Digit 5: Choice list—In a combination code entry, a list of one or more codes in the target system from which one code must be chosen to satisfy the equivalent meaning of a code in the source system. This digit also indicates the possible target system codes that, when combined, satisfies the scenario.

NCHS advises using three basic steps when using the ICD-10-CM GEM files:

Step 1 Extract—Select all rows containing the source system code to be mapped.

Step 2 Analyze—Note any conventions (flags) applied to the codes, and consider the purpose of the code mapping.

Step 3 Refine—Select the most appropriate code mapping based on analysis of all information provided.

The user may encounter the need to make certain decisions when mapping data. For example, ICD-10-CM contains a higher degree of code specificity than was available in ICD-9-CM. If a user has access to the records by which the data gaps can be appropriately filled, and specific codes can be researched and reassigned, the decision is straightforward.

However, other users who do not have access to source data will need to document and apply consistent mapping methods to ensure that the disparity between the systems is handled consistently, ensuring integrity of the data.

Every use of coded data carries with it a specific set of assumptions. For example, if the intended use of the data is reimbursement, the assumption is that the code must group to a specific reimbursement category. For medical necessity, the clinical concepts must align between the two code sets. Outcomes measures may require more specificity. Claims adjudication may require the clinical concept of laterality and encounter identification.

ICD-10-PCS PROCEDURE CODE MAPPINGS

Similar to the diagnosis code mappings, the procedure code mappings do not always provide a one-to-one code linkage relationship due to the expanded capability of the ICD-10-PCS system. In comparison, approximately 73,000 ICD-10-PCS codes will replace the approximate 4,000 ICD-9-CM volume 3 procedure codes effective October 1, 2013. The PCS codes comprise seven alphanumeric digits, allowing for exponentially greater classification specificity. As a result, each I-9 code is commonly linked to more than one PCS code, due to the enhanced specificity of the ICD-10-PCS system. The General Equivalence Mapping (GEM) for procedures cannot possibly provide a direct "crosswalk" in all situations because of the disparity between the two systems. Therefore, the GEM files link the existing codes to all valid coding options from which choices can be made.

As with the diagnosis code mappings, reconciliation methods between the two procedure systems may vary, according to the intended use of the data. Data needs for claims adjudication may not be the same as those for research or statistical analysis. For example:

- One-to-one mapping: Provides a direct code-to code linkage that offers the most likely code choice or "best compromise" between codes
- One-to-many mapping: Provides a comparison of all possible code linkages
- Forward mapping: Translates existing ICD-9-CM coding data into ICD-10-PCS equivalents
- Backward mapping: Translates ICD-10-PCS information back to the previous code set (ICD-9-CM volume 3) for comparison

ICD-10-PCS Code Structure

The ICD-10-PCS was created specifically for enhanced expandability; to have a greater code capacity. In recent years, chapter 00, "Procedures and Interventions, Not Elsewhere Classified," was created because ICD-9-CM has been running out of code capacity; unable to systemically classify and accommodate advances in new technologies within the existing structure. Therefore, the basic code structure was changed, along with a standardization of classification and terminology from which the codes are built.

The structural changes inherent to the PCS system include:

- Seven-digit alphanumeric characters
- Standard "root operations" or "root (procedure) types," which specifically identify the surgical method; eliminating the use of eponyms and Latin terminology
- Standardized levels of specificity whereby all the elements of the procedure are defined (method of procedure, approach, anatomic site, devices used, and assisted technologies employed)

- Method of surgical approach is more clearly differentiated and defined. The terms "open" and "closed" used in ICD-9-CM are further specified in ICD-10-PCS, from which more accurate and complete data capture can be accomplished (e.g., open, percutaneous, percutaneous endoscopic)
- Elimination of "diagnosis" from classification codes
- Translation of ICD-9-CM "adjunct" procedure codes into sixth-digit device or seventh-digit extension characters

Generalizing ICD-9-CM codes resulted in classifications of code "families" or several variations of procedures under single classification codes. This characteristic has been largely eliminated in PCS, and a greater number of highly specific code classifications have been created. Consequently, the majority of ICD-9-CM codes are mapped to multiple ICD-10-PCS coding options from which the most appropriate code linkage can be made. However, there are exceptions. ICD-9-CM volume 3 procedure codes would often incorporate the reason for the procedure (diagnosis) into the code classification or identify anatomical sites and surgical approaches in a way that has been eliminated from ICD-10-PCS structure. As a result, certain ICD-10-PCS codes may be linked to more than one ICD-9-CM code option.

The ICD-10-PCS codes have been classified into single, standardized procedures—therefore, multiple PCS procedure codes may be necessary to fully describe and report the entire scope of the procedure performed. These combination procedures are linked using conventions (flags) that indicate the appropriate choices.

HOW TO USE PROCEDURE CODE GEM FILES

The 2009 version GEM files for procedure code mapping between ICD-9-CM (volume 3) and ICD-10-PCS are posted on the Centers for Medicare and Medicaid Services (CMS) website; along with user's guides that provide the user with information necessary to apply the mappings correctly. GEMs are differentiated from "crosswalks" in that they help the user navigate between systems and translating code meanings. These tools help in data comparison and analysis. From these mappings, users may derive their own mappings suited to their individual needs. The GEM files are formatted as text files which can be downloaded and used to create specific mapping applications.

These files contain a list of ICD-9-CM volume 3 and ICD-10-PCS code pairs. The first column lists the source system codes. The second column lists the target system codes. The direction in which a code is mapped (to or from which code system) determines the "source" or "target" system. For example, if the user is mapping an ICD-9-CM code to an ICD-10-PCS code, then the ICD-9-CM code is her "source" system, and the ICD-10-PCS code is her "target" system. Codes in the source system may be listed on multiple lines if multiple code options exist in the target system or if a combination of codes are linked. The third column in the GEM files consist of conventions referred to as "attributes." They serve a similar purpose to the conventions (flags) in the diagnosis GEM files. These attributes are used to assist in the analysis required to properly link codes together.

These coded conventions appear as single-digit units contained in the third column directly to the left of the code pairing for the source and target systems. For a detailed description of these conventions and their applications, consult the GEM users guide posted on the CMS website at: http://www.cms.hhs.gov/ICD10/01m_2009_ICD10PCS.asp.

The following examples illustrate how the GEM conventions in the third column associate code linkage.

KEY POINT

For a detailed description of these conventions, consult the GEM users guide posted on the CMS website at:

http://www.cms.hhs.gov/ICD10/01m_2009_ICD10PCS.asp.

Example 1: ICD-9-CM to ICD-10-PCS

The ICD-9-CM to ICD-10-PCS GEM maps procedure code 28.3 to the following ICD-10-PCS code options:

Procedure: Tonsillectomy with adenoidectomy, open approach

283	0CTP0ZZ	10111
283	0CTPXZZ	10111
283	0CTQ0ZZ	10112
283	0CTQXZZ	10112

From left to right, the digits in the third column indicate the following GEM conventions. The following table is a magnified version of column three of the GEM files as listed above. Each digit is illustrated in greater detail:

Approximate Flag	No Map Flag	Combination Flag	Scenario	Choice List
1	0	1	1	1
1	0	1	1	1
1	0	1	1	2
1	0	1	1	2

In the example above, the combination code flag is 1, which indicates a combination of codes are necessary to fully report the entire scope of the procedure. Review of PCS table 0CT reveals that resection of the tonsils is reported separately from resection of the adenoids, requiring two codes to report each separate body part resected. A combination option of "tonsils and adenoids" does not exist in ICD-10-PCS as it did in ICD-9-CM. Character 5 indicates the operative approach, which is specified in the procedural statement as "open." Therefore, those codes linked to 28.3 with the fifth character X External are not appropriate code linkage options for the procedure described as "open."

Example 2: ICD-10-PCS to ICD-9-CM

The ICD-10-PCS to ICD-9-CM GEM maps the following procedure from the 027 PCS code table to its ICD-9-CM equivalent procedures.

Procedure: PTCA; Percutaneous dilation of two coronary arteries with insertion of drug-eluting stent, vessel bifurcation

0271346	0041	10112
0271346	0044	10115
0271346	0046	10113
0271346	0066	10111
0271346	3607	10114

From left to right, the digits in the third column indicate the following GEM conventions. The following table is a magnified version of column three of the GEM files as listed above. Each digit is illustrated in greater detail:

Approximate Flag	No Map Flag	Combination Flag	Scenario	Choice List
1	0	1	1	2
1	0	1	1	5
1	0	1	1	3
1	0	1	1	1
1	0	1	1	4

There are five rows in the PCS to I-9 GEM for combination code 0271346. The entry is of the combination type, meaning that code 0271346 must be linked to the following ICD-9-CM codes in the order of the last digit represented to be considered a valid entry.

The combination flag (third digit in third column) is 1 in the table. The scenario number is 1 because there is only one version of the procedure specified in the combination code.

The column headers in the tables above describe the content of each digit of the third column of the GEM mapping files. Each digit represents the following:

Digit 1: Approximate flag—When populated with a "1," indicates that the code entry is not considered direct equivalent clinical translation, but an approximate linkage

Digit 2: No Map flag—When populated with a "1," indicates that a code in the source system is not linked to any code in the target system. Therefore, there is no mapping available.

Digit 3: Combination flag—When populated with a "1," indicates that more than one code in the target system is required to satisfy the full equivalent meaning of a code in the source system

Digit 4: Scenario—In a combination code entry, a collection of codes from the target system contains the necessary codes that when combined as directed, will satisfy the equivalent meaning of a code in the source system. This digit also indicates the number of distinct clinical variations of procedure code combinations included in the source system code.

Digit 5: Choice list—In a combination code entry, a list of one or more codes in the target system from which one code must be chosen to satisfy the equivalent meaning of a code in the source system. This digit also indicates the possible target system codes that when combined, satisfy the scenario.

CMS advises three basic steps when using the ICD-10-PCS Mapping files:

Step 1 Extract—Select all rows containing the source system code to be mapped.

Step 2 Analyze—Note any conventions (flags) applied to the codes and consider the purpose of the code mapping.

Step 3 Refine—Select the most appropriate code mapping based on analysis of all information provided.

The user may encounter the need to make certain decisions when mapping data. For example, ICD-10-PCS contains a higher degree of code specificity than was available in ICD-9-CM. If a user has access to the records by which the data gaps can be appropriately filled and specific codes can be researched and reassigned, the decision is straightforward. However, other users who do not have access to source data will need to document and apply consistent mapping methods to ensure that the disparity between the systems is handled consistently, ensuring integrity of the data.

ICD-10-PCS to ICD-9-CM Reimbursement Mappings

The 2009 procedure code mappings include a separate applied reimbursement map. This map links the ICD-10-CM (diagnosis) and ICD-10-PCS (procedure) code systems to the ICD-9-CM volume 1 (diagnosis) and ICD-9-CM volume 3 (procedure) code systems, respectively. The reimbursement mapping documents include:

- reimb_map_dx_2009.txt – Map from ICD-10-CM diagnoses to ICD-9-CM diagnoses or diagnosis clusters
- reimb_map_pr_2009.txt - Map from ICD-10-PCS procedures to ICD-9-CM (Volume 3) procedures or procedure clusters

Reimbursement maps are separate listings that take the diagnosis into consideration to facilitate code linkage for reimbursement comparison purposes. Therefore, this map is a tool that provides a mechanism whereby claims may be processed using legacy systems during the ICD-10 conversion process, using existing pricing rules to facilitate payment.

The reimbursement mappings are differentiated from the GEMs in that they use a one-to-one translation among codes, selecting the most viable code linkage option. Alternately, The GEMs often indicate multiple code choices between the source and target systems, providing alternate codes or clusters of codes as viable linkage options. To serve reimbursement mapping purposes, only the most representative code linkage is made. However, an important distinction is made in the reimbursement mappings in regard to multiple code listings. If the reimbursement mapping lists multiple I-9 codes as an equivalent option to one ICD-10-PCS code, this indicates that all the I-9 codes linked to the ICD-10-PCS code must be submitted on the translated claim as required codes.

The reimbursement mappings are formatted as text files that can be downloaded and used to create specific mapping applications. These files contain a list of diagnoses and a separate list of procedures, in I-10 code order. Users are advised to download the files and load them into a database or table that facilitates look-up based on the individual ICD-10-PCS code at the beginning of each mapping entry.

The first column lists the source system (ICD-10-PCS) codes. The second column indicates the number of ICD-9-CM codes mapped to the ICD-10-PCS code. The third through the fifth columns list the target (ICD-9-CM) system procedure codes.

Example:

045Y4ZZ	1	3868			
047004Z	4	3950	0040	0055	0045
04700DZ	3	3950	0040	3990	
04700ZZ	2	3950	0040		

Example in table format:

045Y4ZZ	1	3868			
047004Z	4	3950	0040	0055	0045
04700DZ	3	3950	0040	3990	
04700ZZ	2	3950	0040		

Certain ICD-10-PCS reimbursement mapping entries will contain the text "NODX" in the I-9 code field. This text indicates that the ICD-10-PCS codes have no equivalent code in ICD-9-CM.

CMS recommends that the reimbursement mapping be modified to claims systems using the following criteria:

- Reserve space accommodations in the claims system for I-9 cluster mapping; reserve space for up to four ICD-9-CM diagnosis codes and five ICD-9-CM procedure codes
- Map the ICD-10-CM principal diagnosis first. If the mapping contains an ICD-9-CM code cluster, select the first ICD-9-CM diagnosis in the cluster as the principal diagnosis and assign the remaining codes as secondary diagnoses.

- If a "NODX" test appears in the ICD-9-CM mapping when mapping secondary diagnoses, do not include anything in the code list for the ICD-10-CM code being mapped. Track the placement of the ICD-9-CM codes separately from the ICD-10-CM codes, as a one-to-one ratio will not always occur and the mappings may contain more than one ICD-9-CM code.
- There are no ICD-10-PCS procedures without a corresponding ICD-9-CM code. Procedure codes are rarely distinguished as "principal" or "secondary."

If certain ICD-9-CM codes are not used by the reimbursement mapping that are essential to the legacy system, the reimbursement mapping can be customized, as appropriate, to satisfy the requirements of individual claims systems.

DISCUSSION QUESTIONS

1.   How are the GEM files differentiated from code "crosswalks"?

   _____

   _____

   _____

2.   What is some of the information that the conventions (flags) convey about a code entry or code linkage between systems?

   _____

   _____

   _____

3.   How are the reimbursement mappings different from the other GEM files? What purpose do they serve? What are some key characteristics that set them apart from the GEM files?

   _____

   _____

   _____

4.   What are the basic steps to follow when using mapping files? Why are these steps important?

   _____

   _____

   _____

Chapter 6: National Standards

HEALTH INSURANCE PORTABILITY AND ACCOUNTABILITY ACT OF 1996

Provisions to set standards for patient privacy, data security, electronic transactions, and other administrative simplification issues were adopted by Congress as part of the Health Insurance Portability and Accountability Act of 1996 (HIPAA), Public Law 104-191, which was enacted on August 21, 1996. The original intent of the administrative simplification provisions of HIPAA was to develop a single set of standards for the transmission of electronic data to effectively promote widespread reliance on these electronic transactions. From that original intent, HIPAA and its administrative simplification have grown to become much more than that, and will have a significant effect on the way the health care industry uses and transmits data.

Standards of Administrative Simplification

Two years after HIPAA won congressional approval, the secretary of the Department of Health and Human Services began releasing notices of proposed rulemaking (NPRM) regarding various standards pertaining to administrative simplification provisions. Many of these NPRMs have now become final rules, and include the following:

- Standards for Electronic Transactions and Code Sets (issued August 17, 2000)
- Standards for Privacy of Individually Identifiable Health Information (issued December 28, 2000, modified August 14, 2002)
- National Standard Unique Employer Identifier (issued May 31, 2002)
- Health Insurance Reform: Security Standards 45 CFR Parts 160, 162, and 164 [CMS-0049-F] (February 23, 2003)
- HIPAA Administrative Simplification: Standard Unique Health Identifier for Health Care Providers 45 CFR RIN 0938-AH99, Part 162 [CMS-0045-F] (January 23, 2004)
- Health Insurance Reform; Modifications to the Health Insurance Portability and Accountability Act (HIPAA) Electronic Transaction Standards 45 CFR Part 162 [CMS-0009-F] (January 16, 2009), with adoption of X12 version 5010 Technical Reports Type 3 for HIPAA Transactions. Enhancements are expected to be implemented in future versions.
- HIPAA Administrative Simplification: Modifications to Medical Data Code Set Standards to Adopt ICD-10-CM and ICD-10-PCS 45 CFR Part 162 [CMS-0013-F] (January 16, 2009)

FINAL RULE—STANDARDS FOR ELECTRONIC TRANSACTIONS AND CODE SETS

A final rule published in the August 17, 2000 *Federal Register* acted on the standards of electronic health care transactions, as well as established the medical data sets (code sets) that are suitable for use in electronic transactions. Compliance with this rule was required by October 16, 2002. Small health plans were given until October 16, 2003.

According to the January 16, 2009, final rule, CMS is adopting a compliance date for all covered entities for version 5010 and version D.0 on January 1, 2012. Revisions were made to the following rules: § 162.1102, § 162.1202, § 162.1302, § 162.1402, § 162.1502, § 162.1602,

 KEY POINT

National standards for electronic health care transactions are meant to encourage electronic commerce in the health care industry and simplify the processes involved. The anticipated results of a standardized system include savings from the reduction in the administrative burdens of Medicare, Medicaid, and the State Children's Health Insurance Plan on health care providers and health plans. All private sector health plans and government health plans, all health care clearinghouses, and all health care providers must use the standards for electronic transactions when conducting any of the defined transactions covered under the HIPAA. A health care clearinghouse may accept nonstandard transactions from health care providers for translating and sending. The Department of Health and Human Services (HHS) can impose penalties of not more than $100 for each violation of the standard, except that the total amount imposed on any one person in each calendar year may not exceed $25,000 for violations of one requirement. Enforcement procedures will be published in a future regulation. Public Law 107-105, the Administrative Simplification Compliance Act, requires all affected entities to either be in compliance with the rules, or file a timely compliance plan. Failure to comply with this law can result in exclusion from federal health care programs.

§ 162.1702, and § 162.1802. Covered entities will be able to engage in Level 2 testing by allowing for the use of both the old standard and the updated standard.

In final rule 45 CFR part 162, CMS set an effective date of January 1, 2010, for the provisions of 45 CFR Subpart S, in that all covered entities other than small health plans must be in compliance by January 1, 2012. Small health plans will have an additional 12 months, with a compliance date of January 1, 2013.

CMS published the following timeline for implementation of versions 5010/D.0, version 3.0, and ICD-10 in the January 16, 2009, final rule 45 CFR part 162:

Timeline for Implementation of Versions 5010/D.0 and ICD-10

January 2009	Publish final rule
January 2009	Begin Level 1 testing period activities (gap analysis, design, development, internal testing) for versions 5010 and D.0.
January 2010	Begin internal testing for versions 5010 and D.0.
December 2010	Achieve Level 1 compliance (covered entities have completed internal testing and can send and receive compliant transactions) for versions 5010 and D.0
January 2011	Begin Level 2 testing period activities (external testing with trading partners and move into production; dual processing mode) for versions 5010 and D.0.
January 2011	Begin initial compliance activities (gap analysis, design, development, internal testing)
January 2012	Achieve Level 2 compliance; compliance date for all covered entities. This is also the compliance date for version 3.0 for all covered entities except small health plans *
January 2013	Compliance date for version 3.0 for small health plans.
October 2013	Compliance date for all covered entities (subject to the final compliance date in any rule published for the adoption of ICD-10).

* Note: Level 1 and Level 2 compliance requirements apply only to versions 5010 and D.0.

Standards for Electronic Transactions

The final rule lists the following summary of formats acceptable for electronic transactions, selected on the basis of guiding principles that were used to designate a standard as a HIPAA standard. Some of these standards may be altered based on NPRMs awaiting finalization or as ongoing CMS revisions to final rules published in the interim.

CMS published the following HIPAA Standard and Transactions Table in the January 16, 2009, final rule 45 CFR part 162:

HIPAA Standard and Transactions

Standard	Transaction
ASC X12 837 D	Health care claims—Dental
ASC X12 837 P	Health care claims—Professional
ASC X12 837 I	Health care claims—Institutional
NCPDP D.0	Health care claims—Retail pharmacy drug
ASC X12 837 P and NCPDP D.0	Health care claims—Retail pharmacy supplies and professional services

DEFINITIONS

Code set. Any set of codes used for encoding data elements, such as tables of terms, medical concepts, medical diagnosis codes, or medical procedure codes. A code set includes both the codes and the descriptors that accompany the codes.

Covered entity. Any health plan, health care clearinghouse, or health care provider who transmits any health information in electronic form in connection with a HIPAA transaction.

Electronic data interchange (EDI). The electronic transfer of information, such as electronic media health claims, in a standard format that is fast and cost effective. Currently there are about 400 formats for electronic health claims being used in the United States. The lack of standardization makes it difficult and expensive to develop and maintain software.

Health Insurance Portability and Accountability Act of 1996 (HIPAA). Amends the Internal Revenue Code of 1986 to improve portability and continuity of health insurance coverage in the group and individual markets. Among its many provisions, HIPAA addresses improved access to long-term care services and coverage, and simplifies the administration of health insurance.

Standard	Transaction
NCPDP D.0	Coordination of benefits—Retail pharmacy drug
ASC X12 837 D	Coordination of benefits—Dental
ASC X12 837 P	Coordination of benefits—Professional
ASC X12 837 I	Coordination of benefits—Institutional
ASC X12 270/271	Eligibility for a health plan (request and response)—dental, professional and institutional
NCPDP D.0	Eligibility for a health plan (request and response)—Retail pharmacy drugs
ASC X12 276/277	Health care claim status (request and response)
ASC X12 834	Enrollment and disenrollment in a health plan
ASC X12 835	Health care payment and remittance advice
ASC X12 820	Health plan premium payment
ASC X12 278	Referral certification and authorization (request and response)
NCPDP D.0	Referral certification and authorization (request and response)—Retail pharmacy drugs
NCPDP 5.1 and NCPDP D.0	Retail pharmacy drug claims (telecommunication and batch standards)
NCPDP 3.0	Medicaid pharmacy subrogation (batch standard).

Retail Pharmacy Specifications

Health care providers that submit retail pharmacy claims, and health care plans that process retail pharmacy claims, currently use the National Council for Prescription Drug Programs (NCPDP) format. The NCPDP claim and equivalent encounter is used either in online interactive or batch mode. According to the January 16, 2009, CMS 45 CFR Part 162, CMS allows covered entities to use either version 4010/4010A, 5010, 5.1, or D.0 for billing retail pharmacy supplies and services, and reflect that policy in revisions to § 162.1102. CMS acknowledged that version D.0 will facilitate transactions for the Medicare Part D pharmacy benefit.

ASC X12 837 for Submission of Institutional Health Care Claims, Professional Health Care Claims, Dental Claims, and Coordination of Benefits

All health care providers and health plans are required to use the ASC X12 837 for submitting electronic health care claims (hospital, physician/supplier, and dental), and have the option of using a health care clearinghouse to satisfy the HIPAA standard requirements. The ASC X12 837 was selected as the standard for the institutional (hospital, nursing facilities, and similar inpatient institutions) claim and will replace the UB-92 Format developed by CMS for Medicare claims.

ASC X12 835 for Receipt of Health Care Remittance

Health care providers that conduct EDI with health plans and that do not change their internal systems will have to convert the ASC X12 835 transactions received from health plans into a format compatible with their internal systems, either by using a translator or a health care clearinghouse. Health plans that want to transmit remittance advice directly to health care providers and that do not use the ASC X12 835 will also incur costs to convert to the standard.

 KEY POINT

Cost estimates for long-term expenses due to electronic transmission are expected to be negligible since the majority of costs are one-time costs related to implementation. There are on-going costs associated with administrative simplification, such as subscribing to or purchasing documentation and implementation specifications related to code sets and standard formats, and obtaining current health plan and health care provider identifier directories or data files.

HIPAA required standards to be developed, when possible, by private sector organizations accredited by the American National Standards Institute (ANSI). These are not government agencies and all standards are from the Accredited Standards Committee (ASC) X12N except the standards for retail pharmacy transactions, which are from the National Council for Prescription Drug Programs (NCPDP).

ASC X12 276/277 for Health Care Claim Status/Response

Most health care providers that are currently using an electronic format for claim status inquiries may request claim status electronically using the ASC X12 276/277. After implementation, health care providers will be able to request and receive the status of claims in one standard format from all health care plans. Health plans that do not currently directly accept electronic claim status requests and do not directly send electronic claims status responses will have to modify their systems to accept the ASC X12 276 and to send the ASC X12 277. No disruptions in claims processing or payment should occur.

ASC X12 834 for Benefit Enrollment and Maintenance in a Health Plan

Employers may use the ASC X12 834 to electronically enroll or disenroll its subscribers into or out of a health plan. Currently, most small and medium size employers and other sponsors conduct subscriber enrollments using paper forms. In addition, the ASC X12 834 supports detailed enrollment information on the subscriber's dependents, which is often lacking in current practice.

ASC X12 270/271 for Eligibility for a Health Plan

The ASC X12 270/271 transaction may be used by a health care provider to electronically request and receive eligibility information from a health care plan prior to providing or billing for a dental, professional, or institutional health care service.

ASC X12 820 for Payroll Deducted and Other Group Premium Payment for Insurance Product

An employer can respond to a bill by using the ASC X12 820 to electronically transmit a remittance notice and payment for health insurance premiums. Payment may be by paper check or an electronic funds transfer transaction. The ASC X12 820 can be sent with electronic funds transfer instructions that are routed directly to the Federal Reserve System's automated health care clearinghouses or with payments generated directly by the employer's or other sponsor's bank.

ASC X12 278 for Referral Certification and Authorization

A health care provider may use the ASC X12 278 to electronically request and receive authorization for a health care service from a health plan prior to providing a health care service.

Code Sets

In order to be designated as a HIPAA code set, the criteria must be met. According to the *Federal Register* 63, no. 88, May 7, 1998, a code set must do the following:

- Improve the efficiency and effectiveness of the health care system by leading to cost reductions for or improvements in benefits from electronic health care transactions
- Meet the needs of the user community, especially providers, health plans, and clearing-houses
- Be consistent and uniform with other HIPAA standards in data element definitions and privacy requirement
- Have low additional development and implementation costs relative to benefits of using the standard
- Be supported by an ANSI-accredited standards organization or other organization
- Be timely in development, testing, implementation, and updating
- Be technologically independent of computer platforms and transmission protocols
- Be precise, simple, and unambiguous
- Be efficient in terms of paper work burdens on users

- Incorporate flexibility to adapt to change in health care industry infrastructure and information technology

When conducting standard transactions as discussed above, the code sets that have been adopted as the standard medical data code sets are to be used. As new code sets become available, such as ICD-10-CM, and are adequately tested and revised, they are considered for inclusion in the list of standard medical code sets. Effective October 1, 2013, the ICD-10-CM and ICD-10-PCS classification systems will become the standard code set for coding and reporting diagnoses (ICD-10-CM) and inpatient hospital procedures (ICD-10-PCS). This is a decision that would be weighed by the Designated Standard Maintenance Organization and the National Committee on Vital and Health Statistics, and presented to the secretary for the Department of Health and Human Services. It would then normally be submitted through the NPRM process for public comment, and all affected entities would have a minimum of 24 months to become compliant with the new code set once a change becomes final. Following are the code sets as adopted in the August 17, 2000, and January 16, 2009, *Federal Registers*:

- International Classification of Diseases, 9th Edition, Clinical Modification, (ICD-9-CM), volumes 1 and 2 (including The Official ICD-9-CM Guidelines for Coding and Reporting), as updated and distributed by NCHS, for the following conditions:
  1. Diseases
  2. Injuries
  3. Impairments
  4. Other health related problems and their manifestations
  5. Causes of injury, disease, impairment, or other health-related problems
- International Classification of Diseases, 9th Edition, Clinical Modification, (ICD-9-CM), volume 3 Procedures (including The Official ICD-9-CM Guidelines for Coding and Reporting), as updated and distributed by HHS, for the following procedures or other actions taken for diseases, injuries, and impairments on hospital inpatients reported by hospitals:
  1. Prevention
  2. Diagnosis
  3. Treatment
  4. Management
- National Drug Codes (NDC), as updated and distributed by HHS, in collaboration with drug manufacturers, for the following:
  1. Drugs
  2. Biologics
- Code on Dental Procedures and Nomenclature, as updated and distributed by the American Dental Association, for dental services.
- The combination of Healthcare Common Procedure Coding System (HCPCS), as updated and distributed by HHS, and *Physician's Current Procedural Terminology*, Fourth Edition (CPT), as updated and distributed by the American Medical Association, for physician services and other health related services. These services include, but are not limited to, the following:
  1. Physician services
  2. Physical and occupational therapy services
  3. Radiological procedures
  4. Clinical laboratory tests
  5. Other medical diagnostic procedures
  6. Hearing and vision services

 FOR MORE INFO

The implementation guides for the ASC X12N standards are available from the Washington Publishing Company, PMB 161, 5284 Randolph Road, Rockville, MD, 20852-2116; telephone: 301-949-9740; FAX: 301-949-9742. These guides are also available at no cost through the Washington Publishing Company on the Internet at http://www.wpc-edi.com/hipaa/. The implementation guide for retail pharmacy standards is available from the National Council for Prescription Drug Programs, 9240 East Raintree Drive, Scottsdale, AZ, 85260-7518; telephone: 480-477-1000; fax: 480-767-1042. It is also available from the NCPDP's website at http://www.ncpdp.org.

7. Transportation services including ambulance
- The Healthcare Common Procedure Coding System (HCPCS), as updated and distributed by CMS/HHS, for all other substances, equipment, supplies, or other items used in health care services. These items include, but are not limited to, the following:
    1. Medical supplies
    2. Orthotic and prosthetic devices
    3. Durable medical equipment

STANDARDS FOR PRIVACY OF INDIVIDUALLY IDENTIFIABLE HEALTH INFORMATION

HIPAA gave Congress until August 21, 1999, to pass health privacy legislation. However, after three years went by without an act of Congress, HHS used the authority granted by HIPAA regulations to develop privacy protections. The final rule published in December 2000 (*Federal Register*) covers health plans, health care clearinghouses, and those health care providers who conduct certain financial and administrative transactions. The regulations protect all medical records and other identifiable health information held by a covered entity, whether communicated electronically, on paper, or orally. The privacy regulations were effective on April 14, 2001, but most covered entities have until April 14, 2003, to become fully compliant. Several modifications to the final privacy rule were made final on August 14, 2002.

The fundamental purpose of the privacy rule is to set a federal "floor" of basic protections to prevent those who do not need identifiable health information from accessing or using it for purposes never intended or known by the individual who is the subject of that information. It affords certain rights to patients regarding the use of their information, and gives patients the right to file a complaint about any perceived violation of the privacy rule. It also provides covered entities with the ability to use protected health information for treatment, payment, and health care operations, provided that entity has made a good faith effort to notify the patient about these uses.

STANDARD UNIQUE EMPLOYER IDENTIFIER

This rule, published May 28, 2002, adopts the use of the employer identification number (EIN) as assigned by the Internal Revenue Service as a standard identifier for employers in standard transactions. The use of this identifier mainly applies to employers as sponsors of health insurance for employees, and would be used in electronic transactions to enroll employees in a health plan (or remove employees) or make premium payments to health plans on behalf of their employees. Health care providers would only be required to use it on a situational basis, such as with X12N 270/271 eligibility transactions when the employer is the holder of that information.

Standards for Security and Electronic Signatures

An NPRM regarding data security and electronic signatures was published on August 12, 1998. The purpose of the security standards is to address the steps that must be taken by a covered entity to prevent the unintentional disclosure, destruction, or corruption of personal health information maintained or transmitted by health plans, health care providers, and health care clearinghouses. It includes administrative procedures, physical safeguards, technical security services, and technical security mechanisms. A final rule was published in the *Federal Register* as Health Insurance Reform: Security Standards 45 CFR Parts 160, 162, and 164 (CMS-0049-F) on February 23, 2003.

KEY POINT

The privacy regulations provide for a federal minimum standard to be met regarding the protection of individually identifiable health information, which can be preempted by a more stringent state law. Be sure to check the patient privacy laws in your state to determine whether they are more or less stringent than the privacy rule. If they are more stringent than HIPAA, they will be the standard in your state.

National Standard Health Care Provider Identifier (NPI)

The NPI is a proposed 10-position numeric identifier for health care providers submitting claims or conducting other transactions specified by HIPAA. A health care provider is an individual, group, or organization that provides medical or other health services or supplies. This includes physicians and other practitioners, physician/practitioner groups, institutions such as hospitals, laboratories, and nursing homes, organizations such as health maintenance organizations, and suppliers such as pharmacies and medical supply companies. This rule is expected to simplify the cumbersome process of receiving and administering multiple provider identification numbers.

The proposed rule was published in the *Federal Register* on May 7, 1998. Public comment ended July 6, 1998. A final rule was published in the *Federal Register* as HIPAA Administrative Simplification: Standard Unique Health Identifier for Health Care Providers 45 CFR RIN 0938–AH99, Part 162 (CMS–0045–F) on January 23, 2004.

SUMMARY

The Health Insurance Portability and Accountability Act of 1996 (HIPAA) was established to improve health care coverage in individual and group markets. The administrative simplification provisions of HIPAA apply directly to health providers because of the requirements for electronic transmission of health care information and the related issues, such as the privacy of patient and medical information. In past years, final rules in accordance to HIPAA regulations include those establishing formats for electronic transmission, the code sets (diagnostic and procedural) acceptable for electronic transmission, security, provider identifier, and privacy rules to protect the patient and medical record.

DISCUSSION QUESTIONS

1. List the administrative simplification provisions in HIPAA as they apply to the health care provider.

   _____

   _____

   _____

2. Briefly describe the administrative simplification regulations so far approved by final rule.

   _____

   _____

   _____

3. Who must use the electronic transmission requirements, and when did the requirements go into effect?

   _____

   _____

   _____

4. List the code sets adopted as the standard under administrative simplification provisions.

   _____

   _____

   _____

5. If state and federal patient privacy provisions conflict, which set of regulations will prevail?

   _____

   _____

   _____

Chapter 7: Documentation

The ICD-10 classification and coding systems are constructed with future reporting needs in mind. Their architecture has been constructed on a scale that offers incredible potential for growth to meet present and future health care data demands. For our purposes in this chapter, we will focus on the diagnosis coding system (ICD-10-CM), because it will affect both hospital and physician providers in the near future. The documentation principles and concepts, however, may apply to documentation considerations created by the impact of both systems.

In creating the clinical modification for ICD-10 in this country, the National Center for Health Statistics (NCHS) has clearly decided the future is already here. The number of diagnostic codes available for use in the ICD-10-CM coding system is larger than the number available in ICD-9-CM by thousands.

This greater level of detail, called "granularity," is good news for the nosologists and government researchers tracking disease in the United States. Don't underestimate the importance of this work; their statistics help drive healthcare reform, research, payment systems, and social programs. The granularity of ICD-10-CM does indeed provide benefits for everyone in our society.

DOCUMENTATION NEEDS

ICD-10-CM will pose certain significant challenges to coders in both physician and facility settings. As additional detail is to be reported with ICD-10-CM, more detail will be required in the medical records from which the data for coding is extracted. For coders who are already facing these challenges on a daily basis, the increased specificity required to report ICD-10-CM may seem daunting. The following examples illustrate some of the documentation gaps that coders should be prepared to address:

Example 1

Term	Coding Component	Codes
Chalazion	**Specify laterality and anatomic site:** Right upper eyelid Right lower eyelid Right eye, unspecified eyelid Left upper eyelid Left lower eyelid Left eye, unspecified eyelid Unspecified eye, unspecified	H00.11 Chalazion, right upper eyelid H00.12 Chalazion right lower eyelid H00.13 Chalazion right eye, unspecified eyelid H00.14 Chalazion left upper eyelid H00.15 Chalazion left lower eyelid H00.16 Chalazion left eye, unspecified eyelid H00.19 Chalazion unspecified eye, unspecified

A single code, 373.2 Chalazion, was used to classify this diagnosis in ICD-9-CM. In ICD-10-CM, an expanded classification was created to facilitate data capture of specific anatomic site and laterality. Providers should be made aware of the classification specificity of ICD-10-CM so that documentation practices can adjusted before implementation. However, in most cases, specific information about laterality and an anatomic site may be readily available in the patient record.

In this example, the information listed in the coding component column is information that has not been required under ICD-9-CM, but will be required with ICD-10-CM. You may

OBJECTIVES

Iin this chapter, you will learn:
- About preview examples of documentation requirements for ICD-10-CM
- How increased granularity affects documentation, coding, and the reimbursement cycle
- How data collection affects outcomes
- Society's advantage in using a coding system with greater granularity

DEFINITIONS

Nosologist. A scientist who studies the classification of diseases.

find that information not essential to choosing the code in ICD-9-CM, but necessary for selecting the code in ICD-10-CM, may already be present in the medical record, such as laterality and specific site.

Keep in mind, though, that issues like laterality are not documentation issues for ICD-10-CM alone. Physicians must meet the legal and professional standards for documentation that demand a level of granularity in the medical record.

Example 2

Term	Coding Component	Codes
Pregnancy	**With bladder infection, specify trimester:** first second third	O23.10 Infections of bladder in pregnancy, unspecified trimester O23.11 Infections of bladder in pregnancy, first trimester O23.12 Infections of bladder in pregnancy, second trimester O23.13 Infections of bladder in pregnancy, third trimester

In this case, the new documentation component required for ICD-10-CM code selection is one that you would already expect to find in the medical record. In ICD-10-CM, code selection in pregnancy includes a trimester component. One would normally expect medical charts to include this data, or it could be derived from the patient's due date.

Example 3

Term	Coding Component	Codes
Sarcoidosis	**Specify anatomic site and/or nature of manifestation**	D86.0 Sarcoidosis of lung D86.1 Sarcoidosis of lymph nodes D86.2 Sarcoidosis of lung with sarcoidosis of lymph nodes D86.3 Sarcoidosis of skin D86.8 Sarcoidosis of other sites D86.81 Sarcoid meningitis D86.82 Multiple cranial nerve palsies in sarcoidosis D86.83 Sarcoid iridocyclitis D86.84 Sarcoid pyelonephritis D86.85 Sarcoid myocarditis D86.86 Sarcoid arthropathy D86.87 Sarcoid myositis D86.89 Sarcoidosis of other sites D86.9 Sarcoidosis, unspecified

This example shows a case in which information specifying the nature of the manifestation, as well as the site where it is occurring, is necessary for choosing the most appropriate code.

Sometimes the necessary components are not other conditions, complications, or manifestations that the physician may also have documented somewhere in the medical record. In these cases, it becomes especially important to educate medical staff members about the changes in the necessary code components and the documentation requirements for choosing a code. This is also true for conditions that may be classified as different types, or with different nomenclature.

While information about the upcoming changes, given to all medical staff members, is pertinent and important, individual studies that focus on providers' documentation habits and the particular conditions they are likely to report may also be useful in determining areas for improvement.

KEY POINT

One physician, upon hearing a coder from another clinic complain about her doctor's documentation, offered this anecdote:

"My daughter came home from school yesterday with a report card and all subjects were marked with the grade, 'incomplete.' I scheduled an appointment with the teacher, since my daughter said she had turned in all of her homework and felt the tests were very easy. At the meeting with the teacher, I asked how a student who does such sterling work could be awarded 'incomplete' in every class. The teacher looked me straight in the eye and said, with a bit of a chip on his shoulder, 'You know, I didn't get into teaching to do paper work…'

"Doctors," this physician continued, "could learn a lot from that story. Your job isn't done until your paper work is done."

Holding smaller, focused inservices that cover changes in coding components and documentation requirements for conditions often encountered within certain specialties may be another way to improve documentation.

DOCUMENTATION AND THE REIMBURSEMENT PROCESS

No one will deny that documentation plays an important role in the reimbursement process. The lack of it can create bottlenecks at certain points along the way that delay billing and hence payment. While it may seem that the implementation of ICD-10-CM holds only the disadvantages of slowing down your cycle of payment, there are going to be definite advantages that ICD-10-CM will also bring. Before we look at what those advantages are, let's examine some of the potential scenarios that may happen while your facility captures the learning curve on documenting with ICD-10-CM requirements.

The reimbursement process functions something like this in its basic format, although your facility or practice may have other steps along the way:

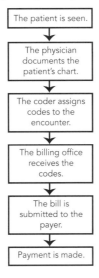

The bottlenecking that can occur because of the increased granularity and documentation requirements of ICD-10-CM is most likely to happen in the early steps. The coder will be the first to recognize that important information is missing. The coder must then query the doctor for more information and the doctor has to ensure that it gets into the medical record before the coding part of the process can proceed.

If the doctor wasn't aware of the components required to assign a code, he or she may not have that information and will have to go back to the patient. Avoiding this last possibility is one of the reasons why disseminating information about ICD-10-CM granularity and the accompanying documentation necessities is so important. By studying the differences in coding components and adjusting documentation habits now, future paperwork bottlenecks can be minimized.

These areas of bottlenecking along the reimbursement process are already very familiar to us now with ICD-9-CM. A certain amount of "documentation chasing" is always going to be in the picture, so it is safe to say that the increase in time until billing that you will experience with the implementation of ICD-10-CM will not remain a constant. As the learning curve is conquered, the time spent on these steps will return to a usual operating level.

CODING AXIOM

Build documentation compliance for physicians into your compliance plan, with provisions for fines or other punitive actions for chronic noncompliance. One New York clinic noted a significant reduction in underdocumentation after a provision for a $100 fine was written into the clinic's compliance plan. The fine was levied at the third documented instance for a documentation mistake (for example, not noting the type of diabetes) found by the same coder. Who were the checks made out to? The coders whose work was hampered by the documentation problems.

QUICK TIP

Start now by auditing your medical records to asses whether current documentation practices will support the level of detail required to code in the new systems. Provide medical staff with examples of where their current practices fall short, and inform them of the resultant backlogs in the deficiency process and revenue cycle.

Advantages of ICD-10-CM Within the Reimbursement Process

There are also some definite advantages to using ICD-10-CM within the reimbursement cycle that occur at the coding stage and beyond. Since the codes are so much more defined in their subclassification, the coder experiences a reduction in the manual processing time of choosing the codes. Coders are also much more likely to choose the correct code the first time. There is much less ambiguity left open for discussion in ICD-10-CM.

The whole billing process is made much more complicated when "extra documentation" has to be mailed in to clarify the situation. This is hard to do electronically and these extra documents have to be read and manually processed in order for the payer to make a decision. ICD-10-CM generates much less of a problem when it comes to submitting paper because the codes intrinsically paint a clearer and more complete picture of the patient's condition.

This leads us into another advantage of ICD-10-CM that happens at the payer's end. There is much less room for denial based on the diagnosis not matching the procedure for medical necessity. With ICD-10-CM, the diagnosis comes much closer to being "married" to the procedure, and since it gives a more complete description of the condition intrinsically, it leaves a smaller gap for denial.

INCREASED GRANULARITY

When we think about the purposes that a coding system fulfills, it seems that we focus only on the billing and reimbursement function for using codes. The primary reason for creating a coding system that assigns a number to the diagnosis or condition is simply to record and retrieve information in an efficient way. One of the main purposes we use this for is—and always has been—to gather data for research and statistics. The awareness of this purpose seems to have fallen into the background against the daily rush to assign codes for billing third party payers.

Nosologists, medical researchers, and epidemiologists are constantly tracking disease in the United States. Where do they get their data? What are their findings doing for the country? Our coding system with its assigned codes for morbidity cases is how they are able to pull their data, whether they are looking at a certain subpopulation, a specific disease or condition, or procedures performed.

A coding system for documenting and reporting cases allows the researchers, the statisticians, and the epidemiologists to gather the information with which they work. Their statistics and their research findings are very important. They help drive healthcare reform, make decisions about the most effective and appropriate treatments, determine what research to be pursuing, and aid in structuring our social programs concerned with health and well-being. For answering these purposes, increased granularity is a mighty tool.

Understanding these crucial functions of a coding system can assuage some of the apprehension surrounding the implementation of ICD-10-CM and our need for it. How can you know where you are going and make informed, educated decisions for the future if you don't know what's happening? To track what is happening, you need data. Data affects your outcomes. Good data can help change our world. Coders are literally building the database that drives our future every time they choose the codes that are used in painting our statistical pictures and conducting research.

The increased granularity, or in other words, the greater level of detail that ICD-10-CM brings with it gives us the better data that we need and it will lead to better clinical outcomes and more cost-effective disease management, which benefits everyone. ICD-10-CM has the power to begin turning medicine from an art into a science.

Improving Treatment Management

Let's look at how ICD-10-CM can improve the management and treatment of disease for the individual.

In ICD-10-CM, code classifications for complications of medical and surgical care have been expanded to include the following categories:

Y62   Failure of sterile precautions during surgical and medical care
Y63   Failure in dosage during surgical and medical care
Y64   Contaminated medical or biological substances
Y70–Y82   Medical devices associated with adverse incidents in diagnostic and therapeutic use

The increased level of detail in this chapter provides a means to improve care by putting forth a mechanism for increased efficiency in tracking nosocomial and iatrogenic incidents that were previously either loosely defined by the code categories 996–999 in ICD-9-CM or missing from classification altogether.

Establishing Better Clinical Outcomes and Treatment Protocols

ICD-10-CM will not only aid in improving disease management and treatment for all individuals within a certain diagnostic group, but it will help us achieve better treatment protocols that yield better clinical outcomes for future cases. In the race against cancer, for instance, there is an advantage waiting to be exploited for research purposes and better treatment outcomes within the ICD-10-CM system for reporting morbidity. This is especially true when combined with the ICD-10-PCS system for documenting procedures.

With the greater granularity that the detail of ICD-10-CM provides, researchers will be able to study diseases, together with the current treatments being used, on a much finer level. They will begin to see patterns emerging and can track those patterns and outcomes to find the critical connections needed to develop new treatments and speed research.

For example, carcinoma in situ of the breast can be tracked by only one code in ICD-9-CM, 233.0. There are 12 separate codes in the rubric for carcinoma in situ of the breast (D05) in ICD-10-CM, with axes for lobular, intraductal, other, and unspecified carcinoma. Together with the ICD-10-PCS system for reporting the procedures with greater detail, researchers can track the specific outcomes of the different types of radioactive materials versus surgical procedures used in treating those cases. They may start discovering certain trends that would have been very difficult, if not impossible, to see with less specific data.

Researchers may discover, for instance, that one particular isotope used for treating lobular cancer results in a better response than other isotopes, or the same treatment doesn't yield the same outcome on intraductal carcinoma, or surgical intervention proves more effective than radiation in females; these are only examples of the kinds of trends and patterns that could be discovered when research is done with better data. Data always affects the outcome. When you can marry the procedure to the diagnosis, you get definitive trackable outcomes. This is also why there will be less room for denial on the reimbursement side of using ICD-10-CM to document medical necessity.

Other Advantages of Increased Granularity

We may see other advantages happen from the sidelines with the implementation of ICD-10-CM. For instance, under ICD-9-CM, there is only one code available for reporting Down syndrome, 758.0. There are, in fact, three different types of Down syndrome: nonmosaicism (meiotic nondisjunction), mosaicism (mitotic nondisjunction), and translocation. With ICD-10-CM, the following are the codes to choose from:

 KEY POINT

The Joint Commission on Accreditation of Healthcare Organizations (JCAHO) has set standards for record-keeping that, if rigorously followed by physicians, would eliminate many of the documentation problems present in the medical record today. Among the elements it requires are the following:

- Progress notes made by medical staff and other authorized staff
- Reports on any diagnostic or therapeutic procedures, such as pathology and clinical laboratory examinations, and radiology and nuclear medicine examinations or treatments
- Medical history
- Impressions and conclusions drawn from history and examination
- Plan for patient care
- Consultation reports
- Final diagnoses
- Discharge instructions

Q90.0	Trisomy 21, nonmosaicism (meiotic nondisjunction)
Q90.1	Trisomy 21, mosaicism (mitotic nondisjunction)
Q90.2	Trisomy 21, translocation
Q90.9	Down syndrome, unspecified

Once the distinction is made in the clinical coding system, it allows for gathering documented data on a much higher level of detail, and researchers will be using that data; ultimately it may prove to be a catalyst in making genetic testing a standard practice rather than leaving such testing undone, as it currently is in so many cases. This could have far-reaching effects for making all kinds of discoveries. The increased granularity of the ICD-10-CM coding system has many deep and extensive advantages that are worth celebrating.

DISCUSSION QUESTIONS

1. What are some action plans that your facility or office can use to educate physicians about documentation requirements?

    _____

    _____

    _____

2. How will better documentation habits help the reimbursement process?

    _____

    _____

    _____

3. Explain how the data we use affects the outcome when establishing protocols for treating disease.

    _____

    _____

    _____

4. Evaluate the importance of increased granularity in the data used and the role that granularity plays in shaping the future.

    _____

    _____

    _____

Chapter 8:
Implementation Issues

It has been more than 20 years since the United States adopted a new medical coding system. Since that time, payment systems have shifted from a system in which physicians and facilities were paid based upon what they charged, to one in which payments are standardized and based upon what is coded. The reliance upon codes for reimbursement has greatly increased the importance of medical coding for everyone in American health care—more than 500,000 physicians and more than 6,000 hospitals. Preparing all professionals at your facility—not just the coders—for the impact of the new coding system is key to the successful implementation of ICD-10-CM. Now is the time to begin baseline training. A heightened awareness of the issues surrounding ICD-10-CM will bring many benefits:

- Prevent your organization from investing in potentially obsolete equipment
- Guide you in cultivating the right skill sets required for ICD-10-CM implementation
- Allow your financial managers to prepare for the added capital and personnel investments required by the change
- Minimize the overall impact of the change for your organization

Within 12 months prior to the official date of implementation, you will want coders at your facility to undergo extensive clinical training in the use of ICD-10-CM. Until then, training should be limited to an overview of ICD-10-CM issues. Early training will result in improved planning within three business categories at your medical office:

- Training and personnel
- Information technology
- Business and finance

TRAINING AND PERSONNEL

There is no avoiding ICD-10. The new diagnostic system provides the detail lacking in the current system. Granularity, the degree to which codes are explicitly defined, is imperative to tracking disease in the United States. The statistics gathered from coding systems are used in many critical ways:

- To drive health care reform
- To measure both the quality and the efficacy of care
- To power payment systems
- To identify public health risks
- To detect fraud
- To monitor clinical trials and epidemics
- To track resource utilization
- To prioritize social programs

The improved data provided by ICD-10 codes combined with today's technology has the potential to turn medicine into a very precise science. Statistics gathered from coded claims on specific illnesses and successful patterns of care lead to medical protocols for disease

OBJECTIVES

In this chapter, you will learn:

- The far-reaching impact of ICD-10-CM on your facility
- How to prepare all departments within your facility for implementation
- How to reduce last-minute crises with IS or budgeting
- How to help your facility or office organize a task force to oversee change

QUICK TIP

Take advantage of the following educational opportunities now:

- Audio and Web-based seminars
- Convention and conference presentations
- Web-based training
- Professional association community networks and publications

management; but medical standards developed from data are only as good as the data itself. Therefore, it is important to the future of our nation's health care system—not just to coders or the business office—that coders are trained and committed to accuracy. Otherwise, poor decisions will result when inaccurate codes are used to track epidemics, to measure the efficacy of care, or for any of the other statistical uses mentioned above.

According to Department of Labor statistics, there are more than 600,000 coders and health information specialists in this country. Because the many uses of codes cross so many medical professions, it is no surprise that many people other than coders will be affected by ICD-10. Among the people who will require education and/or training are the following:

- Senior management
- HIM managers
- Utilization management/case managers
- Risk management
- Registration/patient access
- Medical necessity coordinators
- Contract managers
- Clinical coders
- Physicians
- Compliance officers
- Data analysts
- Auditors
- Software vendors
- Quality assurance management
- Claims reviewers
- Human resources managers
- Accounting managers
- Information systems personnel

Clinical Personnel
Coding Staff

The greater detail found in ICD-10 must be reflected in the medical records coders use for extracting information. Examples of higher clinical coding complexity include the following:

- For pressure ulcer, 15 codes in ICD-9-CM are replaced with a choice from among 60 codes that identify the specific site (lower back, sacral region, left buttock, etc.) and the degree of ulceration (e.g., limited to skin breakdown, fat layer exposure, necrosis of muscle or bone).
- For cardiac arrest, a single code in ICD-9-CM is replaced with choices classifying cardiac arrest due to underlying cardiac conditions, other underlying conditions and as complications following interventions and surgeries.
- For the symptom, abnormal gait, a single code has been replaced by seven codes in ICD-10-CM that identify ataxic gate, paralytic gate, difficulty in walking, falling, unsteadiness, and other abnormalities of gait.

Since coding conventions in ICD-10-CM are similar to those of ICD-9-CM, these conventions will largely be understood by experienced coders. However, be sure to provide office resources such as medical dictionaries, anatomy charts, and "self-help" instructional materials, since the level of anatomic detail is much higher in ICD-10-CM, and coders will be required to translate the language of the medical record into the language of code selection. For example:

Sprain of the long head of the right biceps muscle would be coded in ICD-9-CM as 840.8 Sprains and strains of shoulder and upper arm. In ICD-10-CM, the condition is coded specifically by the nature of the injury, laterality, anatomical site, and specific part of the muscle.

ICD-9-CM

840.8   Sprains and strains of other specified sites of shoulder and upper arm

ICD-10-CM

S46.111   Strain of muscle and tendon of long head of biceps, right arm

Specialty-specific and code-specific training should be reserved for the 12-month period preceding implementation. However, in the interim, some foundation training of clinical coders can prepare them for the change and get them oriented to using ICD-10-CM. These are some of the early training issues that can be addressed with clinical coders:

- Anatomical and physiological literacy training
- Heightened awareness of and sensitivity to documentation requirements
- Exposure to some of the new conventions of ICD-10-CM, including
  - alpha kickers for injuries that identify initial encounter, subsequent encounter, and sequelae
  - alpha kickers for coma that identify the treatment site as being in the field, at arrival to emergency department, upon hospital admission, 24 hours post admission, or an unspecified time
  - "place holding 'x'" to allow for future expansion of the code set

Communication Is Key

Communication with all coders during implementation and pre-implementation is very important. When talk turns to ICD-10-CM, many experienced coders respond by outlining their retirement timetables. In many cases, people who have been coding for 20 years or more may feel threatened by the pending classification system change. They may fear they will be unseated as the resident "experts." It will be a challenge to retain experienced coders in the ICD-9-CM system, but if management presents the right attitudes regarding the change, and if all coders are encouraged to participate in the planning process for implementation, attrition can be lessened. Use the experience and knowledge of your more senior coders as you develop your implementation plans for ICD-10-CM. Your payoff will be a more comprehensive review of the impact ICD-10-CM is going to have, and a satisfied, willing staff with a vested interest in achieving a smooth implementation transition.

Whether you are a compliance officer, an auditor, a coder, or a quality assurance worker, the best early education tool for the transition is a copy of the ICD-10-CM and ICD-10-PCS code books. Ingenix regularly publishes updated drafts of versions of both ICD-10-CM and ICD-10-PCS. These versions should see little change before the final codes are published and adopted. Study the codes affecting your specialty or facility's services and familiarize yourself with the old and new conventions in ICD-10-CM. This will reduce the anxiety you may feel regarding the change. The added perspectives may also provide important insight into potential problem areas that need to be addressed. For example, upon learning about the alpha-numeric composition of the codes in ICD-10-CM, one clinical coder remarked to her manager that the data entry being performed by a 10-key operator would be protracted, since the 10-key operators were accustomed to numeric characters only. This observation led the facility to eliminate 10-key data entry, relying

 QUICK TIP

A higher level of anatomical and clinical knowledge is demanded by ICD-10-CM than by ICD-9-CM. ICD-10-PCS requires even more sophistication from coders. This is because while the ICD-10-CM uses nomenclature common to the medical record, ICD-10-PCS has standardized the medical language to the point where the coder reading the medical record will be required to "translate" the language into the universal nomenclature of ICD-10-PCS. The coder will also be required to "build" the code logically by selecting the individual pieces that make up the code from the standardized available choices.

 KEY POINT

Take measures to include your more experienced coders in your facility's plans for change. Their knowledge can ease the transition to ICD-10, once they are convinced the new coding system is an exciting opportunity, not a conspiracy to make their jobs more difficult.

 KEY POINT

Whenever possible, coordinate work disruptions. For example, schedule an IS upgrade of coder computers for the day when your coding staff will be off-site, attending ICD-10 training.

instead on full typewriter keyboards for data entry. It was expected that by the time ICD-10-CM was implemented, the 10-key operator would be as efficient on the keyboard as she was on the 10-key. A potential stumbling block to implementation was averted.

Do not assume that an encoder product will negate the need for training or reference guides to the new coding systems. Encoders are merely tools whereby codes are assigned. It takes an educated coder to follow encoder logic and interpret documentation within the parameters of coding guidelines to ensure accurate and compliant coding. It is especially imperative with the advent of new coding systems and interfaces that coders have a means to check encoder and grouper logic to ensure that software programs and interfaces are working properly.

Understanding the new coding system, becoming familiar with the codes for their specialty, and knowing the strategic goals of their business department can help coders feel vested in the new system. When it comes to a new challenge, attitude can be the difference between success and failure.

Physicians

Physicians know the consequences of inadequate documentation as Medicare and private payers tighten their reimbursement belts. Even so, documentation continues to be the number one problem in clinical coding and reimbursement. ICD-10-CM represents the first new diagnostic coding system adopted since computers in the medical reimbursement industry raised the standards of accuracy in coding. This may provide coders and office managers with an unprecedented opportunity to train physicians who ask, "What's all this fuss about ICD-10-CM?"

The most important message that can be conveyed to physicians is that lack of compliance with the new documentation requirements of ICD-10-CM will cost them money, and cost them time. We can expect every step in the reimbursement cycle to be extended a bit during the initial stages of implementation. Nobody enjoys delayed payments, so everyone's goal will be to shrink that cycle back to its previous size. If physicians expect their staff to strive to tighten the reimbursement cycle, their best move is to lead by example.

The level of detail required in medical documentation for assignment of ICD-10-CM codes emphasizes physician participation. The patient's chart MUST specify terminology and provide complete documentation according to new standards. For example:

- For osteoporosis with pathological fracture, the origin of osteoporosis as either post-menopausal or other type, such as disuse, drug-induced, idiopathic, or, postsurgical, must be identified together with the specific site of the current fracture.
- For an injury to a nerve of the lower limb (one code in ICD-9-CM), medical documentation must show which nerve (tibial, peroneal, cutaneous sensory, or other nerve), right or left side, and whether the encounter is initial, subsequent, or to treat late effects. There are 45 choices for coding an injury to a nerve at the lower leg level in ICD-10-CM.

Physicians routinely use eponyms to document their procedures. No eponyms are used in ICD-10-PCS, so physicians must learn to document using standard terminology. For example, Steinberg operation will need to be documented as a revision of gastric anastomosis to facilitate coding.

One "hands-on" approach to teaching physicians the issues of ICD-10-CM documentation is to perform audits on physician charts to identify documentation problems relevant to ICD-10-CM. After masking identifying information to preserve the privacy of the patient, photocopy actual medical records that are under-documented. Photocopy the page with ICD-10-CM code selections for that disorder. Highlight the documentation and the

 KEY POINT

ICD-10 provides an unprecedented window of opportunity for physician training. It may be the only time that physicians recognize the need for change, and coders need to be armed to move when that recognition happens. A higher interest in documentation requirements can be generated if you can tie the higher level of documentation needed for ICD-10 to tangible reimbursement issues for the organization and the physician's practice.

appropriate ICD-10-CM code section, and staple the two sheets together. Keep a separate file for each physician in your office, and when your file holds 10 or more examples of underdocumentation for ICD-10-CM, schedule a short meeting with the physician to go over these examples.

Human Resource Managers

Including human resources managers in ICD-10-CM planning may help prevent manpower shortages at implementation time. Some issues are important to HR departments as ICD-10-CM implementation nears:

- Retaining current employees
- Finding new employees

By U.S. government accounts, health care costs in this country topped more than one trillion dollars in 2001, and are expected to double by the end of this decade. More than half of this amount was billed through codes applied to claims at facilities and physician practices. Even without the impact of the new coding system, the Department of Labor is predicting a shortage in health information management professionals, including coders, through the rest of this decade. Qualified, experienced coders are going to be a premium commodity.

The number one goal of human resources personnel should be a successful campaign to retain current coding employees over time. A high retention rate eliminates the high costs of recruitment and training of new employees. By beginning now to measure and ensure the job satisfaction of HIM staff, human resources personnel can reduce the attrition that the new coding system threatens. The coder shortage will create competition among employers. Make sure that wages and benefits at your facility are competitive. The cost of receiving or maintaining credentialing is expensive, and coders will look elsewhere if expected to shoulder that burden at your office.

Begin networking now to develop sources for finding and recruiting new coders—through local professional organizations and placement agencies, training centers, and online employment sources.

Accounting Managers

The immediate issue affecting accounting managers regarding ICD-10-CM implementation is the capital expenditures required by the new system. Medical reimbursement offices may be required to do the following:

- Upgrade computers
- Replace software
- Hire new IS and coding personnel
- Pay for training and for coders' wages as they attend training
- Purchase reference manuals
- Manage losses in productivity

Developing a financial plan is a strategic move that is imperative to successful implementation.

A valid question is, "How will ICD-10-CM affect payment?" ICD codes are the determinants for the DRGs that are the basis for inpatient payment. Another common question is, "What is the expected impact of the change to ICD-10-CM and the potential change to ICD-10-PCS upon inpatient reimbursement?" Today reimbursement rates in the United States are based upon years of aggregate data. No one will want to give up a historically valid payment methodology when a new coding system is implemented. Instead, it is expected that for the first years, ICD-10-CM codes and ICD-10-PCS codes will be

KEY POINT

Don't wait until the month before implementation to discuss with your software and hardware vendors how their products will fare with ICD-10-CM, unless you want to pay a high price for substandard service. It's important to keep communication flowing in the year before implementation. From this point forward, it is also wise not to make new investments without a guarantee that the product will be "ICD-10 compatible."

CODING AXIOM

Do not assume that outside vendors, independent coding contractors, and per diem staff will stay current with the transition. Ensure that all persons performing coding at your facility or office can demonstrate ICD-10-CM and/or ICD-10-PCS literacy.

mapped to their equivalent ICD-9-CM codes for payment determination. When sufficient data has been collected, payment schedules will be modified to reflect the more detailed information available in ICD-10-CM and ICD-10-PCS.

For those paid under CPT, the change to ICD-10-CM will only affect payment as related to medical necessity and the need to be accurate in the selection of codes. It is likely the number of rejected claims will climb during the period shortly after implementation, then settle to previous levels. When hospitals implement ICD-10-PCS, the change will be more dramatic. For the first year or so, codes in ICD-10-PCS and ICD-10-CM will be mapped to ICD-9-CM codes. Once a baseline of data has been developed, new fee schedules will be established for ICD-10-PCS and ICD-10-CM for facilities. The same issues of accuracy and claims rejection will apply at hospitals as in physician offices.

An oft-overlooked and critical factor in implementation of a new code set is its impact upon the reimbursement cycle. Each step in the reimbursement cycle has the potential to be protracted as a result of the code changes. While it is taking longer for your office to file a claim, and for the payer to reimburse you for the services, your office will be facing additional costs associated with the change: new personnel, new reference materials, new computers, training costs, productivity reductions.

No matter how well the provider does its job, it must still rely on the payer for its income. It is critical that providers contact each of their payers to be certain that procedures are coordinated and implementation is synchronized. Campaigns to work with payers can be managed by the accounting office or through the coding and billing office.

INFORMATION SYSTEMS

The move to ICD-10-CM is much bigger in the healthcare industry than Y2K ever was. Information systems (IS) personnel are major resources in the transition. As you begin budgeting and planning, remember the others who will be affected by ICD-10-CM.

Every electronic transaction requiring an ICD-9-CM code will need to be changed under ICD-10-CM or ICD-10-PCS. This includes the following:

- Medical records abstraction
- Data reporting
- Utilization
- Billing
- Fee schedules
- Payment policies
- Provider profiling
- Medical review
- Medical necessity software
- Benefits determination
- Claims submission
- Test ordering systems
- Accounting systems
- Case mix systems
- Groupers
- Abstracting systems
- Clinical systems

The changes will include specific functions, record format, and fields or data location sites, including the following:

- Software interfaces
- Field length formats on screens
- Report formats and layouts
- Expansions of flat files
- Coding edits and logic
- In-house custom applications

If you are using software that has ICD-9-CM codes, make sure that your software vendor and information systems personnel are preparing to accommodate ICD-10-CM codes. Systems are set up to accept code data in specific formats and the structural disparity between ICD-10-CM and ICD-9-CM requires modified software. Do not assume that outside vendors will stay current with the transition.

Planning Issues

IS will want to create a software application or an interface between the two systems. IS can work with the coding department to identify the systems and software using ICD-9-CM codes, such as computer applications in anesthesia, the emergency department, and the intensive care unit. A facility with internally developed software or interfaces needs IS to draw up long-range plans.

Information systems will need examples of the structural changes inherent in I-10 systems to make the necessary modifications. IS will need to ensure that multiple code sets (ICD-9-CM, ICD-10-CM, ICD-10-PCS, and CPT) can be supported. Because of the far-reaching impact and uses of coded data throughout a facility, IS transition strategies are pivotal. IS will need to account for all products and functions that include codes, and create tactics accordingly to support changes in areas such as:

- Programs
- Screens
- Reports
- Interfaces or APIs
- Forms—printed or electronic
- Documentation
- Online help

As well as this, every electronic transaction requiring an ICD-9-CM code needs to be changed to accommodate I-10. This includes software applications for abstraction of coded data, data reporting tools, utilization management tools, billing software, claims editors, groupers, coding edits, and clinical systems.

Storage requirements (hardware/disk space) will need to be increased to accommodate new, larger classification schemes. The size of the I-10 code set will increase nearly tenfold. Fields will need to be modified to accommodate alphanumeric codes, while also being able to differentiate between letters, numbers, and case sensitivity. Hardware, software, materials, and staff must support both old and new code sets.

For some time period, systems will need to be able to run both ICD-9-CM and ICD-10-CM/PCS systems concurrently. Code support for dual systems are necessary in order to code and process both old and new claims, enable trend analysis, and promote code translation for reporting.

 KEY POINT

Make any necessary process, policy, and procedural changes for your department now. Allow your documentation efforts to "multi-task" and function as a training resource, process quality assessment tool, and communication enhancement.

Crosswalks/Data Mapping

To enable data reporting before, during, and after the I-10 transition, code crosswalks or data maps will need to be in place. This includes cross-walking or mapping codes in the following ways:

With "forward mapping" of the old system to the new system:

- ICD-9-CM to ICD-10-CM
- ICD-9-CM to ICD-10-PCS

With "backward mapping" of the new system to the old system:

- ICD-10-CM to ICD-9-CM
- ICD-10-PCS to ICD-9-CM

General equivalence mappings and reimbursement mappings have been made available on the CMS (ICD-10-PCS) and the NCHS websites (ICD-10-CM), along with user's guides to ensure their proper translations and use. These mappings will be updated concurrently with updates to the coding systems. See chapter 5 for further detail.

Information systems will be particularly pivotal in facilitating implementation throughout the organization. The following list provides an example of how data systems throughout the organization will need to be modified:

- Pre-admission, registration
  - Scheduling
  - Intake
  - Pre-certification support
  - Medical necessity software
  - Encounter forms
  - Registration
  - Emergency Room
  - ADT
- During stay or visit
  - Order entry
  - Clinical/ancillary systems
  - Dietary
  - OR Scheduling
  - Clinical protocols
  - Clinical reminder/alerting systems
  - Concurrent coding
- Post discharge
  - HIM/Abstracting/Encoding
  - Data editing software
  - Benefits determination, contract management
  - Billing/AR
  - UR and QM systems
  - Case mix/decision support
  - State and federal reporting
  - Risk management
  - Aggregate data reporting

 KEY POINT

Consult the ICD-10-CM GEM Users Guide posted on the NCHS website at: http://www.cdc.gov/nchs/about/otheract/icd9/icd10cm.htm

For the ICD-10-PCS GEM and Reimbursement User's Guides, see the CMS website at:

http://www.cms.hhs.gov/ICD10/01m_2009_ICD10PCS.asp

Along with these data collection systems, standardized forms and interfaces such as the UB-04, HIPAA 837, 835, HL7, EMC 6, clinical interfaces, any customized interfaces utilizing codes, and APIs will need to make the necessary modifications.

For the IS implementation task force representative, subcommittee, or workgroup, a contextual map of the facility's software and interfaces is helpful for identifying the requirements related to the character changes and storage needs, and for recognizing the interfaces that may be at risk if not checked and updated. For this major undertaking, each area of the facility must be assessed.

On the administrative side, IS can develop a system to access accurate data for longitudinal studies in finance and performance improvement. The system must be capable of creating reports during the transition. Care must be taken, however, in extracting information from longitudinal studies that may compare ICD-9-CM health patterns to ICD-10-CM health patterns. For example, the time frame for classifying myocardial infarct codes in ICD-9-CM to acute MI codes is eight weeks. In ICD-10-CM, it is four weeks. This could result in a statistical drop in the incidence of acute myocardial infarctions. Coders and code analysts would need to understand the nuances between the two coding systems to understand that the decrease was a reflection of changes in data reporting, not in the incidence of MIs.

Elements Affecting Information System (IS)

The following illustrates the differences between ICD-9-CM and ICD-10-CM and addresses issues that your IS department must consider.

Number of Characters

ICD-9-CM	ICD-10-CM	Implementation Issues for ICD-10-CM
3–5	3–7	Any field that reads an ICD-10-CM code needs to be able to accommodate up to seven characters.

Type of Character

ICD-9-CM	ICD-10-CM	Implementation Issues for ICD-10-CM
Numeric only (except V codes and E codes)	Alphanumeric	Make sure all ICD-10-CM code fields allow for both numeric and alpha characters.
		Reprogramming may be necessary to distinguish between numbers (0,1) and alpha characters (O,I). For example, alpha characters may need to be capitalized to distinguish between the letter I and the number one (1). A slash may need to be used with the zero to distinguish between the number and the letter O: Ø.

 KEY POINT

Many fonts are available that use a "European zero," a zero with a line through it: Ø. Your facility may want to consider adopting a European zero to avoid coding confusion:

000.0   Abdominal pregnancy
0Ø0.Ø   Abdominal pregnancy

Some information systems drop the decimal point in ICD-9-CM to save memory space. If this practice continues, some HCPCS Level II codes may be duplicate numbers to ICD-10-CM.

Decimals

ICD-9-CM	ICD-10-CM	Implementation Issues for ICD-10-CM
Decimals are used after the third character	Decimals are used after the third character	If your system currently accommodates decimals, make sure up to four characters can be allowed after the decimal.
		If your system does not accommodate decimals, there should be no implementation issue, other than the total number of characters required for each field.
		Special consideration: If your system accepts both ICD and HCPCS codes, the absence of a decimal may make it difficult for your system to distinguish between HCPCS codes and 5-character ICD-10-CM codes: both have five characters with an alpha character in the first position. Examples:
		E05.00 Thyrotoxicosis with diffuse goiter without thyrotoxic crisis or storm
		E0500 IPPB machine, all types, with built-in nebulization; manual or automatic valves; internal or external power source
		L40.50 Arthropathic psoriasis, unspecified
		L4050 Replace molded calf lacer
		Your system may need to be reprogrammed to place decimals with ICD-10-CM codes or otherwise differentiate between the ICD-10-CM and HCPCS codes.

Descriptions

ICD-9-CM	ICD-10-CM	Implementation Issues for ICD-10-CM
Tabular listing shows partial description for fourth– and fifth-digit codes	Full (stand-alone) descriptions are used for every code.	Even though the ICD-9-CM tabular listing (book) uses partial descriptions for fourth- and fifth-digit codes, data files are available for ICD-9-CM that provide a full description for every code. If your system currently uses such a data file, then there should be no implementation issues.
		Some ICD-9-CM data files provide the code description in multiple fields: the three-digit category description, a 4-digit subcategory description, and a five-digit subclassification description. If your system uses separate fields to accommodate category and subclassification descriptions, then reprogramming may be necessary to accept the ICD-10-CM descriptions.
		Some ICD-9-CM data files provide abbreviated descriptions (e.g., 35-character, 48-character, 150-character). If your description field is set up to accept a specific length of description, make sure that you use a vendor who can provide ICD-10-CM abbreviated descriptions in the length you need.
		Many of the ICD-10-CM descriptions contain several characters. Reprogramming may be necessary to expand the character limit of the description field to accept the ICD-10-CM codes and descriptions.

☞ **KEY POINT**

The complete descriptions provided with ICD-10-CM codes are widely praised as a great improvement over ICD-9-CM.

Hierarchy

ICD-9-CM	ICD-10-CM	Implementation Issues for ICD-10-CM
Fourth- and fifth-character codes have hierarchical relationships within a three-character category.	Fourth-, fifth-, sixth-, and seventh-character codes have hierarchical relationships within a three-character category.	Your system may recognize the hierarchical relationship of fifth-digit codes to fourth-digit codes, and of fourth-digit codes to three-digit categories. If this is the case, then reprogramming may be necessary to accommodate an additional hierarchical relationship — sixth- and seventh-digit codes to the preceding code level.

Conventions

ICD-9-CM	ICD-10-CM	Implementation Issues for ICD-10-CM
The Tabular List may include "excludes" and "includes" notations, instructional notes, essential modifiers, nonessential modifiers, etc., in reference to any code.	The Tabular List may include excludes and includes notations, instructional notes, essential modifiers, nonessential modifiers, etc., in reference to any code.	ICD-10-CM incorporates excludes notes, includes notes, other instructional notes, etc., in the same way as ICD-9-CM. If your program uses this information, you may need to differentiate among the two types of excludes notes.

Quantity of Codes

ICD-9-CM	ICD-10-CM	Implementation Issues for ICD-10-CM
ICD-9-CM contains more than 15,000 Vol. 1 and Vol. 3 codes. For 1999, CPT has nearly 8,000 codes.	ICD-10-CM contains more than 68,000 codes; ICD-10-PCS contains more than 86,000 codes.	ICD-10-CM contains considerably more codes.
		Reprogramming may be necessary to accommodate the increased number of codes and descriptions.
		Make sure your system has sufficient memory to handle the additional data. Increasing memory may handle the increased amount of data.

Format and Availability of Data

ICD-9-CM	ICD-10-CM	Implementation Issues for ICD-10-CM
Codes and descriptions are available both in print and numerous electronic formats (e.g., tab-delimited, fixed-format, etc.)	Codes and descriptions are available in print and electronic formats.	Most systems are set up to accept codes and descriptions electronically. ICD-10-PCS codes and descriptions are available on the CMS website in text and table format. ICD-10-CM codes and descriptions are available on the CMS and NCHS websites in text format.

KEY POINT

If you have data entry personnel who work with ten-keys instead of full keyboards, you may experience a slowdown in productivity when ICD-10-CM or ICD-10-PCS is implemented.

KEY POINT

Reprogramming may be necessary to accommodate the increased number of codes and descriptions in ICD-10-CM or ICD-10-PCS.

KEY POINT

Reprogramming may be necessary to accommodate the increased number of codes and descriptions in ICD-10-CM or ICD-10-PCS. Do you use shortened descriptions?

Take a look at a code like:

S21.441 Puncture wound with foreign body of right back wall of thorax with penetration into thoracic cavity

A 48-character description would read:

Punc wnd w/FB; RT bk thorax, w/pen, thoracic cav

A 35-character description would read:

Pun wd FB RT bk thrx, w pen thor cv

WHAT TO DO NOW

There are a number of ways to structure, organize, and phase in implementation. The following section suggests strategies and tactics for various elements of ICD-10 project management.

Build an ICD-10 Task Force

The first step in developing a solid ICD-10 implementation plan is to create an interdepartmental team or task force. This team's duties should be tailored to fit the size and needs of your facility or office, with interdepartmental/interdisciplinary representation. Smaller facilities or physician practices may divide responsibilities into major working topics and give each member of the task force a job. The group may need to meet monthly or quarterly, depending on its specific needs and government actions.

For larger practices and facilities, another approach may be to create an overall task force to drive the implementation process as a strategic planning or steering committee with subcommittees, subteams, or workgroups that address specific departmental needs or the needs of certain groups. If a multi-team approach is desired, cross-representation in these subgroups is encouraged to ensure smooth transition when responsibilities and data usage overlap or when workflow is interdependent.

Regardless of whether your task force comprises one main group or multi-teams for your facility or practice, some initial decisions should be made or agreed upon by the task force steering committee or by the task force as a group. These decisions include:

- Establishing leadership, including an authoritative chairperson to act as a facilitator to this interdisciplinary process and as a driving force that surmounts obstacles and ensures movement toward the common goal
- Establishing the critical factors in successful implementation
- Formulating a plan and setting goals
- Building an education and training program
- Devising a method for periodic evaluation of milestones
- Devising a method of post-implementation analysis and reporting

Subcommittees and workgroups: Many facilities work toward implementation goals through subcommittees and smaller workgroups—whereby duties and leaderships are delegated for specific tasks to address the challenges in certain sections or departments within the organization, and these groups report back to the main task force group or steering committee. For facilities of this size and/or structure, cross-representation is necessary to ensure that common goals and interdependent, interdepartmental needs are met. Some tips for working with workgroups include:

- Avoid "meeting drag," bogging down the strategic and tactical group with issues that need to be dealt with by specific members of the organization. Working with sub-committees and workgroups keeps the focus on the tasks at hand, while still providing representation and two-way communication.
- Keep the process going forward by minimizing meeting times in large groups. Front-line processes are kept moving by making sure the information is relative to the group.
- Stick to "overall" and inter-related issues. As a rule, large groups should focus on large issues, small groups on specifics. By keeping meetings streamlined and appropriately focused, time and money are conserved.

- Determine critical success factors. Resources should be allocated appropriately to the critical operations with the most need. Those critical factors should be provided with resources and support from the task force to ensure that those factors are priorities.
- Develop an implementation plan with goals. Both the task force and the subcommittees or workgroups should start with specific goals in hand to ensure success.
- Evaluate milestones periodically. To prevent roadblocks, bottlenecks, and other obstacles that result in lost time and money, re-evaluation is necessary, both at the front-line/technical and administrative levels.
- Build an education and training program. Specific areas and players within the organization have specific training needs that should be tailored to their role within the organizational structure. By building its own education and training program, a facility can develop relevant and cost-effective training. Inappropriate or ineffective training wastes time and money just as little or no training does. Two way communication between trainer and trainee is necessary to achieve this aim.

Initiate Project Management Strategies and Tactics

The task force will need to lay organizational groundwork or devise a plan for implementation. A strategy can be defined as "a plan of action intended to accomplish a specific goal." Tactics can be defined as "a procedure or set of maneuvers engaged in to achieve an end, an aim, or a goal." A smooth and effective implementation process depends on both a strategy (plan) and a set of tactics (maneuvers).

Strategic Planning

The scope of strategic planning will be different for different services or organizations. For hospitals, a thorough assessment and planning for the transition's financial impact will be integral to the process due to the nature of hospitals as organizations. Keeping costs contained and using technology judiciously will be key considerations. Vendors' planning will involve capitalizing on identifying new products and services to offer to provide customers across all markets with the tools they need to meet their goals, while ultimately keeping costs down and revenue up.

Tactical Decisions

There are a number of tactical decisions that must be made throughout the organization. The task force must employ tactics on an organizational and front-line level. Some of these decisions include:

- Provide initial or basic staff training
- Identify all products, programs, and forms that need changing
- Identify all integrated third-party software that needs changing
- Design the system changes or select vendors
- Schedule the changes and coordinate with vendors
- Decide whether or not to postpone other upgrades or transitions that would occur during the I-10 implementation period
- Formalize conversion planning; involve vendors, where applicable
- Implement and test the changes
- Integrate and test third-party components
- Train support staff
- Update documentation
- Roll out the changes
- Assist customers with conversion planning
- Maintain and support dual systems (ICD-9, ICD-10)

To get started, the team may want to consider some of these key components:

Write project goals: State the goals of the transition and ensure that key members are moving in the same direction. With these goals in mind, the team can delegate specific duties, roles, or actions appropriately and most effectively throughout the group and ensure that each member has adequate support from other members to meet their goals. Establishing goals early in the process can help identify key stakeholders and their roles in the process, as well as identify priorities.

Assess the impact of coding data: Once the task force or team has been gathered, the flow of coded data and the contributors and users of these data throughout the organization can be analyzed. The team must ensure that all functions and services using the coded data are accounted for to accommodate the system change. It may be necessary to continue with additional team representation in the post-analysis phase. The team may want to assess whether the following processes can accommodate ICD-10:

- DRG algorithms (Medicare, Medicaid, commercial)
- APCs, APGs, ASC groupers
- Claims editing software; claim "scrubbers"
- Code-based pricing rules and contractual software
- Medical necessity tools
- Federal reporting mechanisms
- State reporting mechanisms
- Longitudinal studies requiring common nomenclature
- Decision support systems
- Process improvement opportunities
- Data warehousing
- Tumor registries and other repositories
- Official mapping and modeling rules between coding systems

Assess each area of the facility: Each task force representative should conduct a needs assessment of the areas represented and set in motion the mechanisms to make the needed changes.

For example:

- HIM can conduct a gap analysis, assess educational needs, analyze the current query process, estimate the pace and extent of training, and forecast impact on productivity.
- IS can create a contextual map of the facility's software and interfaces, and assess labor and staffing needs to provide technical resources and support.
- Finance can create a list of reporting issues and contracts that incorporate coded data.
- PFS can analyze the denial management process and assess delay in AR days attributed to the transition.
- Vendors can proactively assess products and services; will the vendors be able to support ICD-10 and accommodate the organization's timeline?
- Management can assess whether it understands the scope, resources, and impact of the transition to I-10.
- Medical staff can determine the documentation and training needs of most clinicians.

Define timeline and stages/phases of implementation: Grand-scale changes are often best phased in over a period of time. A minimum two-year implementation period can be postulated based on notice of proposed rule making (NPRM) or other government mandate. An abbreviated example of a phased implementation structure follows:

First Year (Phase I)
- Form a task force
- Establish IT/IS leadership
- Begin introductory education
- Establish communication
- Evaluate processes

Second Year (Phase II)
- Educate coders and clinicians
- Review financial impact (budget)
- Identify software changes or upgrades
- Begin advanced education

A multi-phase implementation plan may be more realistic for your organization and provide more structure.

Phase Implementation Process Timeline

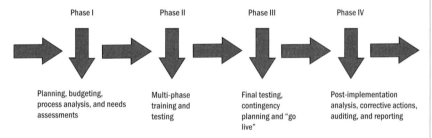

Phase I	Phase II	Phase III	Phase IV
Planning, budgeting, process analysis, and needs assessments	Multi-phase training and testing	Final testing, contingency planning and "go live"	Post-implementation analysis, corrective actions, auditing, and reporting

Phase I

During phase I, it is necessary to establish task force membership, identify key stakeholders, establish timelines, and lay the groundwork for preparation via strategic planning. This phase of work should set goals and responsibilities for the over-arching task force or steering committee and/or the basic goals of the subgroups. The budget should be analyzed as early in the process as possible to ensure compliance with timelines based on government mandates and facility resources. At this point, it is advisable to collect a list of all vendors and assess software/hardware and contracting needs. Also, the team should conduct internal user surveys to estimate the scope of the transition's effect on the organization as a whole, then delegate tasks appropriately and evaluate process improvement opportunities. Means of communications need to be set up to ensure awareness of change throughout the facility. An educational plan can be formulated at this point. The team must initiate measurement and analysis of specific areas: HIM/coding, payers, IS/IT (mapping information flow throughout the organization), PFS, finance, and data collection. For example, the HIM department needs to asses its own needs at this time or work through a subcommittee that includes the coding staff, coding management, and HIM leadership to ensure adequate planning and resources. It could be that contracting services should be budgeted. PFS may need to conduct payer readiness surveys to find out whether claims processing contingency plans are in place. At the end of phase I, surveys and assessments should have been gathered and analyzed and specific actions set into place to address the needs identified.

Phase II

By phase II, the system changes should be well underway, with needs assessment and analysis from the prior phase having prompted development of the mechanisms necessary to incorporate implementation changes. The systems will be ready for testing, confirmation, and/or modification in preparation for going "live" with I-10. Payer claims transactions can be tested, and financial and reimbursement impacts can be analyzed, specifically including testing of IPPS and OPPS grouping mechanisms (DRGs, APCs, etc.). Depending on the needs of the organization, introductory training may be started at phase I, with advanced training for necessary users, such as the coding staff, being introduced in phase II. Phase II is also prime time for conducting inservices and seminars and/or testing the results of preliminary training as well as assessing readiness of the coding staff. At this time, arrangements should be made for additional support staff or contractors. Communication should be thorough and often, including updates on progress and completion of goals, as well as discussion of the remaining steps before going live.

Phase III

By phase III, systems and processes should have been tested and be ready to go live. By now, vendors should have demonstrated readiness and provided testing. Intensive education, training, and testing, although late, will likely still be necessary at this stage of implementation. Contingency planning should be in place for failed processes or services. Open communication should continue, with regular email or newsletter notifications. By phase III, IT/IS should be ready to roll out the live version interdepartmentally—between areas such as IT/IS, HIM/coding, PFS, payers, finance/AR.

Phase IV

Post-implementation assessment and corrective action across all departments and workgroups will be critical in ensuring long-term success. It may be necessary to use adjunct training and education at this point. Communication will be essential between senior management, finance, IT/IS, and payers. Budget and cost reporting should be diligent and judicious. The HIM department will have to monitor and audit coding intensively, report findings, and stay organized for attaining target goals. Correct coding monitoring and reporting with analysis of findings and corrective actions will be essential for long-term success. This is, in essence, the creation of a new coding culture. Lay a firm foundation. Audit and monitor carefully for reimbursement and DRG impact. Track and analyze DRG targets and CMI monthly.

Other Issues

Ensure receptiveness to change: Recognize that each department or group will show some resistance to change. Communication will be key in breaking down this resistance. At this point, the team should be reading and summarizing implementation literature and government notices. In turn, a task force member or subcommittee should be made responsible for communication methods. Interactive, two-way communication with the task force and management will be essential. Team members should set a positive tone and exhibit a can-do attitude to the rest of the organization. Ensuring that the task force's primary goals include successful and smooth transitioning may help to calm certain anxieties, while using this group as a forum to address concerns and difficulties can promote cooperation by providing the rest of the organization with a voice in the process.

IT should adapt to the requirements of the new codes: Information technology will play one of the most vital roles in ensuring that the transition is smooth and successful. The dramatic difference between ICD-9-CM and ICD-10 coding systems will affect nearly every member of the organization in some capacity, via the demands made on the hospital information systems, platforms, interfaces, individual specialized software programs, forms, and individual roles.

Promote physician compliance with increased documentation needs: Transitioning to a new coding system will affect the clinical staff both in their practices and in the facility. The better the clinical staff understands how integral documentation is to coding and how dramatically increased the granularity of the new coding system is, the better the resulting data. This is a golden opportunity to promote quality documentation and illustrate in a very meaningful way to physicians just how dependent upon documentation the new system is. One approach may be to create a clinical staff subcommittee, with cross-representation from HIM and PFS that can provide physicians with examples of how their documentation translates into clinical codes and how these codes are in turn used to reimburse, quantify, and qualify care.

Conduct financial planning for expenses associated with adoption of the new system and revenue cycle impacts: Taking a cue from Australia and Canada's implementation experiences, financial planning for this transition at an early stage can prevent expensive mistakes or delays in the long run. Care should be taken to account for expenses that result from software upgrades, education, decreased productivity, new supplies, changes in business practices, and other transitory expenses.

Employee accountability and job satisfaction: The impact of this transition is greater than HIPAA and Y2K. In fact, it has been stated to be the greatest change since the advent of computers. Due to human nature, some degree of anxiety is to be expected. Depending on individual circumstances and tenure, many coders are dreading the transition to a new coding system. A culture change may be necessary to motivate recalcitrant or ambivalent coders by focusing on the positive impact these new systems will have on their individual careers and skill sets, as well as on the health care industry as a whole by presenting the opportunity to capture and generate better, more useful data. Knowing that they are the cornerstone to this process and that they play a crucial part will help coders do what they are already trained to do, but with better tools to fit today's health care environment. It's important not to encourage coders to demonstrate reactionary behaviors as if this change were a mandate put upon them for their personal inconvenience. Creating a culture of opportunity during this time of massive change may be the task force and the manager's greatest challenge.

Budget Considerations

In the facility or physician practice, major costs are likely to incur in the following areas:

Coder training and education: Every coder will be starting over from scratch with the new system. While experienced coders will have less of a learning curve with the conventions and philosophies behind the new systems, it is likely that inexperienced coders will require additional skill development. The new systems are far more demanding in specificity and require a greater level of knowledge of anatomy, pathophysiology, and a clinical understanding of surgical and procedural technologies. Perhaps for some coders, education and training will require obtaining an increased level of education in the physical sciences. Keep in mind that education will realistically be an ongoing process; however, for the moderate to experienced coders on staff, a basic overview of the new diagnosis and procedure systems will need to be provided as well as more advanced curriculum tailored to the needs of the practice or facility.

Coder staffing: Based on an assessment of the skills of the current staff, it may be necessary to recruit additional coders, or coders with a different educational background or skill set. Some coders may choose to leave the profession during this time, so it is important to retain staff as much as possible. Coders who are experienced in ICD-9-CM will provide a wealth of skills and background in coding conventions, medical and surgical documentation translation skills, and other abilities that are required for effective ICD-10 coding. Employers should be encouraged to provide initiatives to promote job satisfaction and create a culture of continued learning and value of the coder's contribution to the organization.

Physician training and documentation: Due to the absolute reliance on quality documentation that is integral to I-10 coding, the benefits of physician training will far outweigh the costs in long-term returns that can be measured, in part, by accurately coded data that directly correspond to reimbursement. It should be an integral part of the implementation strategy to include physician education through seminars and workshops that orient the medical staff to the new system by illustrating, in a practical way, the impact the new systems will have on their practices and facilities as a whole. Through this investment, the hospital and/or practice can benefit by minimizing rejected claims and by improving their documentation and data.

Information services: Strategic planning is required for the increased IS services, labor, and hardware and software acquisitions integral to the transition.

Communication: Communication across the organization will be necessary for a smooth transition. A task force designee or committee will need to allocate time and resources for keeping the organization informed.

One-time costs: Some expenditures will require a large initial investment. These include:

- Initial training
- System (software) changes and upgrades
- Productivity losses attributed to initial learning curves

Ongoing costs: Expenditures that will have a more lasting organizational impact include:

- Ongoing training as the classification systems continue to evolve
- Productivity losses over the long term
- Process changes as a result of the demands of accommodating the new system

Build Organizational Awareness

Communication is vital to implementation, promoting teamwork and ensuring preparation. The more informed the facility is as a whole, the fewer surprises and hidden budget-busting costs will be encountered. Whether a task force designee or communications workgroup is deemed responsible, solutions and methods for gathering and disseminating information throughout the facility will be instrumental in successful implementation. A point person can be designated to monitor government actions and communicate information on a regular basis. Some successful vehicles for communication include creating and posting or distributing newsletters, designating an intranet site for project news, emailing status reports, and holding town hall or other organizational meetings. These communication tools include all employees across an organization in the process.

Because of the technical nature of medical coding, there may be many people in an organization, regardless of the size, who will need to be educated as to what ICD codes are used for, how that affects the organization, and ultimately, the employees personally. Make sure that the information provided can be assimilated and suited to the targeted audiences.

Some of the goals for communication may include:

- Heighten awareness and get people thinking about how ICD-10 will affect the facility.
- Provide a basic introduction to the value and impact of the new coding systems.
- Foster an understanding of the necessity for any associated process changes that will affect individual jobs.
- Provide a proactive, positive environment for change management; minimize reactionary attitudes and behaviors.

HIM's Role in the Implementation Task Force

It is vital that health information managers understand that the transition to ICD-10 is not merely an upgrade of coding sets but is, in fact, a massive overhaul of the existing coding systems and their associated processes and platforms. This overhaul will require field size expansion, change to alphanumeric composition, and complete redefinition of code values and their interpretation. To put its effect into perspective, the implementation of ICD-10 is expected to be the most significant change in medical coding since the advent of computers and the prospective payment system.

Coding quality—relying on past experience: Due to the magnitude of this change, steps need to be taken to ensure complete and accurate data during and after the transition so that data can be compared. In addition to educational initiatives, coding managers and supervisors need to be sure that improper coding practices are avoided. Experienced and well-trained coders should already be well aware of the standards for ethical coding and the practices that constitute fraud and abuse. Coders may need to be reassured that the same HIPAA standards apply and that the new coding systems do not negate existing ethical practices. Coders may need to be reminded to avoid improper coding practices that are linked to health care fraud and abuse by misrepresenting clinical documentation or services and distorting provider reimbursements and statistics. Now, more than ever, the importance of a coder's role in the health care organizational structure needs to be emphasized. Reinforcing this importance to the coders will help to quell anxieties of obsolescence and build morale and professional pride. This is a golden opportunity to illustrate the coder's role to the organization as a whole.

Along those same lines, coding managers and supervisors will need to watch for undercoding practices. Coders may need to be reminded that undercoding does not eliminate legal risks or financial liabilities. In fact, deliberate undercoding is another form of misrepresentation and carries significant risks to the organization such as:

- Reduces reimbursement under code-based payment systems (DRGs, APCs)
- Increases administrative expenses, including accounts receivable
- Diminishes value of management information systems
- Affects the design of code-based payment systems negatively

Undercoding is often a result of poor education in coding guidelines, or poor physician documentation. If auditing reveals undercoding tendencies in your organization, it likely indicates a need for physician documentation education and query tools. Reassess existing physician query processes and tools for their efficacy with the demands of I-10. Ask the coders for concrete examples for the clinical staff that illustrate where documentation falls short of classification demand, and arrange opportunities to communicate that information.

Coding Productivity—Plan, Test, and Reassess

Certain preliminary studies show that coding with the new systems may initially require at least 25 percent more time than coding with current systems. These delays will need to be communicated to the interdisciplinary team so that the delays can be accommodated.

During the early months of implementation, HIM and coding managers need to evaluate the impact of sufficient documentation on coder productivity. These measures will help to illustrate how vital documentation is to coding and the financial viability of and statistics generated by the facility. This information, including practical examples, will serve a dual purpose in clinical staff education efforts.

One method of estimating the impact on productivity is to perform a gap analysis, whereby medical records are re-coded in ICD-10 to determine where problems will occur. A gap analysis can also be thought of as a period of "test coding." This testing can provide a concrete way of focusing in on areas where education, staffing, and technical resources should be allocated in advance of going live with I-10. This practical exercise can also provide managers with data for estimating productivity problems and the need for staffing support. Delays that occur as a result of a lack of documentation can be used as a point of reference for physician education or refinement of the query process. Delays that are discovered to result from a lack of knowledge in anatomy, for instance, can point to both the current level of skills and the need for education. Coder and physician education and training efforts can be accurately or more efficiently focused based on the results of such analyses.

Along these lines, allowing coders to use a small amount of work time to practice newly learned skills performing gap analysis or shadow coding will give the coders more confidence by virtue of the fact that they will know what to expect, thereby decreasing a degree of uncertainty. During these mock coding exercises, assess the change in pace and productivity and formulate contingency plans for staffing and training.

HIM Education and Training

When building an education and training program for HIM staff, build parallel training for clinical and coding staff as well, and be prepared to educate other areas of the organization. Education should be tailored to suit the needs of the audience. Ensure an understanding of the big picture. Make sure that all coders are aware how coding data affect the organization. Managers may be surprised at what even the most experienced coders take for granted. For example, some coders may have spent a majority of their careers believing that codes are used solely for payment. Take this opportunity to educate coders on the far-reaching effects of coded data. Focus on increasing awareness of the role of medical coding in statistics, research, and reimbursement; introduce the necessity of transition to ICD-10 and how it will affect the facility.

Structure coding education to provide an initial overview or broad base to coders early in the implementation process, and follow up with advances or in-depth seminars. Coding management will need to demonstrate and track efficacy of educational efforts. Follow-up testing, as well as curriculum, will be necessary to provide data on educational efficacy. Keep in mind that, depending on the future of OPPS reporting requirements, outpatient coders will still need to keep current with CPT coding changes. Allow enough funding in your budget to account for the services provided and coded at your facility. Budget for and schedule continuing education, above and beyond the normal annual allocations.

Make sure training time is adequate, along with the training material. Conduct initial assessments of the skills of existing staff early in the process to allow enough time for both basic level and advanced training. Developing ICD-10 coding tests is another way to assess coders' skill level and readiness to begin coding ICD-10 on a daily basis. Through these tests, it may become apparent that some coders require additional remedial anatomy and physiology courses to keep up with the demands of the new systems. During the entire education and training process, ensure that coders have all the references and tools they need to continue learning.

Some of the more challenging learning issues for coders will include:

- Learning to use different main terms to classify procedures. (For a detailed example of this, see chapter 4, "Procedure Coding.")
- Translating procedures documented by eponym into the correct procedure category. This will likely require physicians to change their documentation practices and coders to improve their understanding of surgical procedures and techniques.

- Classifying equipment and devices correctly for PCS coding. Facility coders may have less orientation to coding devices since HCPCS coding has been largely a hard-coded (chargemaster-assigned) process.
- Differentiating and applying coding guidelines to the appropriate system.

Educating the Medical Staff—HIM's Role

Whether your facility forms a medical staff subcommittee, or an HIM representative is designated to act as a liaison, both HIM and PFS need to develop a plan to educate physicians on the importance of documentation as it relates to the new systems. Consider that it will be necessary to educate on an ongoing basis. The implementation process should allow for a learning curve whereby an orientation session or documentation session can be followed with more specifics at a later time. Also, as time passes and clinicians experience working with this system in their practices, they may come up with questions and concerns for the subcommittee or representative to address in forthcoming changes to the new system. Plan to conduct periodic or annual I-10 documentation meetings to cover the educational needs arising from changes in medical staff.

The goals of physician documentation education should include helping physicians understand the requirements for both ICD-10-CM and PCS and how the new systems are even more data driven and documentation demanding than the old systems were. Physicians should be able to readily tie documentation to reimbursement with an understanding of how a lack of adequate documentation directly results in poor or inaccurate code representations of the services provided. Physicians should understand and support the query process, acknowledging that queries are technical questions that can be directly tied to reimbursement and statistics, and that these follow-up questions are not necessary if documentation is adequate to support proper coding in the first place. Queries should be regarded by providers as an alert that documentation processes need to improve.

When writing I-10 documentation seminars or presentations, illustrate how poor data quality harms providers in the following ways, and be sure to include specific examples and supportive data:

- Missing or invalid codes result in claim denials and lost revenue.
- Administrative expenses are inflated.
- Bad data means diminished value of management information systems—"garbage data in equals garbage data out."
- Reimbursement is reduced by either claim rejection, insufficient evidence of medical necessity, or under-representation of acuity of services.

It may be helpful to encourage coders to attend physician training to build rapport and support dialogue. If HIM can allocate resources, helping educate physicians' office staff can benefit both the physician and the facility in the short and long term.

Other HIM implementation tips:

- Plan ahead. Late transition efforts will negatively affect everyone—from inadequate funding to the inability to procure necessary tools on time.
- Responsibility for reading and summarizing implementation literature and government notices should be designated to a member of the task force responsible for communication. However, an HIM designee should also follow the adoption process to help determine timeframes. Keep vigilant watch for regulatory and government notices, and adjust the HIM timeline to comply.
- An HIM designee should act as a liaison between clinical and coding staff to ensure education needs are met.

 QUICK TIP

Your facility compliance officer can play an important role on the task force by providing compliance support, leadership, and representation.

- Cross-representation among task force workgroups from other departments will enable HIM to integrate better with other departments, coordinating mutual or interdependent processes and goals.

Learning from Australia and Canada

Australia's transition to their modification, ICD-10-AM, in July 1998 and Canada's transition to ICD-10-CA in 2001 and 2002 raises several issues that the United States will be facing during the next several years. Two of these, as mentioned, are scheduling and budget. It is important to note that even though it is a good idea to learn from other countries who have already experienced implementing their own clinical modification to I-10, the U.S. may not be able to draw many direct conclusions as to how this country should proceed. Due to the circumstances of socialized medicine in other countries, the parallels may be limited. The central government does much of the coordination and decision-making in socialized medicine.

One of the greatest obstacles to implementing ICD-10-CM in the U.S. is predicted to be the lack of readiness among commercial vendors that won't be prepared for this change with appropriate functioning software and other tools needed by those in the health care industry.

Updating ICD-10-AM is already a priority for the Australian NCCH. During the first year, NCCH stabilized the classification, although changes were anticipated due to Australian Coding Standards and typographical corrections. The NCCH maintained ICD-10 codes for mortality coding in Australia. For future editions, NCCH anticipates a 12-month lead time to publication and another five months to implementation, so that preparations would begin in the February prior to the July start date for new editions.

Procedures for updating subsequent editions in the United States will be similar to the process of updating ICD-9-CM. Revisions to ICD-9-CM are made usually once a year, effective October 1 of each year. Major changes in the time frame are published in the "Prospective Payment System, Final Rule" of the Federal Register. The ICD-9-CM Coordination and Maintenance Committee meets twice each year to discuss coding revisions proposed for the subsequent year.

CONCLUSION

Classification provides order and a certain control of our world. Classifying disease and death is one part of that whole system. But the real test of new coding classifications is neither the implementation process nor the technical problems related to electronic transmission. The real test, according to NCCH director Rosemary Roberts in *Coding Matters*, is a system that "withstands this testing crucible of real time use by real clinical coders."

WHERE TO GO

ICD-10-CM

http://www.cdc.gov/nchs/about/otheract/icd9/icd10cm.htm—This site offers a posting of the downloadable ICD-10-CM current draft of the tabular and index sections and other essential ICD-10-CM files including guidelines, mappings, and code descriptions.

FOR MORE INFO

One-half of Australia changed to ICD-10-Australian Modification (ICD-10-AM) in July 1998. The second half of the country changed in July 1999. Canada changed to ICD-10-Canadian Modification (CA) in 2001 and 2002. To learn more about ICD-10-AM or -CA, search with those terms on the Internet to access many varied websites.

KEY POINT

"Clinical coding is a much more important function in Australia's health care system than it was at the time of the last change, that systems will fail if appropriate resources are not allocated," was the conclusion reached in the report, ICD-10-AM Impact Assessment on Australia by Coopers & Lybrand.

ICD-10-PCS

http://www.cms.hhs.gov/ICD10/01m_2009_ICD10PCS.asp—This site offers a posting of downloadable copies of ICD-10-PCS, instructions, mappings, and a PowerPoint slideshow that provides an overview of the system.

World Health Organization (WHO)

http://www.who.int/aboutwho/en/mission.html—This international agency maintains an international nomenclature of diseases, causes of death, and public health practices. WHO updated diagnostic coding with ICD-10.

National Center for Health Statistics (NCHS)

http://www.cdc.gov/nchs—This U.S. government agency, together with CMS, jointly refines the diagnostic portion of ICD-9-CM and is responsible for the clinical modification of ICD-10-CM. NCHS holds several hearings each year to consider changes or additions in diagnostic coding.

National Center for Vital and Health Statistics (NCVHS)

http://www.ncvhs.hhs.gov—This is the advisory committee to the HHS for health statistics. NCVHS has become increasingly active over the past several years, addressing issues relating to uniform health data sets, medical classification systems, and the need for improved mental health statistics. The NCVHS established the objectives for the new procedural coding system, which are as follows: completeness, expandability, hierarchical structure, standardized terminology, improved accuracy, efficiency of coding, and reduced training time.

Centers for Medicare and Medicaid Services (CMS), Formerly the Health Care Financing Administration (HCFA)

http://www.cms.hhs.gov/—This organization is in charge of the federally funded healthcare programs. Essential information regarding both ICD-10 systems is posted on this website.

National Archives and Records Administration

http://www.gpoaccess.gov/fr/index.html—This is the place for the Federal Register on line, via GPO access. Users can look up specific issues of the Federal Register, which publishes notices by department. Rules and regulations for coding generally can be found under CMS.

Administrative Simplification Rules in HIPAA

http://www.hhs.gov/ocr/privacy/hipaa/administrative/index.html—This site links users to sites related to the Administrative Simplification Provision. For example: http://www.disa.org/x12— This is the Data Interchange Standards Association web site. This site contains information on ASC X12, information on X12N subcommittees, task groups, and workgroups, including their meeting minutes. This site will contain the test conditions and results of HIPAA transactions tested at the workgroup level.

American Health Information Management Association (AHIMA)

http://www.ahima.org/—This is a professional organization for clinical data and information management. AHIMA develops industry standards advocating relevant legislation, and provides education in health information management.

DISCUSSION QUESTIONS

1. Cite the major challenges in implementing ICD-10-CM at your facility or practice.

    _____

    _____

    _____

2. Who at your facility or office will need ICD-10-CM training? ICD-10-CM certification?

    _____

    _____

    _____

3. List the problems IS will face at implementation. How can these problems be solved or mitigated?

    _____

    _____

    _____

4. What groups will you go to for assistance in coding or electronic transmission? Do you subscribe to the appropriate periodicals?

    _____

    _____

    _____

5. What can we learn about implementation from Australia and Canada?

    _____

    _____

6. How will the members of the task force or workgroups work together to ensure that their interdependent process functions and procedures run smoothly? How can delays resulting from process problems be avoided?

    _____

    _____

    _____

7. How will training be delivered to the various departments and staff throughout the facility? Who will conduct the training, and how will it be tailored to specific needs?

    _____

    _____

    _____

8. How will implementation be phased in? Does your facility or practice's timeline account for testing?

    _____

    _____

    _____

9. Does your budget allow for ongoing education and for existing coding systems (such as CPT)? Does the budget account for all materials, supplies, and continuing education necessary as the I-10 systems are updated?

    _____

    _____

    _____

10. If your coders are using an encoder, have you planned to supply sufficient tools for the coders to run a quality check of their codes as opposed to just trusting the answer from the encoder? Will they be able to analyze a DRG or APC for accuracy?

    _____

    _____

    _____

11. How will physician documentation education be conducted? Who will provide ongoing guidance, and how will it be structured? Will the query process be integrated into physician education?

    _____

    _____

    _____

Appendix A: ICD-10-CM Official Guidelines for Coding and Reporting (Draft 2009)

The Centers for Medicare and Medicaid Services (CMS) and the National Center for Health Statistics (NCHS), two departments within the U.S. Federal Government's Department of Health and Human Services (DHHS) provide the following guidelines for coding and reporting using the International Classification of Diseases, 10th Revision, Clinical Modification (ICD-10-CM). These guidelines should be used as a companion document to the official version of the ICD-10-CM as published on the NCHS website. The ICD-10-CM is a morbidity classification published by the United States for classifying diagnoses and reason for visits in all health care settings. The ICD-10-CM is based on the ICD-10, the statistical classification of disease published by the World Health Organization (WHO).

These guidelines have been approved by the four organizations that make up the Cooperating Parties for the ICD-10-CM: the American Hospital Association (AHA), the American Health Information Management Association (AHIMA), CMS, and NCHS.

These guidelines are a set of rules that have been developed to accompany and complement the official conventions and instructions provided within the ICD-10-CM itself. These guidelines are based on the coding and sequencing instructions in Volumes I, and II of ICD-10-CM, but provide additional instruction. Adherence to these guidelines when assigning ICD-10-CM diagnosis and procedure codes is required under the Health Insurance Portability and Accountability Act (HIPAA). The diagnosis codes (Volumes 1-2) have been adopted under HIPAA for all healthcare settings. A joint effort between the healthcare provider and the coder is essential to achieve complete and accurate documentation, code assignment, and reporting of diagnoses and procedures. These guidelines have been developed to assist both the healthcare provider and the coder in identifying those diagnoses and procedures that are to be reported. The importance of consistent, complete documentation in the medical record cannot be overemphasized. Without such documentation accurate coding cannot be achieved. The entire record should be reviewed to determine the specific reason for the encounter and the conditions treated.

The term encounter is used for all settings, including hospital admissions. In the context of these guidelines, the term provider is used throughout the guidelines to mean physician or any qualified health care practitioner who is legally accountable for establishing the patient's diagnosis. Only this set of guidelines, approved by the Cooperating Parties, is official.

The guidelines are organized into sections. Section I includes the structure and conventions of the classification and general guidelines that apply to the entire classification, and chapter-specific guidelines that correspond to the chapters as they are arranged in the classification. Section II includes guidelines for selection of principal diagnosis for non-outpatient settings. Section III includes guidelines for reporting additional diagnoses in non-outpatient settings. Section IV is for outpatient coding and reporting. It is necessary to review all sections of the guidelines to fully understand all of the rules and instructions needed to code properly.

ICD-10-CM Official Guidelines for Coding and Reporting

Section I. Conventions, general coding guidelines and chapter specific guidelines

The conventions, general guidelines and chapter-specific guidelines are applicable to all health care settings unless otherwise indicated.

A. Conventions for the ICD-10-CM

1. The Alphabetic Index and Tabular List

The ICD-10-CM is divided into the Index, an alphabetical list of terms and their corresponding code, and the Tabular List, a chronological list of codes divided into chapters based on body system or condition. The Index is divided into two parts, the Index to Diseases and Injury, and the Index to External Causes of Injury. Within the Index of Diseases and Injury there is a Neoplasm Table and a Table of Drugs and Chemicals.

See Section I.C2. General guidelines
See Section I.C.19. Adverse effects, poisoning, underdosing and toxic effects

The conventions for the ICD-10-CM are the general rules for use of the classification independent of the guidelines. These conventions are incorporated within the Index and Tabular of the ICD-10-CM as instructional notes. The conventions are as follows:

2. Format and Structure:

The ICD-10-CM Tabular List contains categories, subcategories and codes. Characters for categories, subcategories and codes may be either a letter or a number. All categories are 3 characters. A three-character category that has no further subdivision is equivalent to a code. Subcategories are either 4 or 5 characters. Codes may be 4, 5, 6 or 7 characters. That is, each level of subdivision after a category is a subcategory. The final level of subdivision is a code. All codes in the Tabular List of the official version of the ICD-10-CM are in bold. Codes that have applicable 7th characters are still referred to as codes, not subcategories. A code that has an applicable 7th character is considered invalid without the 7th character.

The ICD-10-CM uses an indented format for ease in reference

3. Use of codes for reporting purposes

For reporting purposes only codes are permissible, not categories or subcategories, and any applicable 7th character is required.

4. Placeholder character

The ICD-10-CM utilizes a placeholder character "X". The "X" is used as a 5th character placeholder at certain 6 character codes to allow for future expansion. An example of this is at the poisoning, adverse effect and underdosing codes, categories T36-T50. Where a placeholder exists, the X must be used in order for the code to be considered a valid code.

5. 7th Characters

Certain ICD-10-CM categories have applicable 7th characters. The applicable 7th character is required for all codes within the category, or as the notes in the Tabular List instruct. The 7th character must always be the 7th character in the data field. If a code that requires a 7th character is not 6 characters, a placeholder X must be used to fill in the empty characters.

6. Abbreviations

a. Index abbreviations

NEC "Not elsewhere classifiable"

This abbreviation in the Index represents "other specified" when a specific code is not available for a condition the Index directs the coder to the "other specified" code in the Tabular.

b. Tabular abbreviations

NEC "Not elsewhere classifiable"

This abbreviation in the Tabular represents "other specified". When a specific code is not available for a condition the Tabular includes an NEC entry under a code to identify the code as the "other specified" code.

NOS "Not otherwise specified"

This abbreviation is the equivalent of unspecified.

7. Punctuation

[ ] Brackets are used in the tabular list to enclose synonyms, alternative wording or explanatory phrases. Brackets are used in the Index to identify manifestation codes.

( ) Parentheses are used in both the Index and Tabular to enclose supplementary words that may be present or absent in the statement of a disease or procedure without affecting the code number to which it is assigned. The terms within the parentheses are referred to as nonessential modifiers.

: Colons are used in the Tabular List after an incomplete term which needs one or more of the modifiers following the colon to make it assignable to a given category.

8. Use of "and"

When the term "and" is used in a narrative statement it represents and/or.

9. Other and Unspecified codes

a. "Other" codes

Codes titled "other" or "other specified" are for use when the information in the medical record provides detail for which a specific code does not exist. Index entries with NEC in the line designate "other" codes in the Tabular. These Index entries represent specific disease entities for which no specific code exists so the term is included within an "other" code.

b. "Unspecified" codes

Codes (usually a code with a 4th digit 9 or 5th digit 0 for diagnosis codes) titled "unspecified" are for use when the information in the medical record is insufficient to assign a more specific code. For those categories for which an unspecified code is not provided, the "other specified" code may represent both other and unspecified.

10. Includes Notes

This note appears immediately under a three-digit code title to further define, or give examples of, the content of the category.

11. Inclusion terms

List of terms is included under some codes. These terms are the conditions for which that code number is to be used. The terms may be synonyms of the code title, or, in the case of "other specified" codes, the terms are a list of the various conditions assigned to that code. The inclusion terms are not necessarily exhaustive. Additional terms found only in the Index may also be assigned to a code.

12. Excludes Notes

The ICD-10-CM has two types of excludes notes. Each type of note has a different definition for use but they are all similar in that they indicate that codes excluded from each other are independent of each other.

a. Excludes1

A type 1 Excludes note is a pure excludes note. It means "NOT CODED HERE!" An Excludes1 note indicates that the code excluded should never be used at the same time as the code above the Excludes1 note. An Excludes1 is used when two conditions cannot occur together, such as a congenital form versus an acquired form of the same condition.

b. Excludes2

A type 2 excludes note represents "Not included here". An excludes2 note indicates that the condition excluded is not part of the condition represented by the code, but a patient may have both conditions at the same time. When an Excludes2 note appears under a code, it is acceptable to use both the code and the excluded code together, when appropriate.

13. Etiology/manifestation convention ("code first", "use additional code" and "in diseases classified elsewhere" notes)

Certain conditions have both an underlying etiology and multiple body system manifestations due to the underlying etiology. For such conditions, the ICD-10-CM has a coding convention that requires the underlying condition be sequenced first followed by the manifestation. Wherever such a combination exists, there is a "use additional code" note at the etiology code, and a "code first" note at the manifestation code. These instructional notes indicate the proper sequencing order of the codes, etiology followed by manifestation.

In most cases the manifestation codes will have in the code title, "in diseases classified elsewhere." Codes with this title are a component of the etiology/ manifestation convention. The code title indicates that it is a manifestation code. "In diseases classified elsewhere" codes are never permitted to be used as first listed or principal diagnosis codes. They must be used in conjunction with an underlying condition code and they must be listed following the underlying condition. See category F02, Dementia in other diseases classified elsewhere, for an example of this convention.

There are manifestation codes that do not have "in diseases classified elsewhere" in the title. For such codes a "use additional code" note will still be present and the rules for sequencing apply.

In addition to the notes in the Tabular, these conditions also have a specific Index entry structure. In the Index both conditions are listed together with the etiology code first followed by the manifestation codes in brackets. The code in brackets is always to be sequenced second.

The most commonly used etiology/manifestation combinations are the codes for Diabetes mellitus, categories E08-E13. For each code under categories E08-E13 there is a use additional code note for the manifestation that is specific for that particular diabetic manifestation. Should a patient have more than one manifestation of diabetes, more than one code from categories E08-E13 may be used with as many manifestation codes as are needed to fully describe the patient's complete diabetic condition. The diabetes codes should be sequenced first, followed by the manifestation codes.

"Code first" and "Use additional code" notes are also used as sequencing rules in the classification for certain codes that are not part of an etiology/ manifestation combination.

See Section I.B.7. Multiple coding for a single condition.

14. "And"

The word "and" should be interpreted to mean either "and" or "or" when it appears in a title.

15. "With"

The word "with" in the Alphabetic Index is sequenced immediately following the main term, not in alphabetical order.

16. "See" and "See Also"

The "see" instruction following a main term in the Index indicates that another term should be referenced. It is necessary to go to the main term referenced with the "see" note to locate the correct code.

A "see also" instruction following a main term in the index instructs that there is another main term that may also be referenced that may provide additional index entries that may be useful. It is not necessary to follow the "see also" note when the original main term provides the necessary code.

17. "Code also note"

A "code also" note instructs that two codes may be required to fully describe a condition, but this note does not provide sequencing direction.

18. Default codes

A code listed next to a main term in the ICD-10-CM Index is referred to as a default code. The default code represents that condition that is most commonly associated with the main term, or is the unspecified code for the condition. If a condition is documented in a medical record (for example, appendicitis) without any additional information, such as acute or chronic, the default code should be assigned.

B. General Coding Guidelines

1. Locating a code in the ICD-10-CM

To select a code in the classification that corresponds to a diagnosis or reason for visit documented in a medical record, first locate the term in the Index, and then verify the code in the Tabular List. Read and be guided by instructional notations that appear in both the Index and the Tabular List.

It is essential to use both the Index and Tabular List when locating and assigning a code. The Index does not always provide the full code. Selection of the full code, including laterality and any applicable 7th character can only be done in the Tabular list. A dash (-) at the end of an Index entry indicates that additional characters are required. Even if a dash is not included at the Index entry, it is necessary to refer to the Tabular list to verify that no 7th character is required.

2. Level of Detail in Coding

Diagnosis codes are to be used and reported at their highest number of digits available.

ICD-10-CM diagnosis codes are composed of codes with 3, 4, 5, 6 or 7 digits. Codes with three digits are included in ICD-10-CM as the heading of a category of codes that may be further subdivided by the use of fourth and/or fifth digits, which provide greater detail.

A three-digit code is to be used only if it is not further subdivided. A code is invalid if it has not been coded to the full number of characters required for that code, including the 7th character, if applicable.

3. Code or codes from A00.0 through T88.9, Z00-Z99.8

The appropriate code or codes from A00.0 through T88.9, Z00-Z99.8 must be used to identify diagnoses, symptoms, conditions, problems, complaints or other reason(s) for the encounter/visit.

4. Signs and symptoms

Codes that describe symptoms and signs, as opposed to diagnoses, are acceptable for reporting purposes when a related definitive diagnosis has not been established (confirmed) by the provider. Chapter 18 of ICD-10-CM, Symptoms, Signs, and Abnormal Clinical and Laboratory Findings, Not Elsewhere Classified (codes R00.0 - R99) contains many, but not all codes for symptoms.

5. Conditions that are an integral part of a disease process

Signs and symptoms that are associated routinely with a disease process should not be assigned as additional codes, unless otherwise instructed by the classification.

6. Conditions that are not an integral part of a disease process

Additional signs and symptoms that may not be associated routinely with a disease process should be coded when present.

7. Multiple coding for a single condition

In addition to the etiology/manifestation convention that requires two codes to fully describe a single condition that affects multiple body systems, there are other single conditions that also require more than one code. "Use additional code" notes are found in the Tabular at codes that are not part of an etiology/manifestation pair where a secondary code is useful to fully describe a condition. The sequencing rule is the same as the etiology/manifestation pair, "use additional code" indicates that a secondary code should be added.

For example, for bacterial infections that are not included in chapter 1, a secondary code from category B95, Streptococcus, Staphylococcus, and Enterococcus, as the cause of diseases classified elsewhere, or B96, Other bacterial agents as the cause of diseases classified elsewhere, may be required to identify the bacterial organism causing the infection. A "use additional code" note will normally be found at the infectious disease code, indicating a need for the organism code to be added as a secondary code.

"Code first" notes are also under certain codes that are not specifically manifestation codes but may be due to an underlying cause. When there is a "code first" note and an underlying condition is present, the underlying condition should be sequenced first.

"Code, if applicable, any causal condition first", notes indicate that this code may be assigned as a principal diagnosis when the causal condition is unknown or not applicable. If a causal condition is known, then the code for that condition should be sequenced as the principal or first-listed diagnosis.

Multiple codes may be needed for late effects, complication codes and obstetric codes to more fully describe a condition. See the specific guidelines for these conditions for further instruction.

8. Acute and Chronic Conditions

If the same condition is described as both acute (subacute) and chronic, and separate subentries exist in the Alphabetic Index at the same indentation level, code both and sequence the acute (subacute) code first.

9. Combination Code

A combination code is a single code used to classify: Two diagnoses, or

> A diagnosis with an associated secondary process (manifestation)

> A diagnosis with an associated complication

Combination codes are identified by referring to subterm entries in the Alphabetic Index and by reading the inclusion and exclusion notes in the Tabular List.

Assign only the combination code when that code fully identifies the diagnostic conditions involved or when the Alphabetic Index so directs. Multiple coding should not be used when the classification provides a combination code that clearly identifies all of the elements documented in the diagnosis. When the combination code lacks necessary specificity in describing the manifestation or complication, an additional code should be used as a secondary code.

10. Late Effects (Sequela)

A late effect is the residual effect (condition produced) after the acute phase of an illness or injury has terminated. There is no time limit on when a late effect code can be used. The residual may be apparent early, such as in cerebral infarction, or it may occur months or years later, such as that due to a previous injury. Coding of late effects generally requires two codes sequenced in the following order: The condition or nature of the late effect is sequenced first. The late effect code is sequenced second.

An exception to the above guidelines are those instances where the code for late effect is followed by a manifestation code identified in the Tabular List and title, or the late effect code has been expanded (at the fourth, fifth or sixth character levels) to include the manifestation(s). The code for the acute phase of an illness or injury that led to the late effect is never used with a code for the late effect.
See Section I.C.9. Sequelae of cerebrovascular disease
See Section I.C.15. Sequelae of complication of pregnancy, childbirth and the puerperium
See Section I.C.19. Code extensions

11. Impending or Threatened Condition

Code any condition described at the time of discharge as "impending" or "threatened" as follows:

If it did occur, code as confirmed diagnosis.

If it did not occur, reference the Alphabetic Index to determine if the condition has a subentry term for "impending" or "threatened" and also reference main term entries for "Impending" and for "Threatened."

If the subterms are listed, assign the given code.

If the subterms are not listed, code the existing underlying condition(s) and not the condition described as impending or threatened.

12. Reporting Same Diagnosis Code More than Once

Each unique ICD-10-CM diagnosis code may be reported only once for an encounter. This applies to bilateral conditions or two different conditions classified to the same ICD-10-CM diagnosis code.

13. Laterality

For bilateral sites, the final character of the codes in the ICD-10-CM indicates laterality. An unspecified side code is also provided should the side not be identified in the medical record. If no bilateral code is provided and the condition is bilateral, assign separate codes for both the left and right side.

C. Chapter-Specific Coding Guidelines

In addition to general coding guidelines, there are guidelines for specific diagnoses and/or conditions in the classification. Unless otherwise indicated, these guidelines apply to all health care settings. Please refer to Section II for guidelines on the selection of principal diagnosis.

1. Chapter 1: Certain Infectious and Parasitic Diseases (A00-B99)

a. **Human Immunodeficiency Virus (HIV) Infections**

1) Code only confirmed cases

Code only confirmed cases of HIV infection/illness. This is an exception to the hospital inpatient guideline Section II, H.

In this context, "confirmation" does not require documentation of positive serology or culture for HIV; the provider's diagnostic statement that the patient is HIV positive, or has an HIV-related illness is sufficient.

2) Selection and sequencing of HIV codes

a) **Patient admitted for HIV-related condition**

If a patient is admitted for an HIV-related condition, the principal diagnosis should be B20, followed by additional diagnosis codes for all reported HIV-related conditions.

b) **Patient with HIV disease admitted for unrelated condition**

If a patient with HIV disease is admitted for an unrelated condition (such as a traumatic injury), the code for the unrelated condition (e.g., the nature of injury code) should be the principal diagnosis. Other diagnoses would be B20 followed by additional diagnosis codes for all reported HIV-related conditions.

c) **Whether the patient is newly diagnosed**

Whether the patient is newly diagnosed or has had previous admissions/encounters for HIV conditions is irrelevant to the sequencing decision.

d) **Asymptomatic human immunodeficiency virus**

Z21, Asymptomatic human immunodeficiency virus [HIV] infection status, is to be applied when the patient without any documentation of symptoms is listed as being "HIV positive," "known HIV," "HIV test positive," or similar terminology. Do not use this code if the term "AIDS" is used or if the patient is treated for any HIV-related illness or is described as having any condition(s) resulting from his/her HIV positive status; use B20 in these cases.

e) **Patients with inconclusive HIV serology**

Patients with inconclusive HIV serology, but no definitive diagnosis or manifestations of the illness, may be assigned code R75, Inconclusive laboratory evidence of human immunodeficiency virus [HIV].

f) **Previously diagnosed HIV-related illness**

Patients with any known prior diagnosis of an HIV-related illness should be coded to B20. Once a patient has developed an HIV-related illness, the patient should always be assigned code B20 on every subsequent admission/encounter. Patients previously diagnosed with any HIV illness (B20) should never be assigned to R75 or Z21, Asymptomatic human immunodeficiency virus [HIV] infection status.

g) HIV Infection in Pregnancy, Childbirth and the Puerperium

During pregnancy, childbirth or the puerperium, a patient admitted (or presenting for a health care encounter) because of an HIV-related illness should receive a principal diagnosis code of O98.7-, Human immunodeficiency [HIV] disease complicating pregnancy, childbirth and the puerperium, followed by B20 and the code(s) for the HIV-related illness(es). Codes from Chapter 15 always take sequencing priority.

Patients with asymptomatic HIV infection status admitted (or presenting for a health care encounter) during pregnancy, childbirth, or the puerperium should receive codes of O98.7- and Z21.

h) Encounters for testing for HIV

If a patient is being seen to determine his/her HIV status, use code Z11.4, Encounter for screening for human immunodeficiency virus [HIV]. Use additional codes for any associated high risk behavior.

If a patient with signs or symptoms is being seen for HIV testing, code the signs and symptoms. An additional counseling code Z71.7, Human innunodeficiency virus [HIV] counseling, may be used if counseling is provided during the encounter for the test.

When a patient returns to be informed of his/her HIV test results and the test result is negative, use code Z71.7, Human immunodeficiency virus [HIV] counseling.

If the results are positive, see previous guidelines and assign codes as appropriate.

b. Infectious agents as the cause of diseases classified to other chapters

Certain infections are classified in chapters other than Chapter 1 and no organism is identified as part of the infection code. In these instances, it is necessary to use an additional code from Chapter 1 to identify the organism. A code from category B95, Streptococcus, Staphylococcus, and Enterococcus as the cause of diseases classified to other chapters, B96, Other bacterial agents as the cause of diseases classified to other chapters, or B97, Viral agents as the cause of diseases classified to other chapters, is to be used as an additional code to identify the organism. An instructional note will be found at the

infection code advising that an additional organism code is required.

c. Infections resistant to antibiotics

Many bacterial infections are resistant to current antibiotics. It is necessary to identify all infections documented as antibiotic resistant. Assign code Z16, Infection with drug resistant microorganisms, following the infection code for these cases.

d. Sepsis, Severe Sepsis, and Septic Shock

1) Coding of Sepsis and Severe Sepsis

a) Sepsis

For a diagnosis of sepsis, assign the appropriate code for the underlying systemic infection. If the type of infection or causal organism is not further specified, assign code A41.9, Sepsis, unspecified.

A code from subcategory R65.2, Severe sepsis, should not be assigned unless severe sepsis or an associated acute organ dysfunction is documented.

(i) Negative or inconclusive blood cultures and sepsis

Negative or inconclusive blood cultures do not preclude a diagnosis of sepsis in patients with clinical evidence of the condition, however, the provider should be queried.

(ii) Urosepsis

The term urosepsis is a nonspecific term. It is not to be considered synonymous with sepsis. It has no default code in the Alphabetic Index. Should a provider use this term, he/she must be queried for clarification.

(iii) Sepsis with organ dysfunction

If a patient has sepsis and associated acute organ dysfunction or multiple organ dysfunction (MOD), follow the instructions for coding severe sepsis.

(iv) Acute organ dysfunction that is not clearly associated with the sepsis

If a patient has sepsis and an acute organ dysfunction, but the medical record documentation indicates that the acute organ dysfunction is related to a medical condition other than the sepsis, do not assign a code from subcategory R65.2, Severe sepsis. An acute organ dysfunction must be associated with the sepsis in order to assign the severe sepsis code. If the documentation is not clear as to whether an acute organ dysfunction is related to the sepsis or another medical condition, query the provider.

b) Severe sepsis

The coding of severe sepsis requires a minimum of 2 codes: first a code for the underlying systemic infection, followed by a code from subcategory R65.2, Severe sepsis. If the causal organism is not documented, assign code A41.9, Sepsis, unspecified, for the infection. Additional code(s) for the associated acute organ dysfunction are also required.

Due to the complex nature of severe sepsis, some cases may require querying the provider prior to assignment of the codes.

2) **Septic shock**

Septic shock is circulatory failure associated with severe sepsis, and therefore, it represents a type of acute organ dysfunction. For all cases of septic shock, the code for the underlying systemic infection should be sequenced first, followed by code R65.21, Severe sepsis with septic shock. Any additional codes for the other acute organ dysfunctions should also be assigned.

Septic shock indicates the presence of severe sepsis. Code R65.21, Severe sepsis with septic shock, must be assigned if septic shock is documented in the medical record, even if the term severe sepsis is not documented.

3) **Sequencing of severe sepsis**

If severe sepsis is present on admission, and meets the definition of principal diagnosis, the underlying systemic infection should be assigned as principal diagnosis followed by the appropriate code from subcategory R65.2 as required by the sequencing rules in the Tabular List. A code from subcategory R65.2 can never be assigned as a principal diagnosis.

When severe sepsis develops during an encounter (it was not present on admission) the underlying systemic infection and the appropriate code from subcategory R65.2 should be assigned as secondary diagnoses.

Severe sepsis may be present on admission but the diagnosis may not be confirmed until sometime after admission. If the documentation is not clear whether severe sepsis was present on admission, the provider should be queried.

4) **Sepsis and severe sepsis with a localized infection**

If the reason for admission is both sepsis or severe sepsis and a localized infection, such as pneumonia or cellulitis, a code(s) for the underlying systemic infection should be assigned first and the code for the localized infection should be assigned as a secondary diagnosis. If the patient has severe sepsis, a code from subcategory R65.2 should also be assigned as a secondary diagnosis. If the patient is admitted with a localized infection, such as pneumonia, and sepsis/severe sepsis doesn't develop until after admission, the localized infection should be assigned first, followed by the appropriate sepsis/severe sepsis codes.

5) **Sepsis due to a postprocedural infection**

Sepsis resulting from a postprocedural infection is a complication of medical care. For such cases, the postprocedural infection code, such as, T80.2, Infections following infusion, transfusion, and therapeutic injection, T81.4, Infection following a procedure, T88.0, Infection following immunization, or O86.0, Infection of obstetric surgical wound, should be coded first, followed by the code for the specific infection. If the patient has severe sepsis the appropriate code from subcategory R65.2 should also be assigned with the additional code(s) for any acute organ dysfunction.

6) **Sepsis and severe sepsis associated with a noninfectious process (condition)**

In some cases a noninfectious process (condition), such as trauma, may lead to an infection which can result in sepsis or severe sepsis. If sepsis or severe sepsis is documented as associated with a noninfectious condition, such as a burn or serious injury, and this condition meets the definition for principal diagnosis, the code for the noninfectious condition should be sequenced first, followed by the code for the resulting infection. If severe sepsis, is present a code from subcategory R65.2 should also be assigned with any associated organ dysfunction(s) codes. It is not necessary to assign a code from subcategory R65.1, Systemic inflammatory response syndrome (SIRS) of non-infectious origin, for these cases.

If the infection meets the definition of principal diagnosis it should be sequenced before the non-infectious condition. When both the associated non-infectious condition and the infection meet the definition of principal diagnosis either may be assigned as principal diagnosis.

Only one code from category R65, Symptoms and signs specifically associated with systemic inflammation and infection, should be assigned. Therefore, when a non-infectious condition leads to an infection resulting in severe sepsis, assign the appropriate code from subcategory R65.2, Severe sepsis. Do not additionally assign a code from subcategory R65.1, Systemic inflammatory response syndrome (SIRS) of non-infectious origin. *See Section I.C.18. SIRS due to non-infectious process*

7) **Sepsis and septic shock complicating abortion, pregnancy, childbirth, and the puerperium**

See Section I.C.15. Sepsis and septic shock complicating abortion, pregnancy, childbirth and the puerperium

8) **Newborn sepsis**

See Section I.C.16. Newborn sepsis

2. Chapter 2: Neoplasms (C00-D49)

General guidelines

Chapter 2 of the ICD-10-CM contains the codes for most benign and all malignant neoplasms. Certain benign neoplasms, such as prostatic adenomas, may be found in the specific body system chapters. To properly code a neoplasm it is necessary to determine from the record if the neoplasm is benign, in-situ, malignant, or of uncertain histologic behavior. If malignant, any secondary (metastatic) sites should also be determined.

The neoplasm table in the Alphabetic Index should be referenced first. However, if the histological term is documented, that term should be referenced first, rather than going immediately to the Neoplasm Table, in order to determine which column in the Neoplasm Table is appropriate. For example, if the documentation indicates "adenoma," refer to the term in the Alphabetic Index to review the entries under this term and the instructional note to "see also neoplasm, by site, benign." The table provides the proper code based on the type of neoplasm and the site. It is important to select the proper column in the table that corresponds to the type of neoplasm. The Tabular should then be referenced to verify that the correct code has been selected from the table and that a more specific site code does not exist.

See Section I.C.21. Factors influencing health status and contact with health services, Status, for information regarding Z15.0, codes for genetic susceptibility to cancer.

a. **Treatment directed at the malignancy**

If the treatment is directed at the malignancy, designate the malignancy as the principal diagnosis.

The only exception to this guideline is if a patient admission/encounter is solely for the administration of chemotherapy, immunotherapy or radiation therapy, assign the appropriate Z51.-- code as the first-listed or principal diagnosis, and the diagnosis or problem for which the service is being performed as a secondary diagnosis.

b. **Treatment of secondary site**

When a patient is admitted because of a primary neoplasm with metastasis and treatment is directed toward the secondary site only, the secondary neoplasm is designated as the principal diagnosis even though the primary malignancy is still present.

c. **Coding and sequencing of complications**

Coding and sequencing of complications associated with the malignancies or with the therapy thereof are subject to the following guidelines:

1) **Anemia associated with malignancy**

When admission/encounter is for management of an anemia associated with the malignancy, and the treatment is only for anemia, the appropriate code for the malignancy is sequenced as the principal or first-listed diagnosis (followed by code D63.0, Anemia in neoplastic disease).

2) **Anemia associated with chemotherapy, immunotherapy and radiation therapy**

When the admission/encounter is for management of an anemia associated with chemotherapy, immunotherapy or radiotherapy and the only treatment is for the anemia, the anemia is sequenced first followed by code T45.1x5, Adverse effect of antineoplastic and immunosuppressive drugs. The

appropriate neoplasm code should be assigned as an additional code.

3) **Management of dehydration due to the malignancy**

When the admission/encounter is for management of dehydration due to the malignancy or the therapy, or a combination of both, and only the dehydration is being treated (intravenous rehydration), the dehydration is sequenced first, followed by the code(s) for the malignancy.

4) **Treatment of a complication resulting from a surgical procedure**

When the admission/encounter is for treatment of a complication resulting from a surgical procedure, designate the complication as the principal or first-listed diagnosis if treatment is directed at resolving the complication.

d. **Primary malignancy previously excised**

When a primary malignancy has been previously excised or eradicated from its site and there is no further treatment directed to that site and there is no evidence of any existing primary malignancy, a code from category Z85, Personal history of primary and secondary malignant neoplasm, should be used to indicate the former site of the malignancy. Any mention of extension, invasion, or metastasis to another site is coded as a secondary malignant neoplasm to that site. The secondary site may be the principal or first-listed with the Z85 code used as a secondary code.

e. **Admissions/Encounters involving chemotherapy, immunotherapy and radiation therapy**

1) **Episode of care involves surgical removal of neoplasm**

When an episode of care involves the surgical removal of a neoplasm, primary or secondary site, followed by adjunct chemotherapy or radiation treatment during the same episode of care, the neoplasm code should be assigned as principal or first-listed diagnosis, using codes in the C00-D49 series or where appropriate in the C83-C90 series.

2) **Patient admission/encounter solely for administration of chemotherapy, immunotherapy and radiation therapy**

If a patient admission/encounter is solely for the administration of chemotherapy, immunotherapy or radiation therapy assign code Z51.0, Encounter for antineoplastic radiation therapy, or Z51.11, Encounter for antineoplastic chemotherapy, or Z51.12, Encounter for antineoplastic immunotherapy as the first-listed or principal diagnosis. If a patient receives more than one of these therapies during the same admission more than one of these codes may be assigned, in any sequence.

The malignancy for which the therapy is being administered should be assigned as a secondary diagnosis.

3) **Patient admitted for radiation therapy, chemotherapy or immunotherapy and develops complications**

When a patient is admitted for the purpose of radiotherapy, immunotherapy or chemotherapy and develops complications such as uncontrolled nausea and vomiting or dehydration, the principal or first-listed diagnosis is Z51.0, Encounter for antineoplastic radiation therapy, or Z51.11, Encounter for antineoplastic chemotherapy, or Z51.12, Encounter for antineoplastic immunotherapy followed by any codes for the complications.

f. **Admission/encounter to determine extent of malignancy**

When the reason for admission/encounter is to determine the extent of the malignancy, or for a procedure such as paracentesis or thoracentesis, the primary malignancy or appropriate metastatic site is designated as the principal or first-listed diagnosis, even though chemotherapy or radiotherapy is administered.

g. **Symptoms, signs, and abnormal findings listed in Chapter 18 associated with neoplasms**

Symptoms, signs, and ill-defined conditions listed in Chapter 18 characteristic of, or associated with, an existing primary or secondary site malignancy cannot be used to replace the malignancy as principal or first-listed diagnosis, regardless of the number of admissions or encounters for treatment and care of the neoplasm.

See section I.C.21. Factors influencing health status and contact with health services, Encounter for prophylactic organ removal.

h. **Admission/encounter for pain control/management**

See Section I.C.6. for information on coding admission/encounter for pain control/management.

i. **Malignancy in two or more noncontiguous sites**

A patient may have more than one malignant tumor in the same organ. These tumors may represent different primaries or metastatic disease, depending on the site. Should the documentation be unclear, the provider should be queried as to the status of each tumor so that the correct codes can be assigned.

j. **Disseminated malignant neoplasm, unspecified**

Code C80.0, Disseminated malignant neoplasm, unspecified, is for use only in those cases where the patient has advanced metastatic disease and no known primary or secondary sites are specified. It should not be used in place of assigning codes for the primary site and all known secondary sites.

k. **Malignant neoplasm without specification of site**

Code C80.1, Malignant neoplasm, unspecified, equates to Cancer, unspecified. This code should only be used when no determination can be made as to the primary site of a malignancy. This code should rarely be used in the inpatient setting.

l. **Sequencing of neoplasm codes**

1) **Encounter for treatment of primary malignancy**

If the reason for the encounter is for treatment of a primary malignancy, assign the malignancy as the principal/first listed diagnosis. The primary site is to be sequenced first, followed by any metastatic sites.

2) **Encounter for treatment of secondary malignancy**

When an encounter is for a primary malignancy with metastasis and treatment is directed toward the metastatic (secondary) site(s) only, the metastatic site(s) is designated as the principal/first listed diagnosis. The primary malignancy is coded as an additional code.

3) **Malignant neoplasm in a pregnant patient**

Codes from chapter 15, Pregnancy, childbirth, and the puerperium, are always sequenced first on a medical record. A code from subcategory O94.1-, Malignant neoplasm complicating pregnancy, childbirth, and the puerperium, should be used first, followed by the appropriate code from Chapter 2 to indicate the type of neoplasm.

4) **Encounter for complication associated with a neoplasm**

When an encounter is for management of a complication associated with a neoplasm, such as dehydration, and the treatment is only for the complication, the complication is coded first, followed by the appropriate code(s) for the neoplasm.

5) **Complication from surgical procedure for treatment of a neoplasm**

When an encounter is for treatment of a complication resulting from a surgical procedure performed for the treatment of the neoplasm, designate the complication as the principal/first listed diagnosis. See guideline regarding the coding of a current malignancy versus personal history to determine if the code for the neoplasm should also be assigned.

6) **Pathologic fracture due to a neoplasm**

When an encounter is for a pathological fracture due to a neoplasm, if the focus of treatment is the fracture, a code from subcategory M84.5, Pathological fracture in neoplastic disease, should be sequenced first, followed by the code for the neoplasm.

If the focus of treatment is the neoplasm with an associated pathological fracture, the neoplasm code should be sequenced first, followed by a code from M84.5 for the pathological fracture. The "code also" note at M84.5 provides this sequencing instruction.

m. **Current malignancy versus personal history of malignancy**

When a primary malignancy has been excised but further treatment, such as an additional surgery for the malignancy, radiation therapy or chemotherapy is directed to that site, the primary malignancy code should be used until treatment is completed.

When a primary malignancy has been previously excised or eradicated from its site, there is no further treatment (of the malignancy) directed to that site, and there is no evidence of any existing primary malignancy, a code from category Z85, Personal history of primary and secondary malignant neoplasm, should be used to indicate the former site of the malignancy.

See Section I.C.21. Factors influencing health status and contact with health services, History (of)

n. **Leukemia in remission versus personal history of leukemia**

The categories for leukemia, and category C90, Multiple myeloma, have codes for in remission. There are also codes Z85.6, Personal history of leukemia, and Z85.79, Personal history of other malignant neoplasms of lymphoid, hematopoietic and related tissues. If the documentation is unclear, as to whether the patient is in remission, the provider should be queried.

See Section I.C.21. Factors influencing health status and contact with health services, History (of)

o. **Aftercare following surgery for neoplasm**

See Section I.C.21. Factors influencing health status and contact with health services, Aftercare

p. **Follow-up care for completed treatment of a malignancy**

See Section I.C.21. Factors influencing health status and contact with health services, Follow-up

q. **Prophylactic organ removal for prevention of malignancy**

See Section I.C. 21, Factors influencing health status and contact with health services, Prophylactic organ removal

3. **Chapter 3: Disease of the blood and blood-forming organs and certain disorders involving the immune mechanism (D50-D89)**

Reserved for future guideline expansion

4. **Chapter 4: Endocrine, Nutritional, and Metabolic Diseases (E00-E90)**

a. **Diabetes mellitus**

The diabetes mellitus codes are combination codes that include the type of DM, the body system affected, and the complications affecting that body system. As many codes within a particular category as are necessary to describe all of the complications of the disease may be used. They should be sequenced based on the reason for a particular encounter. Assign as many codes from categories E08 – E13 as needed to identify all of the associated conditions that the patient has.

1) **Type of diabetes**

The age of a patient is not the sole determining factor, though most type 1 diabetics develop the condition before reaching puberty. For this reason type 1 diabetes mellitus is also referred to as juvenile diabetes.

2) **Type of diabetes mellitus not documented**

If the type of diabetes mellitus is not documented in the medical record the default is E11.-, Type 2 diabetes mellitus.

3) **Diabetes mellitus and the use of insulin**

If the documentation in a medical record does not indicate the type of diabetes but does indicate that the patient uses insulin, code E11, Type 2 diabetes mellitus, should be assigned for type 2 patients who routinely use insulin, code Z79.4, Long-term (current) use of insulin, should also be assigned to indicate that the patient uses insulin. Code Z79.4 should not be assigned if insulin is given temporarily to bring a type 2 patient's blood sugar under control during an encounter.

4) **Diabetes mellitus in pregnancy and gestational diabetes**

See Section I.C.15. Diabetes mellitus in pregnancy.
See Section I.C.15. Gestational (pregnancy induced) diabetes

5) **Complications due to insulin pump malfunction**

a. **Underdose of insulin due insulin pump failure**

An underdose of insulin due to an insulin pump failure should be assigned to a code from subcategory T85.6, Mechanical complication of other specified internal and external prosthetic devices, implants and grafts, that specifies the type of pump malfunction, as the principal or first listed code, followed by code T38.3x6-, Underdosing of insulin and oral hypoglycemic [antidiabetic] drugs. Additional codes for the type of diabetes mellitus and any associated complications due to the underdosing should also be assigned.

b. **Overdose of insulin due to insulin pump failure**

The principal or first listed code for an encounter due to an insulin pump malfunction resulting in an overdose of insulin, should also be T85.6-, Mechanical complication of other specified internal and external prosthetic devices, implants and grafts, followed by code T38.3x1-, Poisoning by insulin and oral hypoglycemic [antidiabetic] drugs, accidental (unintentional).

5. **Chapter 5: Mental and behavioral disorders (F01-F99)**

a. **Pain disorders related to psychological factors**

Assign code F45.41, for pain that is exclusively psychological. There is also, generally, a psychological component of any type of acute or chronic pain. Code F45.41, Pain disorder with related psychological factors, should be used following the appropriate code from category G89, Pain, not elsewhere classified, if there is documentation of a psychological component for a patient with acute or chronic pain.

See Section I.C.6. Pain

6. **Chapter 6: Diseases of Nervous System and Sense Organs (G00-G99)**

   a. **Dominant/nondominant side**

   Codes from category G81, Hemiplegia and hemiparesis, and subcategories, G83.1, Monoplegia of lower limb, G83.2, Monoplegia of upper limb, and G83.3, Monoplegia, unspecified, identify whether the dominant or nondominant side is affected. Should this information not be available in the record, the default should be dominant. For ambidextrous patients, the default should also be dominant.

   b. **Pain - Category G89**

   1) **General coding information**

   Codes in category G89, Pain, not elsewhere classified, may be used in conjunction with codes from other categories and chapters to provide more detail about acute or chronic pain and neoplasm-related pain, unless otherwise indicated below.

   If the pain is not specified as acute or chronic, post-thoracotomy, postprocedural, or neoplasm-related, do not assign codes from category G89.

   A code from category G89 should not be assigned if the underlying (definitive) diagnosis is known, unless the reason for the encounter is pain control/management and not management of the underlying condition.

   When an admission or encounter is for a procedure aimed at treating the underlying condition (e.g., spinal fusion, kyphoplasty), a code for the underlying condition (e.g., vertebral fracture, spinal stenosis) should be assigned as the principal diagnosis. No code from category G89 should be assigned.

   a) **Category G89 Codes as Principal or First-Listed Diagnosis**

   Category G89 codes are acceptable as principal diagnosis or the first-listed code:

   - When pain control or pain management is the reason for the admission/encounter (e.g., a patient with displaced intervertebral disc, nerve impingement and severe back pain presents for injection of steroid into the spinal canal). The underlying cause of the pain should be reported as an additional diagnosis, if known.

   - When a patient is admitted for the insertion of a neurostimulator for pain control, assign the appropriate pain code as the principal or first listed diagnosis. When an admission or encounter is for a procedure aimed at treating the underlying condition and a neurostimulator is inserted for pain control during the same admission/encounter, a code for the underlying condition should be assigned as the principal diagnosis and the appropriate pain code should be assigned as a secondary diagnosis.

   b) **Use of Category G89 Codes in Conjunction with Site Specific Pain Codes**

   (i) **Assigning Category G89 and Site-Specific Pain Codes**

   Codes from category G89 may be used in conjunction with codes that identify the site of pain (including codes from chapter 18) if the category G89 code provides additional information. For example, if the code describes the site of the pain, but does not fully describe whether the pain is acute or chronic, then both codes should be assigned.

   (ii) **Sequencing of Category G89 Codes with Site-Specific Pain Codes**

   The sequencing of category G89 codes with site-specific pain codes (including chapter 18 codes), is dependent on the circumstances of the encounter/admission as follows:

   - If the encounter is for pain control or pain management, assign the code from category G89 followed by the code identifying the specific site of pain (e.g., encounter for pain management for acute neck pain from trauma is assigned code G89.11, Acute pain due to trauma, followed by code M54.2, Cervicalgia, to identify the site of pain).

   - If the encounter is for any other reason except pain control or pain management, and a related definitive diagnosis has not been established (confirmed) by the provider, assign the code for the specific site of pain first, followed by the appropriate code from category G89.

   2) **Pain due to devices, implants and grafts**

   See Section I.C.19. Pain due to medical devices

   3) **Postoperative Pain**

   The provider's documentation should be used to guide the coding of postoperative pain, as well as *Section III. Reporting Additional Diagnoses and Section IV. Diagnostic Coding and Reporting in the Outpatient Setting.*

   The default for post-thoracotomy and other postoperative pain not specified as acute or chronic is the code for the acute form.

   Routine or expected postoperative pain immediately after surgery should not be coded.

   (a) **Postoperative pain not associated with specific postoperative complication**

   Postoperative pain not associated with a specific postoperative complication is assigned to the appropriate postoperative pain code in category G89.

   (b) **Postoperative pain associated with specific postoperative complication**

   Postoperative pain associated with a specific postoperative complication (such as painful wire sutures) is assigned to the appropriate code(s) found in Chapter 19, Injury, poisoning, and certain other consequences of external causes. If appropriate, use additional code(s) from category G89 to identify acute or chronic pain (G89.18 or G89.28).

4) **Chronic pain**

Chronic pain is classified to subcategory G89.2. There is no time frame defining when pain becomes chronic pain. The provider's documentation should be used to guide use of these codes.

5) **Neoplasm Related Pain**

Code G89.3 is assigned to pain documented as being related, associated or due to cancer, primary or secondary malignancy, or tumor. This code is assigned regardless of whether the pain is acute or chronic.

This code may be assigned as the principal or first-listed code when the stated reason for the admission/encounter is documented as pain control/pain management. The underlying neoplasm should be reported as an additional diagnosis.

When the reason for the admission/encounter is management of the neoplasm and the pain associated with the neoplasm is also documented, code G89.3 may be assigned as an additional diagnosis. It is not necessary to assign an additional code for the site of the pain.

See Section I.C.2 for instructions on the sequencing of neoplasms for all other stated reasons for the admission/encounter (except for pain control/pain management).

6) **Chronic pain syndrome**

Central pain syndrome (G89.0) and chronic pain syndrome (G89.4) are different than the term "chronic pain," and therefore codes should only be used when the provider has specifically documented this condition.

See Section I.C.5. Pain disorders related to psychological factors

7. Chapter 7: Diseases of Eye and Adnexa (H00-IH59)

Reserved for future guideline expansion

8. Chapter 8: Diseases of Ear and Mastoid Process (H60-H59)

Reserved for future guideline expansion

9. Chapter 9: Diseases of Circulatory System (I00-I99)

a. **Hypertension.**

1) **Hypertension with Heart Disease**

Heart conditions classified to I50.- or I51.4-I51.9, are assigned to, a code from category I11, Hypertensive heart disease, when a causal relationship is stated (due to hypertension) or implied (hypertensive). Use an additional code from category I50, Heart failure, to identify the type of heart failure in those patients with heart failure.

The same heart conditions (I50.-, I51.4-I51.9) with hypertension, but without a stated causal relationship, are coded separately. Sequence according to the circumstances of the admission/encounter.

2) **Hypertensive Chronic Kidney Disease**

Assign codes from category I12, Hypertensive chronic kidney disease, when both hypertension and a condition classifiable to category N18, Chronic kidney disease (CKD), are present. Unlike hypertension with heart disease, ICD-10-CM presumes a cause-and-effect relationship and classifies chronic kidney disease with hypertension as hypertensive chronic kidney disease.

The appropriate code from category N18 should be used as a secondary code with a code from category I12 to identify the stage of chronic kidney disease. *See Section I.C.14. Chronic kidney disease.*

If a patient has hypertensive chronic kidney disease and acute renal failure, an additional code for the acute renal failure is required.

3) **Hypertensive Heart and Chronic Kidney Disease**

Assign codes from combination category I13, Hypertensive heart and chronic kidney disease, when both hypertensive kidney disease and hypertensive heart disease are stated in the diagnosis. Assume a relationship between the hypertension and the chronic kidney disease, whether or not the condition is so designated. If heart failure is present, assign an additional code from category I50 to identify the type of heart failure.

The appropriate code from category N18, Chronic kidney disease, should be used as a secondary code with a code from category I13 to identify the stage of chronic kidney disease. *See Section I.C.14. Chronic kidney disease.*

The codes in category I13, Hypertensive heart and chronic kidney disease, are combination codes that include hypertension, heart disease and chronic kidney disease. The Includes note at I13 specifies that the conditions included at I11 and I12 are included together in I13. If a patient has hypertension, heart disease and chronic kidney disease then a code from I13 should be used, not individual codes for hypertension, heart disease and chronic kidney disease, or codes from I11 or I12.

For patients with both acute renal failure and chronic kidney disease an additional code for acute renal failure is required.

4) **Hypertensive Cerebrovascular Disease**

For hypertensive cerebrovascular disease, first assign the appropriate code from categories I60-I69, followed by the appropriate hypertension code.

5) **Hypertensive Retinopathy**

Code H35.0, Hypertensive retinopathy, should be used with code I10, Essential (primary) hypertension, to include the systemic hypertension. The sequencing is based on the reason for the encounter.

6) **Hypertension, Secondary**

Secondary hypertension is due to an underlying condition. Two codes are required: one to identify the underlying etiology and one from category I15 to identify the hypertension. Sequencing of codes is determined by the reason for admission/encounter.

7) **Hypertension, Transient**

Assign code R03.0, Elevated blood pressure reading without diagnosis of hypertension, unless patient has an established diagnosis of hypertension. Assign code O13.-, Gestational [pregnancy-induced] hypertension without significant proteinuria, or O14.-, Gestational [pregnancy-induced] hypertension with significant proteinuria, for transient hypertension of pregnancy.

8) **Hypertension, Controlled**

This diagnostic statement usually refers to an existing state of hypertension under control by therapy. Assign code I10.

9) **Hypertension, Uncontrolled**

Uncontrolled hypertension may refer to untreated hypertension or hypertension not responding to current therapeutic regimen. In either case, assign code I10.

b. **Atherosclerotic coronary artery disease and angina**

ICD-10-CM has combination codes for atherosclerotic heart disease with angina pectoris. The subcategories for these codes are I25.11, Atherosclerotic heart disease of native coronary artery with angina pectoris and I25.7, Atherosclerosis of coronary artery bypass graft(s) and coronary artery of transplanted heart with angina pectoris.

When using one of these combination codes it is not necessary to use an additional code for angina pectoris. A causal relationship can be assumed in a patient with both atherosclerosis and angina pectoris, unless the documentation indicates the angina is due to something other than the atherosclerosis.

If a patient with coronary artery disease is admitted due to an acute myocardial infarction (AMI), the AMI should be sequenced before the coronary artery disease. *See Section I.C.9. Acute myocardial infarction (AMI)*

c. **Intraoperative and Postprocedural cerebrovascular accident**

Proper code assignment depends on whether it was an infarction or hemorrhage and whether it occurred intraoperatively or postoperatively. If it was a cerebral hemorrhage, code assignment depends on the type of procedure performed. Medical record documentation should clearly specify the cause- and-effect relationship between the medical intervention and the cerebrovascular accident in order to assign this code.

d. **Sequelae of Cerebrovascular Disease**

1) **Category I69, Sequelae of Cerebrovascular disease**

Category I69 is used to indicate conditions classifiable to categories I60-I67 as the causes of late effects (neurologic deficits), themselves classified elsewhere. These "late effects" include neurologic deficits that persist after initial onset of conditions classifiable to categories I60-I67. The neurologic deficits caused by cerebrovascular disease may be present from the onset or may arise at any time after the onset of the condition classifiable to categories I60-I67.

2) **Codes from category I69 with codes from I60-I67**

Codes from category I69 may be assigned on a health care record with codes from I60-I67, if the patient has a current cerebrovascular accident (CVA) and deficits from an old CVA.

3) **Code Z86.73**

Assign code Z86.73, Personal history of transient ischemic attack (TIA), and cerebral infarction without residual deficits (and not a code from category I69) as an additional code for history of cerebrovascular disease when no neurologic deficits are present.

e. **Acute myocardial infarction (AMI)**

1) **ST elevation myocardial infarction (STEMI) and non ST elevation myocardial infarction (NSTEMI)**

The ICD-10-CM codes for acute myocardial infarction (AMI) identify the site, such as anterolateral wall or true posterior wall. Subcategories I21.0-I21.2 and code I21.4 are used for ST elevation myocardial infarction (STEMI). Code I21.4, Non-ST elevation (NSTEMI) myocardial infarction, is used for non ST elevation myocardial infarction (NSTEMI) and nontransmural MIs.

2) **Acute myocardial infarction, unspecified**

Code I21.3, ST elevation (STEMI) myocardial infarction of unspecified site, is the default for the unspecified term acute myocardial infarction. If only STEMI or transmural MI without the site is documented, query the provider as to the site, or assign code I21.3.

3) **AMI documented as nontransmural or subendocardial but site provided**

If an AMI is documented as nontransmural or subendocardial, but the site is provided, it is still coded as a subendocardial AMI. If NSTEMI evolves to STEMI, assign the STEMI code. If STEMI converts to NSTEMI due to thrombolytic therapy, it is still coded as STEMI.

4) **Subsequent acute myocardial infarction**

A code from category I22, Subsequent ST elevation (STEMI) and non ST elevation (NSTEMI) myocardial infarction, is to be used when a patient who has suffered an AMI has a new AMI within the 4 week time frame of the initial AMI. A code from category I22 must be used in conjunction with a code from category I21.

The sequencing of the I22 and I21 codes depends on the circumstances of the encounter. Should a patient who is in the hospital due to an AMI have a subsequent AMI while still in the hospital code I21 would be sequenced first as the reason for admission, with code I22 sequenced as a secondary code. Should a patient have a subsequent AMI after discharge for care of an initial AMI, and the reason for admission is the subsequent AMI, the I22 code should be sequenced first followed by the I21. An I21 code must accompany an I22 code to identify the site of the initial AMI, and to indicate that the patient is still within the 4 week time frame of healing from the initial AMI.

The guidelines for assigning the correct I22 code are the same as for the initial AMI.

10. Chapter 10: Diseases of Respiratory System (J00-J99)

a. **Chronic Obstructive Pulmonary Disease [COPD] and Asthma**

   1) **Acute exacerbation of chronic obstructive bronchitis and asthma**

The codes in categories J44 and J45 distinguish between uncomplicated cases and those in acute exacerbation. An acute exacerbation is a worsening or a decompensation of a chronic condition. An acute exacerbation is not equivalent to an infection superimposed on a chronic condition, though an exacerbation may be triggered by an infection.

b. **Acute Respiratory Failure**

   1) **Acute respiratory failure as principal diagnosis**

Code J96.0, Acute respiratory failure, or code J96.2, Acute and chronic respiratory failure, may be assigned as a principal diagnosis when it is the condition established after study to be chiefly responsible for occasioning the admission to the hospital, and the selection is supported by the Alphabetic Index and Tabular List. However, chapter-specific coding guidelines (such as obstetrics, poisoning, HIV, newborn) that provide sequencing direction take precedence.

   2) **Acute respiratory failure as secondary diagnosis**

Respiratory failure may be listed as a secondary diagnosis if it occurs after admission, or if it is present on admission, but does not meet the definition of principal diagnosis.

   3) **Sequencing of acute respiratory failure and another acute condition**

When a patient is admitted with respiratory failure and another acute condition, (e.g., myocardial infarction, cerebrovascular accident, aspiration pneumonia), the principal diagnosis will not be the same in every situation. This applies whether the other acute condition is a respiratory or nonrespiratory condition. Selection of the principal diagnosis will be dependent on the circumstances of admission. If both the respiratory failure and the other acute condition are equally responsible for occasioning the admission to the hospital, and there are no chapter-specific sequencing rules, the guideline regarding two or more diagnoses that equally meet the definition for principal diagnosis (*Section II, C.*) may be applied in these situations.

If the documentation is not clear as to whether acute respiratory failure and another condition are equally responsible for occasioning the admission, query the provider for clarification.

c. **Influenza due to avian influenza virus (avian influenza)**

Code only confirmed cases of avian influenza. This is an exception to the hospital inpatient guideline Section II, H. (Uncertain Diagnosis).

In this context, "confirmation" does not require documentation of positive laboratory testing specific for avian influenza. However, coding should be based on the provider's diagnostic statement that the patient has avian influenza.

If the provider records "suspected or possible or probable avian influenza," the appropriate influenza code from category J10, Influenza due to other influenza virus, should be assigned. Code J09, Influenza due to avian influenza virus, should not be assigned.

11. Chapter 11: Diseases of Digestive System (K00-K94)

Reserved for future guideline expansion

12. Chapter 12: Diseases of Skin and Subcutaneous Tissue (L00-L99)

Reserved for future guideline expansion

13. Chapter 13: Diseases of the Musculoskeletal System and Connective Tissue (M00-M99)

a. **Site and laterality**

Most of the codes within Chapter 13 have site and laterality designations. The site represents either the bone, joint or the muscle involved. For some conditions where more than one bone, joint or muscle is usually involved, such as osteoarthritis, there is a "multiple sites" code available. For categories where no multiple site code is provided and more than one bone, joint or muscle is involved, multiple codes should be used to indicate the different sites involved.

   1) **Bone versus joint**

For certain conditions, the bone may be affected at the upper or lower end, (e.g., avascular necrosis of bone, M87, Osteoporosis, M80, M81). Though the portion of the bone affected may be at the joint, the site designation will be the bone, not the joint.

b. Acute traumatic versus chronic or recurrent musculoskeletal conditions

Many musculoskeletal conditions are a result of previous injury or trauma to a site, or are recurrent conditions. Bone, joint or muscle conditions that are the result of a healed injury are usually found in chapter 13. Recurrent bone, joint or muscle conditions are also usually found in chapter 13. Any current, acute injury should be coded to the appropriate injury code from chapter 19. Chronic or recurrent conditions should generally be coded with a code from chapter 13. If it is difficult to determine from the documentation in the record which code is best to describe a condition, query the provider.

c. Coding of Pathologic Fractures

7th character A is for use as long as the patient is receiving active treatment for the fracture. Examples of active treatment are: surgical treatment, emergency department encounter, evaluation and treatment by a new physician. 7th character, D is to be used for encounters after the patient has completed active treatment. The other 7th characters, listed under each subcategory in the Tabular List, are to be used for subsequent encounters for treatment of problems associated with the healing, such as malunions and nonunions, and sequelae.

Care for complications of surgical treatment for fracture repairs during the healing or recovery phase should be coded with the appropriate complication codes.
See Section I.C.19. Coding of traumatic fractures.

d. Osteoporosis

Osteoporosis is a systemic condition, meaning that all bones of the musculoskeletal system are affected. Therefore, site is not a component of the codes under category M81, Osteoporosis without current pathological fracture. The site codes under category M80, Osteoporosis with current pathological fracture, identify the site of the fracture, not the osteoporosis.

1) Osteoporosis without pathological fracture

Category M81, Osteoporosis without current pathological fracture, is for use for patients with osteoporosis who do not currently have a pathologic fracture due to the osteoporosis, even if they have had a fracture in the past. For patients with a history of osteoporosis fractures, status code Z87.31, Personal history of osteoporosis fracture, should follow the code from M81.

2) Osteoporosis with current pathological fracture

Category M80, Osteoporosis with current pathological fracture, is for patients who have a current pathologic fracture at the time of an encounter. The codes under M80 identify the site of the fracture. A code from category M80, not a traumatic fracture code, should be used for any patient with known osteoporosis who suffers a fracture, even if the patient had a minor fall or trauma, if that fall or trauma would not usually break a normal, healthy bone.

14. Chapter 14: Diseases of Genitourinary System (N00-N99)

a. Chronic kidney disease

1) Stages of chronic kidney disease (CKD)

The ICD-10-CM classifies CKD based on severity. The severity of CKD is designated by stages I-V. Stage II, code N18.2, equates to mild CKD; stage III, code N18.3, equates to moderate CKD; and stage IV, code N18.4, equates to severe CKD. Code N18.6, End stage renal disease (ESRD), is assigned when the provider has documented end-stage-renal disease (ESRD).

If both a stage of CKD and ESRD are documented, assign code N18.6 only.

2) Chronic kidney disease and kidney transplant status

Patients who have undergone kidney transplant may still have some form of CKD, because the kidney transplant may not fully restore kidney function. Therefore, the presence of CKD alone does not constitute a transplant complication. Assign the appropriate N18 code for the patient's stage of CKD and code Z94.0, Kidney transplant status. If a transplant complication such as failure or rejection is documented, see section I.C.19.g for information on coding complications of a kidney transplant. If the documentation is unclear as to whether the patient has a complication of the transplant, query the provider.

3) Chronic kidney disease with other conditions

Patients with CKD may also suffer from other serious conditions, most commonly diabetes mellitus and hypertension. The sequencing of the CKD code in relationship to codes for other contributing conditions is based on the conventions in the Tabular List.
See I.C.9. Hypertensive chronic kidney disease.
See I.C.19. Chronic kidney disease and kidney transplant complications.

15. Chapter 15: Pregnancy, Childbirth, and the Puerperium (O00-O99)

a. General Rules for Obstetric Cases

1) Codes from chapter 15 and sequencing priority

Obstetric cases require codes from chapter 15, codes in the range O00-O99, Pregnancy, Childbirth, and the Puerperium. Chapter 15 codes have sequencing priority over codes from other chapters. Additional codes from other chapters may be used in conjunction with chapter 15 codes to further specify conditions. Should the provider document that the pregnancy is incidental to the encounter, then code Z33.1, Pregnant state, incidental, should be used in place of any chapter 15 codes. It is the provider's responsibility to state that the condition being treated is not affecting the pregnancy.

2) **Chapter 15 codes used only on the maternal record**

Chapter 15 codes are to be used only on the maternal record, never on the record of the newborn.

3) **Final character for trimester**

The majority of codes in Chapter 15 have a final character indicating the trimester of pregnancy. The timeframes for the trimesters are indicated at the beginning of the chapter. If trimester is not a component of a code it is because the condition always occurs in a specific trimester, or the concept of trimester of pregnancy is not applicable. Certain codes have characters for only certain trimesters because the condition does not occur in all trimesters, but it may occur in more than just one.

4) **Selection of trimester for extended inpatient admissions**

In instances when a patient is admitted to a hospital for complications of pregnancy and remains in the hospital for an extended period of time, it is possible for complications to develop during different trimesters. The antepartum complication code should be assigned on the basis of the trimester when the complication developed.

5) **Unspecified trimester**

Each category that includes codes for trimester has a code for "unspecified trimester." The "unspecified trimester" code should rarely be used, such as when the documentation in the record is insufficient to determine the trimester and it is not possible to obtain clarification.

b. **Selection of OB Principal or First-listed Diagnosis**

1) **Routine outpatient prenatal visits**

For routine outpatient prenatal visits when no complications are present, a code from category Z34, Encounter for supervision of normal pregnancy, should be used as the first-listed diagnosis. These codes should not be used in conjunction with chapter 15 codes.

2) **Prenatal outpatient visits for high-risk patients**

For routine prenatal outpatient visits for patients with high-risk pregnancies, a code from category O09, Supervision of high-risk pregnancy, should be used as the first-listed diagnosis. Secondary chapter 15 codes may be used in conjunction with these codes if appropriate.

3) **Episodes when no delivery occurs**

In episodes when no delivery occurs, the principal diagnosis should correspond to the principal complication of the pregnancy which necessitated the encounter. Should more than one complication exist,

all of which are treated or monitored, any of the complications codes may be sequenced first.

4) **When a delivery occurs**

When a delivery occurs, the principal diagnosis should correspond to the main circumstances or complication of the delivery. In cases of cesarean delivery, the selection of the principal diagnosis should correspond to the reason the cesarean delivery was performed unless the reason for admission/encounter was unrelated to the condition resulting in the cesarean delivery.

5) **Outcome of delivery**

A code from category Z37, Outcome of delivery, should be included on every maternal record when a delivery has occurred. These codes are not to be used on subsequent records or on the newborn record.

c. **Pre-existing conditions versus conditions due to the pregnancy**

Certain categories in Chapter 15 distinguish between conditions of the mother that existed prior to pregnancy (pre-existing) and those that are a direct result of pregnancy. When assigning codes from Chapter 15, it is important to assess if a condition was pre-existing prior to pregnancy or developed during or due to the pregnancy in order to assign the correct code.

Categories that do not distinguish between pre-existing and pregnancy-related conditions may be used for either. It is acceptable to use codes specifically for the puerperium with codes complicating pregnancy and childbirth if a condition arises postpartum during the delivery encounter.

d. **Pre-existing hypertension in pregnancy**

Category O10, Pre-existing hypertension complicating pregnancy, childbirth and the puerperium, includes codes for hypertensive heart and hypertensive chronic kidney disease. When assigning one of the O10 codes that includes hypertensive heart disease or hypertensive chronic kidney disease, it is necessary to add a secondary code from the appropriate hypertension category to specify the type of heart failure or chronic kidney disease.
See Section I.C.9. Hypertension.

e. **Fetal Conditions Affecting the Management of the Mother**

1) **Codes from categories O35 and O36**

Codes from categories O35, Maternal care for known or suspected fetal abnormality and damage, and O36, Maternal care for other fetal problems, are assigned only when the fetal condition is actually responsible for modifying the management of the mother, i.e., by requiring diagnostic studies, additional observation, special care, or termination of pregnancy. The fact that the fetal condition exists does not justify assigning a code from this series to the mother's record.

2) **In utero surgery**

In cases when surgery is performed on the fetus, a diagnosis code from category O35, Maternal care for known or suspected fetal abnormality and damage, should be assigned identifying the fetal condition. Assign the appropriate procedure code for the procedure performed.

No code from Chapter 16, the perinatal codes, should be used on the mother's record to identify fetal conditions. Surgery performed in utero on a fetus is still to be coded as an obstetric encounter.

f. **HIV Infection in Pregnancy, Childbirth and the Puerperium**

During pregnancy, childbirth or the puerperium, a patient admitted because of an HIV-related illness should receive a principal diagnosis from subcategory O98.7-, Human immunodeficiency [HIV] disease complicating pregnancy, childbirth and the puerperium, followed by the code(s) for the HIV-related illness(es).

Patients with asymptomatic HIV infection status admitted during pregnancy, childbirth, or the puerperium should receive codes of O98.7- and Z21, Asymptomatic human immunodeficiency virus [HIV] infection status.

g. **Diabetes mellitus in pregnancy**

Diabetes mellitus is a significant complicating factor in pregnancy. Pregnant women who are diabetic should be assigned a code O24, Diabetes mellitus in pregnancy, childbirth, and the puerperium, first, followed by the appropriate diabetes code(s) (E08-E13) from Chapter 4.

h. **Long term use of insulin**

Code Z79.4, Long-term (current) use of insulin, should also be assigned if the diabetes mellitus is being treated with insulin.

i. **Gestational (pregnancy induced) diabetes**

Gestational (pregnancy induced) diabetes can occur during the second and third trimester of pregnancy in women who were not diabetic prior to pregnancy. Gestational diabetes can cause complications in the pregnancy similar to those of pre-existing diabetes mellitus. It also puts the woman at greater risk of developing diabetes after the pregnancy. Codes for gestational diabetes are in subcategory O24.4, Gestational diabetes mellitus. No other code from category O24, Diabetes mellitus in pregnancy, childbirth, and the puerperium, should be used with a code from O24.4.

The codes under subcategory O24.4 include diet controlled and insulin controlled. If a patient with gestational diabetes is treated with both diet and insulin, only the code for insulin-controlled is required. Code V58.67, Long-term (current) use of insulin, should also be assigned if the gestational diabetes is being treated with insulin.

An abnormal glucose tolerance in pregnancy is assigned a code from subcategory O99.81, Abnormal glucose complicating pregnancy, childbirth, and the puerperium.

j. **Sepsis and septic shock complicating abortion, pregnancy, childbirth and the puerperium**

When assigning a chapter 15 code for sepsis complicating abortion, pregnancy, childbirth, and the puerperium, a code for the specific type of infection should be assigned as an additional diagnosis. If severe sepsis is present, a code from subcategory R65.2, Severe sepsis, and code(s) for associated organ dysfunction(s) should also be assigned as additional diagnoses.

k. **Alcohol and tobacco use during pregnancy, childbirth and the puerperium**

1) **Alcohol use during pregnancy, childbirth and the puerperium**

Codes under subcategory O99.31, Alcohol use complicating pregnancy, childbirth, and the puerperium, should be assigned for any pregnancy case when a mother uses alcohol during the pregnancy or postpartum. A secondary code from category F10, Alcohol related disorders, should also be assigned.

2 **Tobacco use during pregnancy, childbirth and the puerperium**

Codes under subcategory O99.33, Smoking (tobacco) complicating pregnancy, childbirth, and the puerperium, should be assigned for any pregnancy case when a mother uses any type of tobacco product during the pregnancy or postpartum. A secondary code from category F17, Nicotine dependence, or code Z72.0, Tobacco use, should also be assigned.

l. **Poisoning, toxic effects, adverse effects and underdosing in a pregnant patient**

A code from subcategory O9A.2, Injury, poisoning and certain other consequences of external causes complicating pregnancy, childbirth, and the puerperium, should be sequenced first, followed by the appropriate poisoning, toxic effect, adverse effect or underdosing code, and then the additional code(s) that specifies the condition caused by the poisoning, toxic effect, adverse effect or underdosing.
See Section I.C.19. Adverse effects, poisoning, underdosing and toxic effects.

m. **Normal Delivery, Code O80**

1) **Encounter for full term uncomplicated delivery**

Code O80 should be assigned when a woman is admitted for a full-term normal delivery and delivers a single, healthy infant without any complications antepartum, during the delivery, or postpartum during the delivery episode. Code O80 is always a principal diagnosis. It is not to be used if any other code from chapter 15 is needed to describe a current complication of the antenatal, delivery, or perinatal period. Additional codes from other chapters may be used with code O80 if they are not related to or are in any way complicating the pregnancy.

2) **Uncomplicated delivery with resolved antepartum complication**

Code O80 may be used if the patient had a complication at some point during the pregnancy, but the complication is not present at the time of the admission for delivery.

3) **Outcome of delivery for O80**

Z37.0, Single live birth, is the only outcome of delivery code appropriate for use with O80.

n. **The Peripartum and Postpartum Periods**

1) **Peripartum and Postpartum periods**

The postpartum period begins immediately after delivery and continues for six weeks following delivery. The peripartum period is defined as the last month of pregnancy to five months postpartum.

2) **Peripartum and postpartum complication**

A postpartum complication is any complication occurring within the six-week period.

3) **Pregnancy-related complications after 6 week period**

Chapter 15 codes may also be used to describe pregnancy-related complications after the peripartum or postpartum period if the provider document that a condition is pregnancy related.

4) **Admission for routine postpartum care following delivery outside hospital**

When the mother delivers outside the hospital prior to admission and is admitted for routine postpartum care and no complications are noted, code Z39.0, Encounter for care and examination of mother immediately after delivery, should be assigned as the principal diagnosis.

5) **Pregnancy associated cardiomyopathy**

Pregnancy associated cardiomyopathy, code O90.3, is unique in that it may be diagnosed in the third trimester of pregnancy but may continue to progress months after delivery. For this reason, it is referred to as peripartum cardiomyopathy. Code O90.3 is only for use when the cardiomyopathy develops as a result of pregnancy in a woman who did not have pre-existing heart disease.

o. **Code O94, Sequelae of complication pregnancy, childbirth, and the puerperium**

1) **Code O94**

Code O94, Sequelae of complication of pregnancy, childbirth, and the puerperium, is for use in those cases when an initial complication of a pregnancy develops a sequelae requiring care or treatment at a future date.

2) **After the initial postpartum period**

This code may be used at any time after the initial postpartum period.

3) **Sequencing of Code O94**

This code, like all late effect codes, is to be sequenced following the code describing the sequelae of the complication.

p. **Abortions**

1) **Abortion with Liveborn Fetus**

When an attempted termination of pregnancy results in a liveborn fetus assign a code from subcategory O60.1, Preterm labor with preterm delivery, category Z37, Outcome of Delivery. The procedure code for the attempted termination of pregnancy should also be assigned.

2) **Retained Products of Conception following an abortion**

Subsequent encounters for retained products of conception following a spontaneous abortion or elective termination of pregnancy are assigned the appropriate code from category O03, Spontaneous abortion, or code Z33.2, Encounter for elective termination of pregnancy. This advice is appropriate even when the patient was discharged previously with a discharge diagnosis of complete abortion.

16. Chapter 16: Newborn (Perinatal) Guidelines (P00-P96)

For coding and reporting purposes the perinatal period is defined as before birth through the 28th day following birth. The following guidelines are provided for reporting purposes.

a. **General Perinatal Rules**

1) **Use of Chapter 16 Codes**

Codes in this chapter are **never** for use on the maternal record. Codes from Chapter 15, the obstetric chapter, are never permitted on the newborn record. Chapter 16 code may be used throughout the life of the patient if the condition is still present.

2) **Principal Diagnosis for Birth Record**

When coding the birth episode in a newborn record, assign a code from category Z38, Liveborn according to place of birth and type of delivery, as the principal diagnosis. A code from category Z38 is assigned only once, to a newborn at the time of birth. If a newborn is transferred to another institution, a code from category Z38 should not be used at the receiving hospital.

A code from category Z38 is used only on the newborn record, not on the mother's record.

3) **Use of Codes from other Chapters with Codes from Chapter 16**

Codes from other chapters may be used with codes from chapter 16 if the codes from the other chapters provide more specific detail. Codes for signs and symptoms may be assigned when a definitive diagnosis has not been established. If the reason for the encounter is a perinatal condition, the code from chapter 16 should be sequenced first.

4) **Use of Chapter 16 Codes after the Perinatal Period**

Should a condition originate in the perinatal period, and continue throughout the life of the patient, the perinatal code should continue to be used regardless of the patient's age.

5) **Birth process or community acquired conditions**

If a newborn has a condition that may be either due to the birth process or community acquired and the documentation does not indicate which it is, the default is due to the birth process and the code from Chapter 16 should be used. If the condition is community-acquired, a code from Chapter 16 should not be assigned.

6) **Code all clinically significant conditions**

All clinically significant conditions noted on routine newborn examination should be coded. A condition is clinically significant if it requires:

- clinical evaluation; or
- therapeutic treatment; or
- diagnostic procedures; or
- extended length of hospital stay; or
- increased nursing care and/or monitoring; or
- has implications for future health care needs

Note: The perinatal guidelines listed above are the same as the general coding guidelines for "additional diagnoses", except for the final point regarding implications for future health care needs. Codes should be assigned for conditions that have been specified by the provider as having implications for future health care needs.

b. **Observation and Evaluation of Newborns for Suspected Conditions not Found**

Assign a code from categories P00-P04 to identify those instances when a healthy newborn is evaluated for a suspected condition that is determined after study not to be present. Do not use a code from categories P00-P04 when the patient has identified signs or symptoms of a suspected problem; in such cases, code the sign or symptom.

c. **Coding Additional Perinatal Diagnoses**

1) **Assigning codes for conditions that require treatment**

Assign codes for conditions that require treatment or further investigation, prolong the length of stay, or require resource utilization.

2) **Codes for conditions specified as having implications for future health care needs**

Assign codes for conditions that have been specified by the provider as having implications for future health care needs.

Note: This guideline should not be used for adult patients.

d. **Prematurity and Fetal Growth Retardation**

Providers utilize different criteria in determining prematurity. A code for prematurity should not be assigned unless it is documented. Assignment of codes in categories P05, Disorders of newborn related to slow fetal growth and fetal malnutrition, and P07, Disorders of newborn related to short gestation and low birth weight, not elsewhere classified, should be based on the recorded birth weight and estimated gestational age. Codes from category P05 should not be assigned with codes from category P07.

When both birth weight and gestational age are available, two codes from category P07 should be assigned, with the code for birth weight sequenced before the code for gestational age.

e. **Low birth weight and immaturity status**

Codes from subcategory Z91.7, Low birth weight and immaturity status, are for use as personal status codes for a child or adult who was premature or had a low birth weight as a newborn and this is affecting the patient's current health status.
See Section I.C.21. Factors influencing health status and contact with health services, Status.

f. **Bacterial Sepsis of Newborn**

Category P36, Bacterial sepsis of newborn, includes congenital sepsis. If a perinate is documented as having sepsis without documentation of congenital or community acquired, the default is congenital and a code from category P36 should be assigned. If the P36 code includes the causal organism, an additional code from category B95, Streptococcus, Staphylococcus, and Enterococcus as the cause of diseases classified elsewhere, or B96, Other bacterial agents as the cause of diseases classified elsewhere, should not be assigned. If the P36 code does not include the causal organism, assign an additional code from category B96. If applicable, use additional codes to identify severe sepsis (R65.2-) and any associated acute organ dysfunction.

g. **Stillbirth**

Code P95, Stillbirth, is only for use in institutions that maintain separate records for stillbirths. No other code should be used with P95. Code P95 should not be used on the mother's record.

17. Chapter 17: Congenital malformations, deformations, and chromosomal abnormalities (Q00-Q99)

Assign an appropriate code(s) from categories Q00-Q99, Congenital malformations, deformations, and chromosomal abnormalities when a malformation/deformation/or chromosomal abnormality is documented. A malformation/deformation/or chromosomal abnormality may be the principal/first listed diagnosis on a record or a secondary diagnosis.

When a malformation/deformation/or chromosomal abnormality does not have a unique code assignment, assign additional code(s) for any manifestations that may be present.

When the code assignment specifically identifies the malformation/deformation/or chromosomal abnormality, manifestations that are an inherent component of the anomaly should not be coded separately. Additional codes should be assigned for manifestations that are not an inherent component.

Codes from Chapter 17 may be used throughout the life of the patient. If a congenital malformation or deformity has been corrected, a personal history code should be used to identify the history of the malformation or deformity. Although present at birth, malformation/deformation/or chromosomal abnormality may not be identified until later in life. Whenever the condition is diagnosed by the physician, it is appropriate to assign a code from codes Q00-Q99.

For the birth admission, the appropriate code from category Z38, Liveborn infants, according to place of birth and type of delivery, should be sequenced as the principal diagnosis, followed by any congenital anomaly codes, Q00-Q89.

18. Chapter 18: Symptoms, signs, and abnormal clinical and laboratory findings, not elsewhere classified (R00-R99)

Chapter 18 includes symptoms, signs, abnormal results of clinical or other investigative procedures, and ill-defined conditions regarding which no diagnosis classifiable elsewhere is recorded. Signs and symptoms that point rather definitely to a given diagnosis have been assigned to a category in other chapters of the classification.

a. Use of symptom codes

Codes that describe symptoms and signs are acceptable for reporting purposes when a related definitive diagnosis has not been established (confirmed) by the provider.

b. Use of a symptom code with a definitive diagnosis code

Codes for signs and symptoms may be reported in addition to a related definitive diagnosis when the sign or symptom is not routinely associated with that diagnosis, such as the various signs and symptoms associated with complex syndromes. The definitive diagnosis code should be sequenced before the symptom code.

Signs or symptoms that are associated routinely with a disease process should not be assigned as additional codes, unless otherwise instructed by the classification.

c. Combination codes that include symptoms

ICD-10-CM contains a number of combination codes that identify both the definitive diagnosis and common symptoms of that diagnosis. When using one of these combination codes, an additional code should not be assigned for the symptom

d. Repeated falls

Code R29.6, Repeated falls, is for use for encounters when a patient has recently fallen and the reason for the fall is being investigated.

Code Z91.81, History of falling, is for use when a patient has fallen in the past and is at risk for future falls. When

appropriate, both codes R29.6 and Z91.81 may be assigned together.

e. Glasgow coma scale

The Glasgow coma scale codes (R40.2-) can be used in conjunction with traumatic brain injury codes or sequelae of cerebrovascular accident codes. These codes are primarily for use by trauma registries, but they may be used in any setting where this information is collected. The coma scale codes should be sequenced after the diagnosis code.

Three codes, one from each subcategory, are needed to complete the scale. The 7th character indicates when the scale was recorded. The 7th character should match for all three codes.

f. Functional quadriplegia

Functional quadriplegia (code R53.2) is the lack of ability to use one's limbs or to ambulate due to extreme debility. It is not associated with neurologic deficit or injury, and code R53.2 should not be used for cases of neurologic quadriplegia. It should only be assigned if functional quadriplegia is specifically documented in the medical record.

g. SIRS due to Non-Infectious Process

The systemic inflammatory response syndrome (SIRS) can develop as a result of certain non-infectious disease processes, such as trauma, malignant neoplasm, or pancreatitis. When SIRS is documented with a noninfectious condition, and no subsequent infection is documented, the code for the underlying condition, such as an injury, should be assigned, followed by code R65.10, Systemic inflammatory response syndrome (SIRS) of non-infectious origin without acute organ dysfunction, or code R65.11, Systemic inflammatory response syndrome (SIRS) of non-infectious origin with acute organ dysfunction. If an associated acute organ dysfunction is documented, the appropriate code(s) for the specific type of organ dysfunction(s) should be assigned in addition to code R65.11. If acute organ dysfunction is documented, but it cannot be determined if the acute organ dysfunction is associated with SIRS or due to another condition (e.g., directly due to the trauma), the provider should be queried.

h. Death NOS

Code R99, Ill-defined and unknown cause of mortality, is only for use in the very limited circumstance when a patient who has already died is brought into an emergency department or other healthcare facility and is pronounced dead upon arrival. It does not represent the discharge disposition of death.

19. Chapter 19: Injury, poisoning, and certain other consequences of external causes (S00-T88)

a. Code Extensions

Most categories in chapter 19 have 7th character extensions that are required for each applicable code. Most categories in this chapter have three extensions (with the exception of fractures): A, initial encounter, D, subsequent encounter and S, sequela.

Extension "A", initial encounter is used while the patient is receiving active treatment for the injury. Examples of active treatment are: surgical treatment, emergency department encounter, and evaluation and treatment by a new physician.

Extension "D" subsequent encounter is used for encounters after the patient has received active treatment of the injury and is receiving routine care for the injury during the healing or recovery phase. Examples of subsequent care are: cast change or removal, removal of external of internal fixation device, medication adjustment, other aftercare and follow up visits following injury treatment.

The aftercare Z codes should not be used for aftercare for injuries. For aftercare of an injury, assign the acute injury code with the 7th character "D" (subsequent encounter).

Extension "S", sequela, is for use for complications or conditions that arise as a direct result of an injury, such as scar formation after a burn. The scars are sequelae of the burn. When using extension "S", it is necessary to use both the injury code that precipitated the sequela and the code for the sequela itself. The "S" is added only to the injury code, not the sequela code. The "S" extension identifies the injury responsible for the sequela. The specific type of sequela (e.g. scar) is sequenced first, followed by the injury code.

b. Coding of Injuries

When coding injuries, assign separate codes for each injury unless a combination code is provided, in which case the combination code is assigned. Multiple injury codes are provided in ICD-10-CM, but should not be assigned unless information for a more specific code is not available. These codes (S00-T14.9) are not to be used for normal, healing surgical wounds or to identify complications of surgical wounds.

The code for the most serious injury, as determined by the provider and the focus of treatment, is sequenced first.

1) Superficial injuries

Superficial injuries such as abrasions or contusions are not coded when associated with more severe injuries of the same site.

2) Primary injury with damage to nerves/blood vessels

When a primary injury results in minor damage to peripheral nerves or blood vessels, the primary injury is sequenced first with additional code(s) for injuries to nerves and spinal cord (such as category S04), and/or injury to blood vessels (such as category S15). When the primary injury is to the blood vessels or nerves, that injury should be sequenced first.

c. Coding of Traumatic Fractures

The principles of multiple coding of injuries should be followed in coding fractures. Fractures of specified sites are coded individually by site in accordance with both the

provisions within categories S02, S12, S22, S32, S42, S52, S62, S72, S82, S92 and the level of detail furnished by medical record content.

A fracture not indicated as open or closed should be coded to closed. A fracture not indicated whether displaced or not displaced should be coded to displaced.

More specific guidelines are as follows:

1) Initial vs. Subsequent Encounter for Fractures

Traumatic fractures are coded using the appropriate 7th character extension for initial encounter (A, B, C) while the patient is receiving active treatment for the fracture. Examples of active treatment are: surgical treatment, emergency department encounter, and evaluation and treatment by a new physician.

Fractures are coded using the appropriate 7th character extension for subsequent care for encounters after the patient has completed active treatment of the fracture and is receiving routine care for the fracture during the healing or recovery phase. Examples of fracture aftercare are: cast change or removal, removal of external or internal fixation device, medication adjustment, and follow up visits following fracture treatment.

Care for complications of surgical treatment for fracture repairs during the healing or recovery phase should be coded with the appropriate complication codes.

Care of complications of fractures, such as malunion and nonunion, should be reported with the appropriate 7th character extensions for subsequent care with nonunion (K, M, N,) or subsequent care with malunion (P, Q, R).

A code from category M80, not a traumatic fracture code, should be used for any patient with known osteoporosis who suffers a fracture.
See Section I.C.13. Osteoporosis.

The aftercare Z codes should not be used for aftercare for injuries. For aftercare of an injury, assign the acute injury code with the 7th character "D" (subsequent encounter).

2) Multiple fractures sequencing

Multiple fractures are sequenced in accordance with the severity of the fracture. The provider should be asked to list the fracture diagnoses in the order of severity.

d. Coding of Burns and Corrosions

The ICD-10-CM distinguishes between burns and corrosions. The burn codes are for thermal burns, except sunburns, that come from a heat source, such as a fire or hot appliance. The burn codes are also for burns resulting from electricity and radiation. Corrosions are burns due to chemicals. The guidelines are the same for burns and corrosions.

Current burns (T20-T25) are classified by depth, extent and by agent (X code). Burns are classified by depth as first degree (erythema), second degree (blistering), and third degree (full-thickness involvement). Burns of the eye and internal organs (T26-T28) are classified by site, but not by degree.

1) **Sequencing of burn and related condition codes**

Sequence first the code that reflects the highest degree of burn when more than one burn is present.

a. When the reason for the admission or encounter is for treatment of external multiple burns, sequence first the code that reflects the burn of the highest degree.

b. When a patient has both internal and external burns, the circumstances of admission govern the selection of the principal diagnosis or first-listed diagnosis.

c. When a patient is admitted for burn injuries and other related conditions such as smoke inhalation and/or respiratory failure, the circumstances of admission govern the selection of the principal or first-listed diagnosis.

2) **Burns of the same local site**

Classify burns of the same local site (three-digit category level, T20-T28) but of different degrees to the subcategory identifying the highest degree recorded in the diagnosis.

3) **Non-healing burns**

Non-healing burns are coded as acute burns.

Necrosis of burned skin should be coded as a non-healed burn.

4) **Infected Burn**

For any documented infected burn site, use an additional code for the infection.

5) **Assign separate codes for each burn site**

When coding burns, assign separate codes for each burn site. Category T30, Burn and corrosion, body region unspecified is extremely vague and should rarely be used.

6) **Burns and Corrosions Classified According to Extent of Body Surface Involved**

Assign codes from category T31, Burns classified according to extent of body surface involved, or T32, Corrosions classified according to extent of body surface involved, when the site of the burn is not specified or when there is a need for additional data. It is advisable to use category T31 as additional coding when needed to provide data for evaluating burn mortality, such as that needed by burn units. It is also advisable to use category T31 as an additional code for reporting purposes when there is mention of a third-degree burn involving 20 percent or more of the body surface.

Categories T31 and T32 are based on the classic "rule of nines" in estimating body surface involved: head and neck are assigned nine percent, each arm nine

percent, each leg 18 percent, the anterior trunk 18 percent, posterior trunk 18 percent, and genitalia one percent. Providers may change these percentage assignments where necessary to accommodate infants and children who have proportionately larger heads than adults, and patients who have large buttocks, thighs, or abdomen that involve burns.

7) **Encounters for treatment of late effects of burns**

Encounters for the treatment of the late effects of burns or corrosions (i.e., scars or joint contractures) should be coded with a burn or corrosion code with the 7th character "S" or sequela.

8) **Sequelae with a late effect code and current burn**

When appropriate, both a code for a current burn or corrosion with 7th character extension "A" or "D" and a burn or corrosion code with extension "S" may be assigned on the same record (when both a current burn and sequelae of an old burn exist). Burns and corrosions do not heal at the same rate and a current healing wound may still exist with sequela of a healed burn or corrosion.

9) **Use of an external cause code with burns and corrosions**

An external cause code should be used with burns and corrosions to identify the source and intent of the burn, as well as the place where it occurred.

e. **Adverse Effects, Poisoning, Underdosing and Toxic Effects**

Codes in categories T36-T65 are combination codes that include the substances related to adverse effects, poisonings, toxic effects and underdosing, as well as the external cause. No additional external cause code is required for poisonings, toxic effects, adverse effects and underdosing codes.

A code from categories T36-T65 is sequenced first, followed by the code(s) that specify the nature of the adverse effect, poisoning, or toxic effect.

1) **Do not code directly from the Table of Drugs**

Do not code directly from the Table of Drugs and Chemicals. Always refer back to the Tabular List.

2) **Use as many codes as necessary to describe**

Use as many codes as necessary to describe completely all drugs, medicinal or biological substances.

3) **If the same code would describe the causative agent**

If the same code would describe the causative agent for more than one adverse reaction, poisoning, toxic effect or underdosing, assign the code only once.

4) **If two or more drugs, medicinal or biological substances**

If two or more drugs, medicinal or biological substances are reported, code each individually unless the combination code is listed in the Table of Drugs and Chemicals.

5) **The occurrence of drug toxicity is classified in ICD-10-CM as follows:**

(a) **Adverse Effect**

Assign the appropriate code for adverse effect (for example, T36.0x5-) when the drug was correctly prescribed and properly administered. Use additional code(s) for all manifestations of adverse effects. Examples of manifestations are tachycardia, delirium, gastrointestinal hemorrhaging, vomiting, hypokalemia, hepatitis, renal failure, or respiratory failure.

(b) **Poisoning**

When coding a poisoning or reaction to the improper use of a medication (e.g., overdose, wrong substance given or taken in error, wrong route of administration), assign the appropriate code from categories T36-T50. Poisoning codes have an associated intent: accidental, intentional self-harm, assault and undetermined. Use additional code(s) for all manifestations of poisonings.

If there is also a diagnosis of drug abuse or dependence to the substance, the abuse or dependence is coded as an additional code.

Examples of poisoning include:

(i) Error was made in drug prescription

Errors made in drug prescription or in the administration of the drug by provider, nurse, patient, or other person.

(ii) Overdose of a drug intentionally taken

If an overdose of a drug was intentionally taken or administered and resulted in drug toxicity, it would be coded as a poisoning.

(iii) Nonprescribed drug taken with correctly prescribed and properly administered drug

If a nonprescribed drug or medicinal agent was taken in combination with a correctly prescribed and properly administered drug, any drug toxicity or other reaction resulting from the 7 interaction of the two drugs would be classified as a poisoning.

(iv) Interaction of drug(s) and alcohol

When a reaction results from the interaction of a drug(s) and alcohol, this would be classified as poisoning.

See Section I.C.4. if poisoning is the result of insulin pump malfunctions.

(c) **Underdosing**

Underdosing refers to taking less of a medication than is prescribed by a physician or a manufacturer's instruction. For underdosing, assign the code from categories T36-T50.

Noncompliance (Z91.12-, Z91.13-) or complication of care (Y63.61, Y63.8-Y63.9) codes are to be used with an underdosing code to indicate intent, if known.

(d) **Toxic Effects**

When a harmful substance is ingested or comes in contact with a person, this is classified as a toxic effect. The toxic effect codes are in categories T51-T65.

Toxic effect codes have an associated intent: accidental, intentional self-harm, assault and undetermined.

f. **Adult and child abuse, neglect and other maltreatment**

Sequence first the appropriate code from categories T74.- or T76.- for abuse, neglect and other maltreatment, followed by any accompanying mental health or injury code(s).

If the documentation in the medical record states abuse or neglect it is coded as confirmed. It is coded as suspected if it is documented as suspected.

For cases of confirmed abuse or neglect an external cause code from the assault section (X92-Y08) should be added to identify the cause of any physical injuries. A perpetrator code (Y07) should be added when the perpetrator of the abuse is known. For suspected cases of abuse or neglect, do not report external cause or perpetrator code.

If a suspected case of abuse, neglect or mistreatment is ruled out during an encounter code Z04.71, Suspected adult physical and sexual abuse, ruled out, or code Z04.72, Suspected child physical and sexual abuse, ruled out, should be used, not a code from T76.

g. **Complications of care**

1) **Complications of care**

(a) **Documentation of complications of care**

As with all procedural or postprocedural complications, code assignment is based on the provider's documentation of the relationship between the condition and the procedure.

2) **Pain due to medical devices**

Pain associated with devices, implants or grafts left in a surgical site (for example painful hip prosthesis) is assigned to the appropriate code(s) found in Chapter 19, Injury, poisoning, and certain other consequences of external causes. Specific codes for pain due to medical devices are found in the T code section of the ICD-10-CM. Use additional code(s) from category G89 to identify acute or chronic pain due to presence of the device, implant or graft (G89.18 or G89.28).

3) **Transplant complications**

(a) **Transplant complications other than kidney**

Codes under category T86, Complications of transplanted organs and tissues, are for use for both complications and rejection of transplanted organs.

A transplant complication code is only assigned if the complication affects the function of the transplanted organ. Two codes are required to fully describe a transplant complication, the appropriate code from category T86 and a secondary code that identifies the complication.

Pre-existing conditions or conditions that develop after the transplant are not coded as complications unless they affect the function of the transplanted organs.

(b) Chronic kidney disease and kidney transplant complications

Patients who have undergone kidney transplant may still have some form of chronic kidney disease (CKD) because the kidney transplant may not fully restore kidney function. Code T86.1- should be assigned for documented complications of a kidney transplant, such as transplant failure or rejection or other transplant complication. Code T86.1- should not be assigned for post kidney transplant patients who have chronic kidney (CKD) unless a transplant complication such as transplant failure or rejection is documented. If the documentation is unclear as to whether the patient has a complication of the transplant, query the provider.

For patients with CKD following a kidney transplant, but who do not have a complication such as failure or rejection, see *section I.C.14. Chronic kidney disease and kidney transplant status*.

4) **Complication codes that include the external cause**

As with certain other T codes, some of the complications of care codes have the external cause included in the code. The code includes the nature of the complication as well as the type of procedure that caused the complication. No external cause code indicating the type of procedure is necessary for these codes.

5) **Complications of care codes within the body system chapters**

Intraoperative and postprocedural complication codes are found within the body system chapters with codes specific to the organs and structures of that body system. These codes should be sequenced first, followed by a code(s) for the specific complication, if applicable.

20. Chapter 20: External Causes of Morbidity (V01-Y95)

Introduction: These guidelines are provided for the reporting of external causes of morbidity codes in order that there will be standardization in the process. These codes are secondary codes for use in any health care setting. External cause codes are not required for reporting to some third-party payers, for example, CMS.

External cause codes are intended to provide data for injury research and evaluation of injury prevention strategies. These codes

capture how the injury or health condition happened (cause), the intent (unintentional or accidental; or intentional, such as suicide or assault), the place where the event occurred and the activity of the patient at the time of the event.

a. General External Cause Coding Guidelines

1) **Used with any code in the range of A00.0-T88.9, Z00-Z99**

An external cause code may be used with any code in the range of A00.0-T88.9, Z00-Z99, classification that is a health condition due to an external cause. Though they are most applicable to injuries, they are also valid for use with such things as infections or diseases due to an external source, and other health conditions, such as a heart attack that occurs during strenuous physical activity.

2) **External cause code used for length of treatment**

Assign the external cause code, with the appropriate 7th character (initial encounter, subsequent encounter or sequela) for each encounter for which the injury or condition is being treated.

3) **Use the full range of external cause codes**

Use the full range of external cause codes to completely describe the cause, the intent, the place of occurrence, if applicable, and the activity of the patient at the time of the event, for all injuries, and other health conditions due to an external cause.

4) **Assign as many external cause codes as necessary**

Assign as many external cause codes as necessary to fully explain each cause. If only one external code can be recorded, assign the code most related to the principal diagnosis.

5) **The selection of the appropriate external cause code**

The selection of the appropriate external cause code is guided by the Index to External Causes, which is located after the Alphabetical Index to diseases and by Inclusion and Exclusion notes in the Tabular List.

6) **External cause code can never be a principal diagnosis**

An external cause code can never be a principal (first listed) diagnosis.

7) **Combination external cause codes**

Certain of the external cause codes are combination codes that identify sequential events that result in an injury, such as a fall which results in striking against an object. The injury may be due to either event or both. The combination external cause code used should correspond to the sequence of events regardless of which caused the most serious injury.

8) **No external cause code needed in certain circumstances**

No external cause code from Chapter 20 is needed if the external cause and intent are included in a code from another chapter (e.g. T360x1- Poisoning by penicillins, accidental (unintentional)).

b. Place of Occurrence Guideline

Codes from category Y92, Place of occurrence of the external cause, are secondary codes for use after other external cause codes to identify the location of the patient at the time of injury or other condition.

A place of occurrence code is used only once, at the initial encounter for treatment. No 7th characters are used for Y92. Only one code from Y92 should be recorded on a medical record. A place of occurrence code should be used in conjunction with an activity code, Y93.

Use place of occurrence code Y92.9 if the place is not stated or is not applicable.

c. Activity Code

Codes from category Y93, Activity code, are secondary codes for use with other external cause codes to identify the activity of the patient at the time of the injury.

An activity code is used only once, at the initial encounter for treatment. Only one code from Y93 should be recorded on a medical record. An activity code should be used in conjunction with a place of occurrence code, Y92.

If a patient is a student but is injured while performing an activity for income, use 7th character "2", work related activity.

A work related activity is any activity for which payment or income is received.

Use activity code Y93.9 if the activity of the patient is not stated or is not applicable.

d. Place of Occurrence and Activity Code Used with other External Cause Code

When applicable, a place of occurrence and an activity code are sequenced after the main external cause code(s). Regardless of the number of external cause codes assigned there should be only one place of occurrence code and one activity code assigned to an encounter.

e. If the Reporting Format Limits the Number of External Cause Codes

If the reporting format limits the number of external cause codes that can be used in reporting clinical data, code the one most related to the principal diagnosis.

f. Multiple External Cause Coding Guidelines

If two or more events cause separate injuries, an external cause code should be assigned for each cause. The first listed external cause code will be selected in the following order:

External cause codes for child and adult abuse take priority over all other external cause codes.
See Section I.C.19. Child and Adult abuse guidelines.

External cause codes for terrorism events take priority over all other E codes except child and adult abuse

External cause codes for cataclysmic events take priority over all other E codes except child and adult abuse and terrorism.

External cause codes for transport accidents take priority over all other external cause codes except cataclysmic events and child and adult abuse and terrorism.

The first-listed external cause code should correspond to the cause of the most serious diagnosis due to an assault, accident, or self-harm, following the order of hierarchy listed above.

g. Child and Adult Abuse Guideline

Adult and child abuse, neglect and maltreatment are classified as assault. Any of the assault codes may be used to indicate the external cause of any injury resulting from the confirmed abuse.

For confirmed cases of abuse, neglect and maltreatment, when the perpetrator is known, a code from Y07, Perpetrator of maltreatment and neglect, should accompany any other assault codes.
See Section I.C.19. Adult and child abuse, neglect and other maltreatment

h. Unknown or Undetermined Intent Guideline

If the intent (accident, self-harm, assault) of the cause of an injury or other condition is unknown or unspecified, code the intent as accidental intent. All transport accident categories assume accidental intent.

1) **Use of undetermined intent**

   External cause codes for events of undetermined intent are only for use if the documentation in the record specifies that the intent cannot be determined.

i. Late Effects of External Cause Guidelines

1) **Late effect external cause codes**

   Late effects are reported using the external cause code with the 7th character extension "S" for sequela. These codes should be used with any report of a late effect or sequela resulting from a previous injury.

2) **Late effect external cause code with a related current injury**

   A late effect external cause code should never be used with a related current nature of injury code.

3) **Use of late effect external cause codes for subsequent visits**

   Use a late effect external cause code for subsequent visits when a late effect of the initial injury is being treated. Do not use a late effect external cause code for subsequent visits for follow-up care (e.g., to assess healing, to receive rehabilitative therapy) of the injury or poisoning when no late effect of the injury has been documented.

j. Terrorism Guidelines

1) **Cause of injury identified by the Federal Government (FBI) as terrorism**

   When the cause of an injury is identified by the Federal Government (FBI) as terrorism, the first-listed external cause code should be a code from category Y38, Terrorism. The definition of terrorism employed by the FBI is found at the inclusion note at the beginning of category Y38. Use additional code for place of occurrence (Y92.-). More than one Y38 code may be assigned if the injury is the result of more than one mechanism of terrorism.

2) Cause of an injury is suspected to be the result of terrorism

When the cause of an injury is suspected to be the result of terrorism a code from category Y38 should not be assigned. Suspected cases should be classified as assault.

3) Code Y38.9, Terrorism, secondary effects

Assign code Y38.9, Terrorism, secondary effects, for conditions occurring subsequent to the terrorist event. This code should not be assigned for conditions that are due to the initial terrorist act.

It is acceptable to assign code Y38.9 with another code from Y38 if there is an injury due to the initial terrorist event and an injury that is a subsequent result of the terrorist event.

21. Chapter 21: Factors influencing health status and contact with health services (Z00-Z99)

Note: The chapter specific guidelines provide additional information about the use of Z codes for specified encounters.

a. Use of Z codes in any healthcare setting

Z codes are for use in any healthcare setting. Z codes may be used as either a first listed (principal diagnosis code in the inpatient setting) or secondary code, depending on the circumstances of the encounter. Certain z codes may only be used as first listed or principal diagnosis.

b. Z Codes indicate a reason for an encounter

Z codes are not procedure codes. A corresponding procedure code must accompany a Z code to describe the procedure performed.

c. Categories of Z Codes

1) Contact/Exposure

Category Z20 indicates contact with, or exposure to, communicable diseases. These codes are for patients who do not show any sign or symptom of a disease but have been exposed to it by close personal contact with an infected individual or are in an area where a disease is epidemic. These codes may be used as a first listed code to explain an encounter for testing, or, more commonly, as a secondary code to identify a potential risk.

2) Inoculations and vaccinations

Code Z23 is for encounters for inoculations and vaccinations. It indicates that a patient is being seen to receive a prophylactic inoculation against a disease. Procedure codes are required to identify the actual administration of the injection and the type(s) of immunizations given. Code Z23 may be used as a secondary code if the inoculation is given as a routine part of preventive health care, such as a well-baby visit.

3) Status

Status codes indicate that a patient is either a carrier of a disease or has the sequelae or residual of a past disease or condition. This includes such things as the presence of prosthetic or mechanical devices resulting from past treatment. A status code is informative, because the status may affect the course of treatment and its outcome. A status code is distinct from a history code. The history code indicates that the patient no longer has the condition.

A status code should not be used with a diagnosis code from one of the body system chapters, if the diagnosis code includes the information provided by the status code. For example, code Z94.1, Heart transplant status, should not be used with a code from subcategory T86.2, Complications of heart transplant. The status code does not provide additional information. The complication code indicates that the patient is a heart transplant patient.

For encounters for weaning from a mechanical ventilator, assign code J96.1, Chronic respiratory failure, followed by code Z99.11, Dependence on respirator [ventilator] status.

The status Z codes/categories are:

Z14   Genetic carrier

Genetic carrier status indicates that a person carries a gene, associated with a particular disease, which may be passed to offspring who may develop that disease. The person does not have the disease and is not at risk of developing the disease.

Z15   Genetic susceptibility to disease

Genetic susceptibility indicates that a person has a gene that increases the risk of that person developing the disease.

Codes from category Z15 should not be used as principal or first-listed codes. If the patient has the condition to which he/she is susceptible, and that condition is the reason for the encounter, the code for the current condition should be sequenced first. If the patient is being seen for follow-up after completed treatment for this condition, and the condition no longer exists, a follow-up code should be sequenced first, followed by the appropriate personal history and genetic susceptibility codes. If the purpose of the encounter is genetic counseling associated with procreative management, code Z31.5, Encounter for genetic counseling, should be assigned as the first-listed code, followed by a code from category Z15. Additional codes should be assigned for any applicable family or personal history.

Z16   Infection with drug-resistant microorganisms

This code indicates that a patient has an infection that is resistant to drug treatment. Sequence the infection code first.

Z17 Estrogen receptor status

Z21 Asymptomatic HIV infection status

This code indicates that a patient has tested positive for HIV but has manifested no signs or symptoms of the disease.

Z22 Carrier of infectious disease

Carrier status indicates that a person harbors the specific organisms of a disease without manifest symptoms and is capable of transmitting the infection.

Z33.1 Pregnant state, incidental

This code is a secondary code only for use when the pregnancy is in no way complicating the reason for visit. Otherwise, a code from the obstetric chapter is required.

Z66 Do not resuscitate

Z67 Blood type

Z68 Body mass index (BMI)

Z74.01 Bed confinement status

Z76.82 Awaiting organ transplant status

Z79 Long-term (current) drug therapy

Codes from this category indicate a patient's continuous use of a prescribed drug (including such things as aspirin therapy) for the long-term treatment of a condition or for prophylactic use. It is not for use for patients who have addictions to drugs. This subcategory is not for use of medications for detoxification or maintenance programs to prevent withdrawal symptoms in patients with drug dependence (e.g., methadone maintenance for opiate dependence). Assign the appropriate code for the drug dependence instead.

Assign a code from Z79 if the patient is receiving a medication for an extended period as a prophylactic measure (such as for the prevention of deep vein thrombosis) or as treatment of a chronic condition (such as arthritis) or a disease requiring a lengthy course of treatment (such as cancer). Do not assign a code from category Z79 for medication being administered for a brief period of time to treat an acute illness or injury (such as a course of antibiotics to treat acute bronchitis).

Z88 Allergy status to drugs, medicaments and biological substances

Except: Z88.9, Allergy status to unspecified drugs, medicaments and biological substances status

Z89 Acquired absence of limb

Z90 Acquired absence of organs, not elsewhere classified

Z91.0- Allergy status, other than to drugs and biological substances

Z91.7- Low birth weight and immaturity status

Z93 Artificial opening status

Z94 Transplanted organ and tissue status

Z95 Presence of cardiac and vascular implants and grafts

Z96 Presence of other functional implants

Z97 Presence of other devices

Z98 Other postprocedural states

Z99 Dependence on enabling machines and devices, not elsewhere classified

Note: Categories Z89-Z90 and Z93-Z99 are for use only if there are no complications or malfunctions of the organ or tissue replaced, the amputation site or the equipment on which the patient is dependent.

4) **History (of)**

There are two types of history Z codes, personal and family. Personal history codes explain a patient's past medical condition that no longer exists and is not receiving any treatment, but that has the potential for recurrence, and therefore may require continued monitoring.

Family history codes are for use when a patient has a family member(s) who has had a particular disease that causes the patient to be at higher risk of also contracting the disease.

Personal history codes may be used in conjunction with follow-up codes and family history codes may be used in conjunction with screening codes to explain the need for a test or procedure. History codes are also acceptable on any medical record regardless of the reason for visit. A history of an illness, even if no longer present, is important information that may alter the type of treatment ordered.

The history Z code categories are:

Z61.81- Personal history of abuse in childhood

Z80 Family history of primary malignant neoplasm

Z81 Family history of mental and behavioral disorders

Z82 Family history of certain disabilities and chronic diseases (leading to disablement)

Z83 Family history of other specific disorders

Z84	Family history of other conditions
Z85	Personal history of primary and secondary malignant neoplasm
Z86	Personal history of certain other diseases
Z87	Personal history of other diseases and conditions
Z91.4-	Personal history of psychological trauma, not elsewhere classified
Z91.5	Personal history of self-harm
Z91.6-	Personal history of other physical trauma
Z91.8-	Other specified personal risk factors, not elsewhere classified
Z92	Personal history of medical treatment Except: Z92.0 Personal history of contraception

5) **Screening**

Screening is the testing for disease or disease precursors in seemingly well individuals so that early detection and treatment can be provided for those who test positive for the disease (e.g., screening mammogram).

The testing of a person to rule out or confirm a suspected diagnosis because the patient has some sign or symptom is a diagnostic examination, not a screening. In these cases, the sign or symptom is used to explain the reason for the test.

A screening code may be a first listed code if the reason for the visit is specifically the screening exam. It may also be used as an additional code if the screening is done during an office visit for other health problems. A screening code is not necessary if the screening is inherent to a routine examination, such as a pap smear done during a routine pelvic examination.

Should a condition be discovered during the screening then the code for the condition may be assigned as an additional diagnosis.

The Z code indicates that a screening exam is planned. A procedure code is required to confirm that the screening was performed.

The screening Z codes/categories:

Z11	Encounter for screening for infectious and parasitic diseases
Z12	Encounter for screening for malignant neoplasms
Z13	Encounter for screening for other diseases and disorders Except: Z13.9, Encounter for screening, unspecified
Z36	Encounter for antenatal screening for mother

6) **Observation**

There are two observation Z code categories. They are for use in very limited circumstances when a

person is being observed for a suspected condition that is ruled out. The observation codes are not for use if an injury or illness or any signs or symptoms related to the suspected condition are present. In such cases the diagnosis/symptom code is used with the corresponding external cause code.

The observation codes are to be used as principal diagnosis only. Additional codes may be used in addition to the observation code but only if they are unrelated to the suspected condition being observed.

The observation Z code categories:

Z03	Encounter for medical observation for suspected diseases and conditions ruled out
Z04	Encounter for examination and observation for other reasons Except: Z04.9, Encounter for examination and observation for unspecified reason

Aftercare

Aftercare visit codes cover situations when the initial treatment of a disease has been performed and the patient requires continued care during the healing or recovery phase, or for the long-term consequences of the disease. The aftercare Z code should not be used if treatment is directed at a current, acute disease. The diagnosis code is to be used in these cases.

The aftercare Z codes should also not be used for aftercare for injuries. For aftercare of an injury, assign the acute injury code with the 7th character "D" (subsequent encounter). Exceptions to this rule are codes Z51.0, Encounter for antineoplastic radiation therapy, and codes from subcategory Z51.1, Encounter for antineoplastic chemotherapy and immunotherapy. These codes are to be first listed, followed by the diagnosis code when a patient's encounter is solely to receive radiation therapy or chemotherapy for the treatment of a neoplasm. If the reason for the encounter is more than one type of antineoplastic therapy, code Z51.0 and a code from subcategory Z51.1 may be assigned together, in which case one of these codes would be reported as a secondary diagnosis.

The aftercare codes are generally first listed to explain the specific reason for the encounter. An aftercare code may be used as an additional code when some type of aftercare is provided in addition to the reason for admission and no diagnosis code is applicable. An example of this would be the closure of a colostomy during an encounter for treatment of another condition.

Aftercare codes should be used in conjunction with any other aftercare codes or other diagnosis codes to provide better detail on the specifics of an aftercare encounter visit, unless otherwise directed by the classification. Should a patient receive multiple types of antineoplastic therapy during the same encounter, code Z51.0, Encounter for antineoplastic radiation therapy, and codes from subcategory Z51.1, Encounter for antineoplastic chemotherapy and immunotherapy, may be used together on a record. The sequencing of multiple aftercare codes is discretionary.

Certain aftercare Z code categories need a secondary diagnosis code to describe the resolving condition or sequelae, for others, the condition is inherent in the code title.

Additional Z code aftercare category terms include fitting and adjustment, and attention to artificial openings.

Status Z codes may be used with aftercare Z codes to indicate the nature of the aftercare. For example code Z95.1, Presence of aortocoronary bypass graft, may be used with code Z48.812, Encounter for surgical aftercare following surgery on the circulatory system, to indicate the surgery for which the aftercare is being performed. A status code should not be used when the aftercare code indicates the type of status, such as using Z43.0, Encounter for attention to tracheostomy, with Z93.0, Tracheostomy status.

The aftercare Z category/codes:

Z43	Encounter for attention to artificial openings
Z44	Encounter for fitting and adjustment of external prosthetic device
Z45	Encounter for adjustment and management of implanted device
Z46	Encounter for fitting and adjustment of other devices
Z47	Orthopedic aftercare
Z48	Encounter for other postprocedural aftercare
Z49	Encounter for care involving renal dialysis
Z51	Encounter for other aftercare

7) **Follow-up**

The follow-up codes are used to explain continuing surveillance following completed treatment of a disease, condition, or injury. They imply that the condition has been fully treated and no longer exists. They should not be confused with aftercare codes, or injury codes with 7th character "D," that explain ongoing care of a healing condition or its sequelae. Follow-up codes may be used in conjunction with history codes to provide the full picture of the healed condition and its treatment. The follow-up code is sequenced first, followed by the history code.

A follow-up code may be used to explain repeated visits. Should a condition be found to have recurred on the follow-up visit, then the code for the condition should be assigned as an additional diagnosis.

The follow-up Z code categories:

Z08	Encounter for follow-up examination after completed treatment for malignant neoplasm
Z09	Encounter for follow-up examination after completed treatment for conditions other than malignant neoplasm
Z39	Encounter for maternal postpartum care and examination

8) **Donor**

Codes in category Z52, Donors of organs and tissues, are used for living individuals who are donating blood or other body tissue. These codes are only for individuals donating for others, not for self donations. They are not for use to identify cadaveric donations.

9) **Counseling**

Counseling Z codes are used when a patient or family member receives assistance in the aftermath of an illness or injury, or when support is required in coping with family or social problems. They are not necessary for use in conjunction with a diagnosis code when the counseling component of care is considered integral to standard treatment.

The counseling Z codes/categories:

Z30.0-	Encounter for general counseling and advice on contraception
Z31.5	Encounter for genetic counseling
Z31.6-	Encounter for general counseling and advice on procreation
Z32.2	Encounter for childbirth instruction
Z32.3	Encounter for childcare instruction
Z69	Encounter for mental health services for victim and perpetrator of abuse
Z70	Counseling related to sexual attitude, behavior and orientation
Z71	Persons encountering health services for other counseling and medical advice, not elsewhere classified
Z76.81	Expectant mother prebirth pediatrician visit

10) **Encounters for Obstetrical and Reproductive Services**

See Section I.C.15. Pregnancy, Childbirth, and the Puerperium, for further instruction on the use of these codes.

Z codes for pregnancy are for use in those circumstances when none of the problems or complications included in the codes from the Obstetrics chapter exist (a routine prenatal visit or postpartum care). Codes in category Z34, Encounter for supervision of normal pregnancy, are always first listed and are not to be used with any other code from the OB chapter.

The outcome of delivery, category Z37, should be included on all maternal delivery records. It is always a secondary code. Codes in category Z37 should not be used on the newborn record.

Z codes for family planning (contraceptive) or procreative management and counseling should be included on an obstetric record either during the pregnancy or the postpartum stage, if applicable.

Z codes/categories for obstetrical and reproductive services:

Z30	Encounter for contraceptive management
Z31	Encounter for procreative management
Z32.2	Encounter for childbirth instruction
Z32.3	Encounter for childcare instruction
Z33	Pregnant state
Z34	Encounter for supervision of normal pregnancy
Z36	Encounter for antenatal screening of mother
Z37	Outcome of delivery
Z39	Encounter for maternal postpartum care and examination
Z76.81	Expectant mother prebirth pediatrician visit

11) Newborns and Infants

See Section I.C.16. Newborn (Perinatal) Guidelines, for further instruction on the use of these codes.

Newborn Z codes/categories:

Z00.1-	Encounter for routine child health examination
Z38	Liveborn infants according to place of birth and type of delivery
Z76.1	Encounter for health supervision and care of foundling

12) Routine and administrative examinations

The Z codes allow for the description of encounters for routine examinations, such as, a general check-up, or, examinations for administrative purposes, such as, a pre-employment physical. The codes are not to be used if the examination is for diagnosis of a suspected condition or for treatment purposes. In such cases the diagnosis code is used. During a routine exam, should a diagnosis or condition be discovered, it should be coded as an additional code. Pre-existing and chronic conditions and history codes may also be included as additional codes as long as the examination is for administrative purposes and not focused on any particular condition.

Some of the codes for routine health examinations distinguish between "with" and "without" abnormal findings. Code assignment depends on the information that is known at the time the encounter is being coded. For example, if no abnormal findings were found during the examination, but the encounter is being coded before test results are back,

it is acceptable to assign the code for "without abnormal findings." When assigning a code for "with abnormal findings," additional code(s) should be assigned to identify the specific abnormal finding(s).

Pre-operative examination Z codes are for use only in those situations when a patient is being cleared for surgery and no treatment is given.

The Z codes/categories for routine and administrative examinations:

Z00	Encounter for general examination without complaint, suspected or reported diagnosis
Z01	Encounter for other special examination without complaint, suspected or reported diagnosis
Z02	Encounter for administrative examination Except: Z02.9, Encounter for administrative examinations, unspecified
Z32.0-	Encounter for pregnancy test

13) Miscellaneous Z codes

The miscellaneous Z codes capture a number of other health care encounters that do not fall into one of the other categories. Certain of these codes identify the reason for the encounter; others are for use as additional codes that provide useful information on circumstances that may affect a patient's care and treatment.

Prophylactic Organ Removal

For encounters specifically for prophylactic removal of an organ (such as prophylactic removal of breasts due to a genetic susceptibility to cancer or a family history of cancer), the principal or first listed code should be a code from category Z40, Encounter for prophylactic surgery, followed by the appropriate codes to identify the associated risk factor (such as genetic susceptibility or family history).

If the patient has a malignancy of one site and is having prophylactic removal at another site to prevent either a new primary malignancy or metastatic disease, a code for the malignancy should also be assigned in addition to a code from subcategory Z40.0, Encounter for prophylactic surgery for risk factors related to malignant neoplasms. A Z40.0 code should not be assigned if the patient is having organ removal for treatment of a malignancy, such as the removal of the testes for the treatment of prostate cancer.

Miscellaneous Z codes/categories:

Z28	Immunization not carried out
Z40	Encounter for prophylactic surgery
Z41	Encounter for procedures for purposes other than remedying health state Except: Z41.9, Encounter for procedure for purposes other than remedying health state, unspecified

Z53   Persons encountering health services for specific procedures and treatment, not carried out

Z55   Problems related to education and literacy

Z56   Problems related to employment and unemployment

Z57   Occupational exposure to risk factors

Z58   Problems related to physical environment

Z59   Problems related to housing and economic circumstances

Z60   Problems related to social environment

Z61   Problems related to negative life events in childhood
        Except: Z61.81-, Personal history of abuse in childhood

Z62   Other problems related to upbringing

Z63   Other problems related to primary support group, including family circumstances

Z64   Problems related to certain psychosocial circumstances

Z65   Problems related to other psychosocial circumstances

Z72   Problems related to lifestyle

Z73   Problems related to life management difficulty

Z74   Problems related to care provider dependency
        Except: Z74.01, Bed confinement status

Z75   Problems related to medical facilities and other health care

Z76.0   Encounter for issue of repeat prescription

Z76.3   Healthy person accompanying sick person

Z76.4   Other boarder to healthcare facility

Z76.5   Malingerer [conscious simulation]

Z76.89 Persons encountering health services in other specified circumstances

Z91.1- Patient's noncompliance with medical treatment and regimen

Z91.89 Other specified personal risk factors, not elsewhere classified

14) Nonspecific Z codes

Certain Z codes are so non-specific, or potentially redundant with other codes in the classification, that there can be little justification for their use in the inpatient setting. Their use in the outpatient setting should be limited to those instances when there is no further documentation to permit more precise coding. Otherwise, any sign or symptom or any other reason for visit that is captured in another code should be used.

Nonspecific Z codes/categories:

Z02.9   Encounter for administrative examinations, unspecified

Z04.9   Encounter for examination and observation for unspecified reason

Z13.9   Encounter for screening, unspecified

Z41.9   Encounter for procedure for purposes other than remedying health state, unspecified

Z52.9   Donor of unspecified organ or tissue

Z88.9   Allergy status to unspecified drugs, medicaments and biological substances status

Z92.0   Personal history of contraception

15) Z Codes That May Only be Principal/First-Listed Diagnosis

The following Z codes/categories may only be reported as the principal/first-listed diagnosis, except when there are multiple encounters on the same day and the medical records for the encounters are combined:

Z00   Encounter for general examination without complaint, suspected or reported diagnosis

Z01   Encounter for other special examination without complaint, suspected or reported diagnosis

Z02   Encounter for administrative examination

Z03   Encounter for medical observation for suspected diseases and conditions ruled out

Z33.2   Encounter for elective termination of pregnancy

Z31.81 Encounter for male factor infertility in female patient

Z31.82 Encounter for Rh incompatibility status

Z31.83 Encounter for assisted reproductive fertility procedure cycle

Z34   Encounter for supervision of normal pregnancy

Z38   Liveborn infants according to place of birth and type of delivery

Z39   Encounter for maternal postpartum care and examination

Z51.0   Encounter for antineoplastic radiation therapy

Z51.1- Encounter for antineoplastic chemotherapy and immunotherapy

Z52   Donors of organs and tissues
        Except: Z52.9, Donor of unspecified organ or tissue

Z76.1   Encounter for health supervision and care of foundling

Z76.2   Encounter for health supervision and care of other healthy infant and child

Z99.12   Encounter for respirator [ventilator] dependence during power failure

SECTION II. SELECTION OF PRINCIPAL DIAGNOSIS

The circumstances of inpatient admission always govern the selection of principal diagnosis. The principal diagnosis is defined in the Uniform Hospital Discharge Data Set (UHDDS) as "that condition established after study to be chiefly responsible for occasioning the admission of the patient to the hospital for care."

The UHDDS definitions are used by hospitals to report inpatient data elements in a standardized manner. These data elements and their definitions can be found in the July 31, 1985, Federal Register (Vol. 50, No, 147), pp. 31038-40.

Since that time the application of the UHDDS definitions has been expanded to include all non-outpatient settings (acute care, short term, long term care and psychiatric hospitals; home health agencies; rehab facilities; nursing homes, etc).

In determining principal diagnosis the coding conventions in the ICD-10-CM, Volumes I and II take precedence over these official coding guidelines.
(See Section I.A., Conventions for the ICD-10-CM)

The importance of consistent, complete documentation in the medical record cannot be overemphasized. Without such documentation the application of all coding guidelines is a difficult, if not impossible, task.

A.   Codes for symptoms, signs, and ill-defined conditions

Codes for symptoms, signs, and ill-defined conditions from Chapter 18 are not to be used as principal diagnosis when a related definitive diagnosis has been established.

B.   Two or more interrelated conditions, each potentially meeting the definition for principal diagnosis.

When there are two or more interrelated conditions (such as diseases in the same ICD-10-CM chapter or manifestations characteristically associated with a certain disease) potentially meeting the definition of principal diagnosis, either condition may be sequenced first, unless the circumstances of the admission, the therapy provided, the Tabular List, or the Alphabetic Index indicate otherwise.

C.   Two or more diagnoses that equally meet the definition for principal diagnosis

In the unusual instance when two or more diagnoses equally meet the criteria for principal diagnosis as determined by the circumstances of admission, diagnostic workup and/or therapy provided, and the Alphabetic Index, Tabular List, or another coding guidelines does not provide sequencing direction, any one of the diagnoses may be sequenced first.

D.   Two or more comparative or contrasting conditions.

In those rare instances when two or more contrasting or comparative diagnoses are documented as "either/or" (or similar terminology), they are coded as if the diagnoses were confirmed and the diagnoses are sequenced according to the circumstances of the admission. If no further determination can be made as to which diagnosis should be principal, either diagnosis may be sequenced first.

E.   A symptom(s) followed by contrasting/comparative diagnoses

When a symptom(s) is followed by contrasting/comparative diagnoses, the symptom code is sequenced first. All the contrasting/comparative diagnoses should be coded as additional diagnoses.

F.   Original treatment plan not carried out

Sequence as the principal diagnosis the condition, which after study occasioned the admission to the hospital, even though treatment may not have been carried out due to unforeseen circumstances.

G.   Complications of surgery and other medical care

When the admission is for treatment of a complication resulting from surgery or other medical care, the complication code is sequenced as the principal diagnosis. If the complication is classified to the T80-T88 series and the code lacks the necessary specificity in describing the complication, an additional code for the specific complication should be assigned.

H.   Uncertain Diagnosis

If the diagnosis documented at the time of discharge is qualified as "probable", "suspected", "likely", "questionable", "possible", or "still to be ruled out", or other similar terms indicating uncertainty, code the condition as if it existed or was established. The bases for these guidelines are the diagnostic workup, arrangements for further workup or observation, and initial therapeutic approach that correspond most closely with the established diagnosis.

Note: This guideline is applicable only to inpatient admissions to short-term, acute, long-term care and psychiatric hospitals.

I.   Admission from Observation Unit

1)   **Admission Following Medical Observation**

When a patient is admitted to an observation unit for a medical condition, which either worsens or does not improve, and is subsequently admitted as an inpatient of the same hospital for this same medical condition, the principal diagnosis would be the medical condition which led to the hospital admission.

2)   **Admission Following Post-Operative Observation**

When a patient is admitted to an observation unit to monitor a condition (or complication) that develops following outpatient surgery, and then is subsequently admitted as an inpatient of the same hospital, hospitals should apply the Uniform Hospital Discharge Data Set (UHDDS) definition of principal diagnosis as "that condition established after study to be chiefly responsible for occasioning the admission of the patient to the hospital for care."

J. Admission from Outpatient Surgery

When a patient receives surgery in the hospital's outpatient surgery department and is subsequently admitted for continuing inpatient care at the same hospital, the following guidelines should be followed in selecting the principal diagnosis for the inpatient admission:

- If the reason for the inpatient admission is a complication, assign the complication as the principal diagnosis.

- If no complication, or other condition, is documented as the reason for the inpatient admission, assign the reason for the outpatient surgery as the principal diagnosis.

- If the reason for the inpatient admission is another condition unrelated to the surgery, assign the unrelated condition as the principal diagnosis.

SECTION III. REPORTING ADDITIONAL DIAGNOSES

GENERAL RULES FOR OTHER (ADDITIONAL) DIAGNOSES

For reporting purposes the definition for "other diagnoses" is interpreted as additional conditions that affect patient care in terms of requiring:

> clinical evaluation; or
>
> therapeutic treatment; or
>
> diagnostic procedures; or
>
> extended length of hospital stay; or
>
> increased nursing care and/or monitoring.

The UHDDS item #11-b defines Other Diagnoses as "all conditions that coexist at the time of admission, that develop subsequently, or that affect the treatment received and/or the length of stay. Diagnoses that relate to an earlier episode which have no bearing on the current hospital stay are to be excluded." UHDDS definitions apply to inpatients in acute care, short-term, long term care and psychiatric hospital setting. The UHDDS definitions are used by acute care short-term hospitals to report inpatient data elements in a standardized manner. These data elements and their definitions can be found in the July 31, 1985, *Federal Register* (Vol. 50, No, 147), pp. 31038-40.

Since that time the application of the UHDDS definitions has been expanded to include all non-outpatient settings (acute care, short term, long term care and psychiatric hospitals; home health agencies; rehab facilities; nursing homes, etc).

The following guidelines are to be applied in designating "other diagnoses" when neither the Alphabetic Index nor the Tabular List in ICD-10-CM provide direction. The listing of the diagnoses in the patient record is the responsibility of the attending provider.

A. Previous conditions

If the provider has included a diagnosis in the final diagnostic statement, such as the discharge summary or the face sheet, it should ordinarily be coded. Some providers include in the diagnostic statement resolved conditions or diagnoses and status-post procedures from previous admission that have no bearing on the current stay. Such conditions are not to be reported and are coded only if required by hospital policy.

However, history codes (categories Z80-Z87) may be used as secondary codes if the historical condition or family history has an impact on current care or influences treatment.

B. Abnormal findings

Abnormal findings (laboratory, x-ray, pathologic, and other diagnostic results) are not coded and reported unless the provider indicates their clinical significance. If the findings are outside the normal range and the attending provider has ordered other tests to evaluate the condition or prescribed treatment, it is appropriate to ask the provider whether the abnormal finding should be added.

Please note: This differs from the coding practices in the outpatient setting for coding encounters for diagnostic tests that have been interpreted by a provider.

C. Uncertain Diagnosis

If the diagnosis documented at the time of discharge is qualified as "probable", "suspected", "likely", "questionable", "possible", or "still to be ruled out" or other similar terms indicating uncertainty, code the condition as if it existed or was established. The bases for these guidelines are the diagnostic workup, arrangements for further workup or observation, and initial therapeutic approach that correspond most closely with the established diagnosis.

Note: This guideline is applicable only to inpatient admissions to short-term, acute, long-term care and psychiatric hospitals.

SECTION IV. DIAGNOSTIC CODING AND REPORTING GUIDELINES FOR OUTPATIENT SERVICES

These coding guidelines for outpatient diagnoses have been approved for use by hospitals/ providers in coding and reporting hospital-based outpatient services and provider-based office visits.

Information about the use of certain abbreviations, punctuation, symbols, and other conventions used in the ICD-10-CM Tabular List (code numbers and titles), can be found in Section IA of these guidelines, under "Conventions Used in the Tabular List." Information about the correct sequence to use in finding a code is also described in Section I.

The terms encounter and visit are often used interchangeably in describing outpatient service contacts and, therefore, appear together in these guidelines without distinguishing one from the other.

Though the conventions and general guidelines apply to all settings, coding guidelines for outpatient and provider reporting of diagnoses will vary in a number of instances from those for inpatient diagnoses, recognizing that:

The Uniform Hospital Discharge Data Set (UHDDS) definition of principal diagnosis applies only to inpatients in acute, short-term, long-term care and psychiatric hospitals.

Coding guidelines for inconclusive diagnoses (probable, suspected, rule out, etc.) were developed for inpatient reporting and do not apply to outpatients.

A. Selection of first-listed condition

In the outpatient setting, the term first-listed diagnosis is used in lieu of principal diagnosis.

In determining the first-listed diagnosis the coding conventions of ICD-10-CM, as well as the general and disease specific guidelines take precedence over the outpatient guidelines.

Diagnoses often are not established at the time of the initial encounter/visit. It may take two or more visits before the diagnosis is confirmed.

The most critical rule involves beginning the search for the correct code assignment through the Alphabetic Index. Never begin searching initially in the Tabular List as this will lead to coding errors.

1. Outpatient Surgery

When a patient presents for outpatient surgery (same day surgery), code the reason for the surgery as the first-listed diagnosis (reason for the encounter), even if the surgery is not performed due to a contraindication.

2. Observation Stay

When a patient is admitted for observation for a medical condition, assign a code for the medical condition as the first-listed diagnosis.

When a patient presents for outpatient surgery and develops complications requiring admission to observation, code the reason for the surgery as the first reported diagnosis (reason for the encounter), followed by codes for the complications as secondary diagnoses.

B. Codes from A00.0 through T88.9, Z00-Z99

The appropriate code(s) from A00.0 through T88.9, Z00-Z99 must be used to identify diagnoses, symptoms, conditions, problems, complaints, or other reason(s) for the encounter/visit.

C. Accurate reporting of ICD-10-CM diagnosis codes

For accurate reporting of ICD-10-CM diagnosis codes, the documentation should describe the patient's condition, using terminology which includes specific diagnoses as well as symptoms, problems, or reasons for the encounter. There are ICD-10-CM codes to describe all of these.

D. Codes that describe symptoms and signs

Codes that describe symptoms and signs, as opposed to diagnoses, are acceptable for reporting purposes when a diagnosis has not been established (confirmed) by the provider. Chapter 18 of ICD-10-CM, Symptoms, Signs, and Abnormal Clinical and Laboratory Findings Not Elsewhere Classified (codes R00-R99) contain many, but not all codes for symptoms.

E. Encounters for circumstances other than a disease or injury

ICD-10-CM provides codes to deal with encounters for circumstances other than a disease or injury. The Factors Influencing Health Status and Contact with Health Services codes (Z00-99) is provided to deal with occasions when circumstances other than a disease or injury are recorded as diagnosis or problems.
See Section I.C.21. Factors influencing health status and contact with health services.

F. Level of Detail in Coding

1. ICD-10-CM codes with 3, 4, or 5 digits

ICD-10-CM is composed of codes with either 3, 4, 5, 6 or 7 digits. Codes with three digits are included in ICD-10-CM as the heading of a category of codes that may be further subdivided by the use of fourth fifth digits, sixth or seventh digits which provide greater specificity.

2. Use of full number of digits required for a code

A three-digit code is to be used only if it is not further subdivided. A code is invalid if it has not been coded to the full number of characters required for that code, including the 7th character extension, if applicable.

G. ICD-10-CM code for the diagnosis, condition, problem, or other reason for encounter/visit

List first the ICD-10-CM code for the diagnosis, condition, problem, or other reason for encounter/visit shown in the medical record to be chiefly responsible for the services provided. List additional codes that describe any coexisting conditions. In some cases the first-listed diagnosis may be a symptom when a diagnosis has not been established (confirmed) by the physician.

H. Uncertain diagnosis

Do not code diagnoses documented as "probable," "suspected," "questionable," "rule out," or "working diagnosis" or other similar terms indicating uncertainty. Rather, code the condition(s) to the highest degree of certainty for that encounter/visit, such as symptoms, signs, abnormal test results, or other reason for the visit.

Please note: This differs from the coding practices used by short-term, acute care, long-term care and psychiatric hospitals.

I. Chronic diseases

Chronic diseases treated on an ongoing basis may be coded and reported as many times as the patient receives treatment and care for the condition(s)

J. Code all documented conditions that coexist

Code all documented conditions that coexist at the time of the encounter/visit, and require or affect patient care treatment or management. Do not code conditions that were previously treated and no longer exist. However, history codes (categories Z80-Z87) may be used as secondary codes if the historical condition or family history has an impact on current care or influences treatment.

K. Patients receiving diagnostic services only

For patients receiving diagnostic services only during an encounter/visit, sequence first the diagnosis, condition, problem, or other reason for encounter/visit shown in the medical record to be chiefly responsible for the outpatient services provided during the encounter/visit. Codes for other diagnoses (e.g., chronic conditions) may be sequenced as additional diagnoses.

For encounters for routine laboratory/radiology testing in the absence of any signs, symptoms, or associated diagnosis, assign Z01.89, Encounter for other specified special examinations. If routine testing is performed during the same encounter as a test to evaluate a sign, symptom, or diagnosis, it is appropriate to assign both the V code and the code describing the reason for the non-routine test.

For outpatient encounters for diagnostic tests that have been interpreted by a physician, and the final report is available at the time of coding, code any confirmed or definitive diagnosis(es) documented in the interpretation. Do not code related signs and symptoms as additional diagnoses.

Please note: This differs from the coding practice in the hospital inpatient setting regarding abnormal findings on test results.

L. Patients receiving therapeutic services only

For patients receiving therapeutic services only during an encounter/visit, sequence first the diagnosis, condition, problem, or other reason for encounter/visit shown in the medical record to be chiefly responsible for the outpatient services provided during the encounter/visit. Codes for other diagnoses (e.g., chronic conditions) may be sequenced as additional diagnoses.

The only exception to this rule is that when the primary reason for the admission/encounter is chemotherapy or radiation therapy, the appropriate Z code for the service is listed first, and the diagnosis or problem for which the service is being performed listed second.

M. Patients receiving preoperative evaluations only

For patients receiving preoperative evaluations only, sequence first a code from subcategory Z01.81, Encounter for pre-procedural examinations, to describe the pre-op consultations. Assign a code for the condition to describe the reason for the surgery as an additional diagnosis. Code also any findings related to the pre-op evaluation.

N. Ambulatory surgery

For ambulatory surgery, code the diagnosis for which the surgery was performed. If the postoperative diagnosis is known to be different from the preoperative diagnosis at the time the diagnosis is confirmed, select the postoperative diagnosis for coding, since it is the most definitive.

O. Routine outpatient prenatal visits

See Section I.C.15. Routine outpatient prenatal visits.

P. Encounters for general medical examinations with abnormal findings

The subcategories for encounters for general medical examinations, Z00.0-, provide codes for with and without abnormal findings. Should a general medical examination result in an abnormal finding, the code for general medical examination with abnormal finding should be assigned as the first listed diagnosis. A secondary code for the abnormal finding should also be coded.

Q. Encounters for routine health screenings

See Section I.C.21. Factors influencing health status and contact with health services, Screening

Appendix B: ICD-10-PCS Draft Coding Guidelines

These are the current draft ICD-10-PCS guidelines. They are grouped into categories, including general guidelines and guidelines that apply to a section or sections. Guidelines for the Medical and Surgical section are further grouped by character. The guidelines are numbered sequentially within each category.

A. General

A.1. It is not possible to construct a procedure code from the alphabetic index. The purpose of the alphabetic index is to locate the appropriate table that contains all information necessary to construct a procedure code.

A.2. The ICD-10-PCS tables and the definitions that accompany them, the body part key, and the draft guidelines contain the complete information for correct coding. While the index contains a hierarchical lookup for finding a table and supplemental procedure terms that refer the user to the corresponding root operation options, the index does not contain exclusive coding instruction unavailable elsewhere. The user is not required to consult the index before proceeding to the tables to complete the code. The user may choose a valid code directly from the tables.

A.3. All seven characters must contain valid values to be a valid procedure code. If the documentation is incomplete for coding purposes, the physician should be queried for the necessary information.

A.4. The columns in the Tables contain the values for characters four through seven. The rows delineate the valid combinations of values. Any combination of values not contained in a single row of the Tables is invalid.

A.5. "And," when used in a code description, means "and/or."

Example: Lower Arm and Wrist Muscle means lower arm and/or wrist muscle.

B. MEDICAL AND SURGICAL SECTION (SECTION 0)

Body system guidelines

B2.1. Body systems contain body-part values that include contiguous body parts. These general body-part values are used:

a. When a procedure is performed on the general body part as a whole.

b. When the specific body part cannot be determined.

c. In the root operations *Change, Removal* and *Revision*, when the specific body-part value is not in the table.

Example: Esophagus is a general body-part value; *Esophagus, Upper* is a specific body-part value.

B2.2. Three body systems contain body-part values that represent general anatomical regions, upper extremity anatomical regions, and lower extremity anatomical regions respectively. These body-part values are used when a procedure is performed on body layers that span more than one body system.

Example: Debridement of skin, muscle, and bone at a procedure site is coded to the anatomical regions body systems.

Exception: Composite tissue transfers are coded to the specific body systems (*Muscles or Subcutaneous Tissue and Fascia*). In these body systems, qualifiers delineate the body layers involved.

B2.3. Body systems designated as upper or lower contain body parts located above or below the diaphragm respectively.

Example: Upper Veins body parts are above the diaphragm; *Lower Veins* body parts are below the diaphragm.

Root operation guidelines

B3.1. In order to determine the appropriate root operation, the full definition of the root operation as contained in the Tables must be applied.

B3.2. Components of a procedure necessary to complete the objective of the procedure specified in the root operation are considered integral to the procedure and are not coded separately.

Example: Resection of a joint is integral to joint replacement.

Multiple procedures

B3.3. During the same operative episode, multiple procedures are coded if:

a. The same root operation is performed on different body parts as defined by distinct values of the body-part character.

    Example: Diagnostic excision of liver and pancreas are coded separately.

b. The same root operation is repeated at different body sites that are included in the same body-part value.

    Example: Excision of the sartorius muscle and excision of the gracilis muscle are both included in the *Upper Leg Muscle* body-part value, and multiple procedures are coded. Destruction of separate skin body sites on the face are all included in the body-part value *Skin, Face*, and multiple procedures are coded.

c. Multiple root operations with distinct objectives are performed on the same body part.

Example: Destruction of sigmoid lesion and bypass of sigmoid colon are coded separately.

d. The intended root operation is attempted using one approach, but is converted to a different approach.

Example: Laparoscopic cholecystectomy converted to an open cholecystectomy is coded as *Endoscopic Inspection* and *Open Resection*.

Discontinued procedures

B3.4. If the intended procedure is discontinued, code the procedure to the root operation performed. If a procedure is discontinued before any other root operation is performed, code the root operation Inspection of the body part or anatomical region inspected.

Example: Ureteroscopy with unsuccessful extirpation of ureteral stone is coded to Inspection of ureter.

Bypass

B3.5. Bypass procedures are coded according to the direction of flow of the contents of a tubular body part: the body-part value identifies the origin of the bypass and the qualifier identifies the destination of the bypass.

Example: Bypass from stomach to jejunum, *Stomach* (origin) is the body part and *Jejunum* (destination) is the qualifier.

Note: Coronary arteries are coded differently. The body-part value identifies the number of coronary artery sites bypassed. The qualifier identifies the origin of the bypass.

B3.6. If multiple coronary artery sites are bypassed, a separate procedure is coded for each coronary artery site that uses a different device and/or qualifier.

Example: Aortocoronary artery bypass and internal mammary coronary artery bypass are coded separately.

Control

B3.7. If an attempt to stop postprocedural bleeding is unsuccessful and requires performing *Bypass, Detachment, Excision, Extraction, Reposition, Replacement,* or *Resection* to stop the bleeding, then that root operation is coded instead of *Control.*

Example: Resection of spleen to stop postprocedural bleeding is coded to *Resection* instead of *Control.*

Diagnostic excision

B3.8. If a diagnostic excision (biopsy) is followed by a therapeutic excision at the same procedure site, or by resection of the body part during the same operative episode, code only the therapeutic excision or resection.

Example: Biopsy of breast followed by partial mastectomy at the same procedure site, only the partial mastectomy procedure is coded.

Excision vs. resection

B3.9. *Resection* is coded whenever "all of a body part" is cut out or off without replacement. "All of a body part" includes any anatomical

subdivision that has its own body part value. Therefore, *Resection* of a specific anatomical subdivision body part is coded whenever possible, rather than *Excision* of the less specific body part.

Example: Left upper lung lobectomy is coded to *Resection* of upper lung lobe, left and not to *Excision* of lung, left.

Inspection

B3.10. Inspection of a body part(s) integral to the performance of the procedure is not coded separately.

Example: Fiberoptic bronchoscopy with irrigation of bronchus, only the irrigation procedure is coded.

B3.11. If multiple body parts are inspected, the body-part character is defined as the general body-part value that identifies the entire area inspected. If no general body-part value is provided, the body-part character is defined as the most distal body part inspected.

Example: Laparoscopy of pelvic organs is coded to the *pelvic region* body-part value. Cystoureteroscopy with inspection of bladder and ureters is coded to the *Ureter* body-part value.

B3.12. When both an *Inspection* procedure and another procedure are performed on the same body part during the same episode, if the *Inspection* procedure is performed using a different approach than the other procedure, the *Inspection* procedure is coded separately.

Example: Percutaneous endoscopic inspection of the small intestine during a procedure in which open excision of the duodenum is performed is coded separately.

Division and release

B3.13. If the sole objective of the procedure is separating a nontubular body part, the root operation is *Division.* If the sole objective of the procedure is freeing a body part without cutting the body part, the root operation is *Release.*

B3.14. In the root operation *Release,* the body-part value coded is the body part being freed and not the tissue being manipulated or cut to free the body part.

Example: Lysis of intestinal adhesions is coded to one of the intestine body-part values.

Fusion of vertebral joints

B3.15. If multiple vertebral joints included in the same body-part value are fused, a separate procedure is coded for each joint that uses a different device and/or qualifier. Joints between two areas of the spine (e.g., cervicothoracic vertebral joint) have their own body-part values and are coded separately.

Example: Fusion of C-4/5 with fixation device and C-5/6 with bone graft are coded separately. Fusion of the C-5/6 joint and the C7-T1 joint are coded separately.

Fracture treatment

B3.16. Reduction of a displaced fracture is coded to the root operation *Reposition.* Treatment of a nondisplaced fracture is coded to the procedure performed.

Example: Putting a pin in a nondisplaced fracture is coded to the root operation *Insertion*. Casting of a nondisplaced fracture is coded to the root operation *Immobilization* in the Placement section.

Transplantation

B3.17. Putting in a mature and functioning living body part taken from another individual or animal is coded to the root operation *Transplantation*. Putting in autologous or nonautologous cells is coded to the Administration section.

Example: Putting in autologous or nonautologous bone marrow, pancreatic islet cells or stem cells is coded to the Administration section.

Body part guidelines

B4.1. If a procedure is performed on a portion of a body part that does not have a separate body-part value, code the body-part value corresponding to the whole body part.

Example: A procedure performed on the alveolar process of the mandible is coded to the *Mandible* body part.

B4.2. If the prefix "peri" is used with a body part to identify the site of the procedure, the body-part value is defined as the body part named.

Example: A procedure site identified as perirenal is coded to the *Kidney* body part.

B4.3. If the procedure documentation uses a body part to further specify the site of the procedure, the body-part value is defined as the body part on which the procedure is performed.

Example: A procedure site identified as the prostatic urethra is coded to the *Urethra* body part.

Coronary arteries

B4.4. The coronary arteries are classified as a single body part. They are further specified by number of sites treated, not by name or number of arteries. Separate body-part values are provided to indicate the number of sites treated when the same procedure is performed on multiple sites in the coronary arteries.

Example: Two dilations with stents of a coronary artery are coded as dilation of *Coronary Artery, Two Sites*, with intraluminal device. Two dilations, one with stent and one without, are coded separately as dilation of *Coronary Artery, One Site*, with intraluminal device, and dilation of *Coronary Artery, One Site*, with no device.

Bilateral body-part values

B4.5. Bilateral body-part values are available for a limited number of body parts. They are included in the system on the basis of frequency and common practice. If the identical procedure is performed on contralateral body parts, and a bilateral body-part value exists for that body part, a single procedure is coded using the bilateral body-part value. If no bilateral body-part value exists, code each procedure separately using the appropriate body-part value.

Example: The identical procedure performed on both fallopian tubes is coded once using the body-part value *Fallopian Tube, Bilateral*. The identical procedure performed on both knee joints is

coded twice using the body-part values *Knee Joint, Right* and *Knee Joint, Left*.

Body parts near a joint

B4.6. Procedures performed on tendons, ligaments, bursae and fascia supporting a joint are coded to the body part that is the focus of the procedure, in the respective body system. Procedures performed on joint structures are coded to the body part in the joint body systems.

Example: Repair of the anterior cruciate ligament of the knee is coded to the *Knee* body part in the *Bursae and Ligaments* body system. Shoulder arthroscopy with shaving of articular cartilage is coded to the *Shoulder Joint* body part.

B4.7. In body systems containing skin, subcutaneous tissue, muscle, and tendon body-part values, where a specific body-part value does not exist for the area surrounding a joint, the corresponding body part is coded as follows:

- Shoulder is coded to *Upper Arm*
- Elbow is coded to *Lower Arm*
- Wrist is coded to *Lower Arm*
- Hip is coded to *Upper Leg*
- Knee is coded to *Lower Leg*
- Ankle is coded to *Foot*

Fingers and toes

B4.8. If a body system does not contain a separate body-part value for fingers, procedures performed on the fingers are coded to the body-part value for the hand. If a body system does not contain a separate body-part value for toes, procedures performed on the toes are coded to the body-part value for the foot.

Example: Excision of finger muscle is coded to the *Hand Muscle* body-part value.

Humerus

B4.9. Procedures performed on the distal (elbow) end of the humerus are coded to the *Humeral Shaft* body-part value.

Skin glands and ducts

B4.10. Procedures performed on skin and breast glands and ducts are coded to body-part values in the body system *Skin* and *Breast*.

Forequarter and hindquarter

B4.11. In the anatomical regions body system containing lower extremities body parts, the body-part value *Forequarter* describes the entire upper limb plus the scapula and clavicle, and the body-part value *Hindquarter* describes the entire lower limb including all of the pelvic girdle and the buttock.

Nerves and vessels

B4.12. Nerves and vessels that are not identified by a separate body-part value are coded to the closest proximal branch identified by a body-part value.

Example: A procedure performed on the mandibular branch of the trigeminal nerve is coded to the *Trigeminal Nerve* body-part value.

Approach guidelines

Endoscopic assistance

B5.1. Procedures performed using the open approach with percutaneous endoscopic assistance are coded to approach value 0, *Open*.

Example: Laparoscopic-assisted sigmoidectomy is coded to approach value 0, *Open*.

B5.2. Procedures performed via natural or artificial opening with percutaneous endoscopic assistance are coded to approach value F, *Via Natural or Artificial Opening with Percutaneous Endoscopic Assistance*.

Example: Laparoscopic-assisted vaginal hysterectomy (LAVH) is coded to approach value F, *Via Natural or Artificial Opening with Percutaneous Endoscopic Assistance*.

External approach

B5.3a. Procedures performed within an orifice on structures that are visible without the aid of any instrumentation are coded to approach value X, *External*.

Example: Resection of tonsils is coded to approach value X, *External*.

B5.3b. Procedures performed indirectly by the application of external force through the intervening body layers are coded to approach value X, *External*.

Example: Closed reduction of fracture is coded to approach value X, *External*.

Indwelling device

B5.4a. Procedures performed via indwelling devices are coded to approach value 3, *Percutaneous*.

Example: Fragmentation of kidney stone performed via percutaneous nephrostomy is coded to approach value 3, *Percutaneous*.

B5.4b. Procedures performed on a device, as defined in the root operations *Change, Irrigation, Removal and Revision*, are coded to the procedure performed.

Example: Irrigation of percutaneous nephrostomy tube is coded to the root operation *Irrigation of Indwelling Device* in the Administration section.

Device guidelines

B6.1. A device is coded only if a device remains after the procedure is completed. If no device remains, the device value *No Device* is coded.

B6.2. Materials such as sutures, ligatures, radiological markers and temporary post-operative wound drains are considered integral to the performance of a procedure and are not coded as devices.

B6.3. A separate procedure to put in a drainage device is coded to the root operation *Drainage* with the device value *Drainage Device*.

B6.4. If, as part of a procedure, an autograft is obtained from a different body part, a separate procedure is coded.

Example: Coronary bypass with excision of saphenous vein graft, excision of saphenous vein is coded separately.

C. OTHER MEDICAL AND SURGICAL-RELATED SECTIONS (SECTIONS 1–9)

C.1. The Obstetrics section includes only the procedures performed on the products of conception. Procedures performed on the pregnant female, other than the products of conception, are coded to a root operation in the Medical and Surgical section.

Example: Episiotomy is coded to a root operation in the Medical and Surgical section.

Glossary

A/S, A.S., or AS. See Administrative simplification.

AAPCC. Adjusted average per capita cost.

Abstractor. A person who selects and extracts specific data from the medical record and enters the information into computer files.

Accredited record technician (ART). A former certification describing medical records practitioners; now known as a registered health information technician (RHIT).

Accredited Standards Committee (ASC). An organization that has been accredited by ANSI for the development of American national standards.

Add-on codes. A procedure performed in addition to the primary procedure and designated with a + in the CPT book. Add-on codes are never reported for stand-alone services but are reported secondarily in addition to the primary procedure.

Adjudication (claims). The completion of a processed claim that results in a payment, rejection, or denial.

Administrative code sets. Code sets that characterize a general business situation, rather than a medical condition or service. Under HIPAA, these are sometimes referred to as nonclinical or nonmedical code sets. Compare with medical code sets.

Administrative simplification (A/S). Title II, subtitle of HIPAA, which gives HHS the authority to mandate the use of standards for the electronic exchange of health care data; to specify what medical and administrative code sets should be used within those standards; to require the use of national identification systems for health care patients, providers, payers (or plans), and employers (or sponsors); and to specify the types of measures required to protect the security and privacy of personally identifiable health care information. This is also the name of Title II, subtitle F, part C of HIPAA.

AHA. See American Hospital Association.

AHIMA. See American Health Information Management Association.

AMA. See American Medical Association.

Amendments and corrections. In the final privacy rule, an amendment to a record would indicate that the data are in dispute while retaining the original information, while a correction to a record would alter or replace the original record.

American Academy of Professional Coders (AAPC). A national organization for coders and billers offering certification based upon physician- or facility-specific guidelines.

American Health Information Management Association (AHIMA). An association of health information management professionals. AHIMA sponsors some HIPAA educational seminars.

American Hospital Association (AHA). A health care industry association that represents the concerns of institutional providers. The AHA hosts the NUBC, which has a formal consultative role under HIPAA.

American Hospital Association (AHA) Central Office. The central office of the AHA works in partnership with the National Center for Health Statistics (NCHS), American Health Information Management Association (AHIMA), and Centers for Medicare and Medicaid Services (CMS) to maintain the integrity of and develop education regarding the ICD-9-CM coding system.

American Medical Association (AMA). A professional organization for physicians. The AMA is the secretariat of the NUCC, which has a formal consultative role under HIPAA. The AMA also maintains the Physician's Current Procedural Terminology (CPT) coding system.

American Medical Informatics Association (AMIA). A professional organization that promotes the development and use of medical informatics for patient care, teaching, research, and health care administration.

American national standards (ANS). Standards developed and approved by organizations accredited by ANSI.

American National Standards Institute (ANSI). An organization that accredits various standards-setting committees and monitors their compliance with the open rule-making process that they must follow to qualify for ANSI accreditation. HIPAA prescribes that the standards mandated under it be developed by ANSI-accredited bodies whenever practical.

ASC. Accredited Standards Committee.

Association for Electronic Health Care Transactions (AFEHCT). An organization that promotes the use of EDI in the health care industry.

Biller. A person who submits claims for services provided by a health care provider or supplier to payers.

Case manager. A clinical professional (e.g., nurse, doctor, or social worker) who works with patients, health care providers, physicians, and insurers to determine and coordinate a plan of medically necessary and appropriate health care; also known as a care coordinator.

Case mix index. Sum of all DRG relative weights, divided by the number of Medicare cases.

Centers for Disease Control and Prevention (CDC). An organization that maintains several code sets included in the HIPAA standards, including the ICD-9-CM codes. The ICD-9-CM codes are created by the World Health Organization. The clinical modifications that occur in the United States. are made by the CM committee. The CDC participates in the committee.

Centers for Medicare and Medicaid Services (CMS). CMS is charged with the responsibility of maintaining, controlling, and enforcing the Health Insurance Portability and Accountability Act (HIPAA) transaction standards. CMS is also the federal agency that oversees all of the fiscal and legislative requirements related to Medicare and Medicaid and that is also responsible for maintaining ICD-9-CM and HCPCS codes.

Character. In ICD-10-PCS, one of the seven component alphanumeric digits that make up an ICD-10-PCS procedure code.

Code set. Under HIPAA, this is any set of codes used to encode data elements, such as tables of terms, medical concepts, medical diagnosis codes, or medical procedure codes. This includes both the codes and their descriptions. Also see 45 CFR, part II, 162.103.

Coder. A trained professional who translates written or transcribed oral diagnoses and procedures into numeric and alphanumeric medical codes for reimbursement and/or statistical purposes.

Coding conventions. Each space, typeface, indentation, and punctuation mark determining how ICD-9-CM codes are interpreted when the diagnoses and procedures performed are reported.

Coding guidelines. Official guidelines that specify how procedure, diagnosis, or durable medical equipment codes are to be translated and listed for various purposes.

Coding rules. Official rules and coding conventions used for diagnosis and procedure coding.

Coding specificity. The codes assigned are the most specific available; i.e., a three-digit disease code is assigned only when there are no four-digit codes within that category, a four-digit code is assigned only when there is no fifth-digit subclassification within that category, or a fifth digit is assigned for any category for which a fifth-digit subclassification is provided.

Compliance audits. Internal or external monitoring and review of activities to ensure compliance with all laws, regulations, and guidelines related to health care.

Compliance committee. Individuals assigned to help the compliance officer teach and comply with all laws, regulations, and guidelines related to health care.

Compliance officer. Individual with authority, funding, and staff to perform all necessary compliance activities, including planning, implementing, and monitoring the compliance program.

Crosswalk. The cross-referencing of codes between coding systems.

Current Procedural Terminology coding system (CPT). A medical code set maintained and copyrighted by the AMA and selected for use under HIPAA for noninstitutional and nondental professional transactions.

Department of Health and Human Services (HHS or DHHS). The cabinet department that oversees the operating divisions of the federal government responsible for health and welfare. HHS oversees the Centers for Medicare and Medicaid Services, Food and Drug Administration, Public Health Service, and other such entities.

Descriptor. The text defining a code in a code set. Also see 45 CFR, part II, 162.103.

Designated code set. A medical code set or an administrative code set that the Department of Health and Human Services has designated for use in one or more of the HIPAA standards.

Designated standard. A standard that HHS designated for use under the authority provided by HIPAA.

Diagnosis code. An ICD-9-CM code that describes the patient's medical condition, symptoms, or the reason for the encounter as documented in the patient record.

Diagnosis-related group (DRG). The inpatient classification scheme used for Medicare's hospital inpatient reimbursement system.

Diagnosis. Determination or confirmation of a condition, disease, or syndrome and its implications.

Diagnostic procedures. A procedure performed on a patient to obtain information to assess the medical condition of the patient or to identify a disease and to determine the nature and severity of an illness or injury.

Electronic data interchange (EDI). Usually means X12 and similar variable-length formats for the electronic exchange of structured data. It is sometimes used more broadly to mean any electronic exchange of formatted data.

Electronic Healthcare Network Accreditation Commission (EHNAC). An organization that tests transactions for consistency with the HIPAA requirements and that accredits health care clearinghouses.

Facility. A building, house, or a place of patient care, including inpatient and outpatient, for acute or long-term care.

Federal Register. A government publication listing changes in regulations and federally mandated standards, including coding standards such as HCPCS Level II and ICD-9-CM.

Fourth and fifth digits. Digits used in the ICD-9-CM coding system to provide more specific information about the diagnosis or procedure being coded. Certain ICD-9-CM codes require a fourth and fifth digit to satisfy Medicare coding guidelines and edits during claims processing.

Health Informatics Standards Board (HISB). A standards group accredited by the American National Standards Institute that has developed an inventory of candidate standards for consideration as possible HIPAA standards.

Health information. According to HIPAA, any information, whether oral or recorded in any form or medium, that is created or received by a covered entity; relates to the past, present, or future physical or mental health or condition of an individual; the provision of health care to an individual; or the past, present, or future payment for the provision of health care to an individual. See 45 CFR, part II, 160.103.

General Equivalence Mappings (GEM). Relationships between corresponding code sets in which the most likely code linkages are provided for the user to navigate between and assist in translation of codes between systems.

Granularity. Level of detail or specificity in regard to code assignment.

Health information. See 45 CFR, part II, 160.103.

Health Insurance Portability and Accountability Act of 1996 (HIPAA). A federal law that allows persons to qualify immediately for comparable health insurance coverage when they change their employment relationships. Title II, subtitle F, of HIPAA gives the Department of Health and Human Services the authority to mandate the use of standards for the electronic exchange of health care data; to specify what medical and administrative code sets should be used within those standards; to require the use of national identification systems for health care patients, providers, payers (or plans), and employers (or sponsors); and to specify the types of measures required to protect the security and privacy of personally identifiable health care information. Also known as the Kennedy-Kassenbaum Bill, the Kassenbaum-Kennedy Bill, K2, or Public Law 104-191.

Healthcare Common Procedure Coding System (HCPCS). Two levels of codes used by Medicare and other payers to describe procedures and supplies. Level I includes of all of the codes listed in CPT, and Level II are alphanumeric supply and procedure codes.

ICD-9-CM. See International Classification of Diseases, Ninth Edition, Clinical Modification.

ICD-10-CM. See International Classification of Diseases, Tenth Edition, Clinical Modification.

ICD-10-PCS. See International Classification of Diseases, Tenth Edition, Procedure Coding System.

Imaging. Radiologic means of producing pictures for clinical study of the internal structures and functions of the body, such as x-ray, ultrasound, magnetic resonance, or positron emission tomography.

Inpatient services. Items and services furnished to an inpatient, including room and board, nursing care and related services, diagnostic and therapeutic services, and medical and surgical services. An inpatient service requires the beneficiary to reside in a specific institutional setting during treatment (Medicare Pub. 100-04, trans #25, October 31, 2003).

International Classification of Diseases (ICD). A medical code set maintained by the World Health Organization (WHO). The primary purpose was to classify causes of death. A U.S. extension, maintained by the National Center for Health Statistics within the Centers for Disease Control and Prevention, identifies morbidity factors, or diagnoses. The ICD-9-CM codes have been selected for use in the HIPAA transactions.

International Classification of Diseases, Ninth Edition, Clinical Modification (ICD-9-CM). A clinical modification of the international statistical coding system used to report, compile, and compare health care data, using numeric and alphanumeric codes to help plan, deliver, reimburse, and quantify medical care in the United States.

International Classification of Diseases, Tenth Edition (ICD-10). Classification of diseases by alphanumeric code, used by the World Health Organization but not yet adopted in the United States.

International Classification of Diseases, Tenth Edition, Clinical Modification (ICD-10-CM). Clinical modification of ICD-10 developed for use in the United States.

International Classification of Diseases, Tenth Edition, Procedure Coding System (ICD-10-PCS). A procedure coding system developed by 3M HIS under contract with the Centers for Medicare and Medicaid Services.

Invalid ICD-9-CM code. A diagnosis code that is incorrect or not specific because one or more digits are missing, numbers have been transposed, or numbers presented are not listed in the ICD-9-CM listing.

JCAHO. Joint Commission on Accreditation of Healthcare Organizations.

Level of specificity. Refers to diagnosis coding specificity; i.e., a three-digit disease code is assigned only when there are no four-digit codes within that category, a four-digit code is assigned only when there is no fifth-digit subclassification within that category, or a fifth digit is assigned for any category for which a fifth-digit subclassification is provided.

Linking codes. To establish medical necessity, CPT and HCPCS Level II codes must be supported by the ICD-9-CM diagnosis and injury codes submitted on the claim form and supported by the documentation.

Medical code sets. Codes that characterize a medical condition or treatment. These code sets are usually maintained by professional societies and public health organizations.

Medical documentation. Patient care records, including operative notes; physical, occupational, and speech-language pathology notes; progress notes; physician certification and recertifications; emergency room records; or the patient's medical record in its entirety.

Medical necessity. The evaluation of health care services to determine if they are medically appropriate and necessary to meet basic health needs; consistent with the diagnosis or condition and rendered in a cost-effective manner; and consistent with national medical practice guidelines regarding type, frequency, and duration of treatment.

National Center for Health Statistics (NCHS). A division of the Centers for Disease Control and Prevention that compiles statistical information used to guide actions and policies to improve the public health of U.S. citizens. The NCHS maintains the ICD-9-CM coding system.

National Committee on Vital and Health Statistics (NCVHS). A federal advisory body within the Department of Health and Human Services that advises the secretary regarding potential changes to the HIPAA standards.

National Council for Prescription Drug Programs (NCPDP). An group accredited by the American National Standards Institute that maintains a number of standard formats for use by the retail pharmacy industry, some of which are included in the HIPAA mandates.

Nomenclature. The assignment of a name or the description of a term or procedure such as an ICD-9 code description.

Nonspecific code. A catchall code that specifies the diagnosis as ill defined, other, or unspecified and may be a valid choice if no other code closely describes the diagnosis.

Not Elsewhere Classifiable (NEC). The condition or diagnosis is not provided with its own specified code in ICD-9-CM, but included in a more broadly defined code for other specified conditions.

Not Otherwise Specified (NOS). The condition or diagnosis remains ill defined and is unspecified without the necessary information for selecting a more specific code.

Office of Inspector General (OIG). An agency within the Department of Health and Human Services that is ultimately responsible for investigating instances of fraud and abuse in the Medicare and Medicaid and other government health care programs.

Outcome measures. Standards assessing the quality of patient care by measuring the change in a patient's performance following health services.

Outcomes. The condition, behavior, or attributes of a patient at the end of therapy or of a disease process, including the degree of wellness and the need for continuing care, medication, support, counseling, or education.

Outpatient services. Medical and other services provided by the hospital or other qualified supplier that are either diagnostic or help the physician treat the patient.

Peer review organization (PRO). An organization that contracts with the Centers for Medicare and Medicaid Services to conduct preadmission, preprocedure, and postdischarge medical reviews and determine medical necessity, appropriateness, and quality of certain inpatient and outpatient surgical procedures for which payment may be made in whole or in part under the Medicare program. (Now known as a quality improvement organization, or QIO. See Quality improvement organization [QIO].)

Principal diagnosis. The condition established after study to be chiefly responsible for occasioning the admission of the patient to the hospital for care.

Principal diagnosis code. The code that identifies the condition established after study to be chiefly responsible for occasioning the patient's visit to the facility for care. The principal diagnosis exists at the time of admission or develops subsequently and has an effect on the length of stay and the resources used to treat the patient.

Principal procedure code. An ICD-9-CM code that describes a procedure performed for the treatment of an illness or injury and not for diagnostic, testing, or assessment purposes. The principal procedure is usually related to the principal diagnosis.

Problem-oriented V codes. ICD-9-CM codes that identify circumstances that could affect the patient in the future but that do not currently constitute an illness or injury.

Procedure. A diagnostic or therapeutic service provided for the care and treatment of a patient, usually conforming to a specific set of steps or instructions.

Prospective payment system (PPS). A reimbursement methodology that uses predetermined rates for each type of discharge, procedure, service, or item based on a standard type of case.

Qualifier. In ICD-10-PCS, the seventh character within a code which represents an additional attribute or component of the procedure, which may be applicable.

Quality assurance (QA). Monitoring and maintenance of established standards of quality for patient care.

Quality improvement organization (QIO). Formerly peer review organization (PRO). An entity established by TEFRA to review, monitor, educate, and improve the care given to patients. A QIO primarily performs this function for Medicare, but may also review Medicaid and private insurers under separate contracts.

Registered health information administrator (RHIA). An accreditation for medical record administrators, previously known as a registered records administrator (RRA).

Registered health information technician (RHIT). An accreditation for medical records practitioners, previously known as accredited records technician (ART).

Reimbursement mappings. Maps which link the ICD-10-CM diagnosis and the ICD-10-PCS procedure code systems to the ICD-9-CM diagnosis and procedure systems. These mappings facilitate code linkage for reimbursement comparison purposes, providing a mechanism by which claims may be processed by providing the most appropriate code choice based on frequency data.

Risk manager. The person charged with keeping financial risk low, including malpractice cases.

Root operation. In ICD-10-PCS, the third character within a code that represents the procedural objective.

Scenario. In General Equivalence Mappings, the scenario is the digit that indicates that a combination code entry exists to satisfy the equivalent meaning of a code in the source system. In procedure mappings, this digit also indicates the number of distinct clinical variations of procedure code combinations included in the source system code.

Secretary. Under HIPAA, this refers to the secretary of the Department of Health and Human Services or his or her designated representatives. Also see 45 CFR, part II, 160.103.

Sequencing codes. Codes reported according to ranking guidelines defining severity, time, and skill required to treat the diagnosed condition and cost of the service for procedures.

Service-oriented V codes. ICD-9-CM codes that identify or define examinations, aftercare, ancillary services, or therapy; or the patient who is not currently ill but seeks medical services for some specific purpose such as follow-up or screening visits.

Severity of illness. The relative levels of loss of function and mortality that may be experienced by patients with a particular disease.

SNOMED. Systematized nomenclature of medicine.

Source. In General Equivalence Mappings, the source is the system from which the mapping is originating. For example, if mapping from ICD-9-CM to ICD-10-CM, the source system is ICD-9-CM.

Standard transaction. Under HIPAA, a transaction that complies with the applicable HIPAA standard. Also see 45 CFR, part II, 162.103.

Strategic national implementation process (SNIP). A Workgroup for Electronic Data Interchange program for helping the health care industry identify and resolve HIPAA implementation issues.

Target. In General Equivalence Mappings, the target is the system being mapped to. For example, if mapping from ICD-9-CM to ICD-10-CM, the target system is ICD-10-CM.

TEFRA. Tax Equity and Fiscal Responsibility Act.

Therapeutic procedures. Treatment of a pathological or traumatic condition through the use of activities performed to treat or heal the cause or to effect change through the application of clinical skills or services that attempt to improve function.

Three-digit diagnosis codes. One of approximately 100 diagnosis codes used alone (without zero filler) only when no fourth or fifth digit is available.

Transaction. Under HIPAA, the exchange of information between two parties to carry out financial or administrative activities related to health care. Also see 45 CFR, part II, 160.103.

Transaction standards. A defined set of rules for the transmission of electronic claims.

Uniform hospital discharge data set (UHDDS). A minimum data set that acute-care, short-term hospitals are required to complete and report for Medicare and Medicaid discharges.

United Nations Rules for Electronic Data Interchange for Administration, Commerce, and Transport (UN/ EDIFACT). An international electronic data interchange format. Interactive X12 transactions use the EDIFACT message syntax.

Unspecified. A diagnostic description when more information is necessary to code the term more specifically.

Utilization management (UM). A process of integrating clinical review and case management of services in a cooperative effort with other parties, including patients, employers, providers, and payers.

Utilization review (UR). A formal assessment of the medical necessity, efficiency, and/or appropriateness of health care services and treatment plans on a prospective, concurrent, or retrospective basis.

V codes. Codes that describe circumstances that influence a patient's health status and identify reasons for medical encounters resulting from circumstances other than a disease or injury already classified in the main part of ICD-9-CM; also known as supplementary classification of factors influencing health status and contact with health services.

Value. In ICD-10-PCS, individual alphanumeric digits specifically defined for each character.

WEDI. See Workgroup for Electronic Data Interchange.

WHO. See World Health Organization.

Work Group (WG1) of the Health Care Task Group (TG2) of the Insurance Subcommittee (N) of X12. This group maintains the X12 270 "Health Care Eligibility & Benefit Inquiry" and the X12 271 "Health Care Eligibility & Benefit

Response" transactions, and is also responsible for maintaining the IHCEBI and IHCEBR transactions.

Workgroup for Electronic Data Interchange (WEDI). A health care industry group that lobbied for HIPAA A/S, and that has a formal consultative role under the HIPAA legislation. WEDI also sponsors the strategic national implementation process (SNIP).

World Health Organization (WHO). International agency comprising UN members to promote the physical, mental, and emotional health of the people of the world and to track morbidity and mortality statistics worldwide. Maintains the International Classification of Diseases (ICD) medical code set.

X12. A group accredited by the American National Standards Institute that defines electronic data interchange standards for many American industries, including health care insurance. Most of the electronic transaction standards mandated or proposed under HIPAA are X12 standards.

X12 Standard. The term currently used for any X12 standard that has been approved since the most recent release of X12 American National Standards. Since a full set of X12 American National Standards is released only about once every five years, it is the X12 standards that are most likely to be in active use. These standards were previously called "draft standards for trial use."

Index